D1575976

# TRAINING
# THE
# DEVELOPMENTALLY
# YOUNG

# TRAINING THE DEVELOPMENTALLY YOUNG

Beth Stephens, Editor

JOHN DAY BOOKS IN

**S** **E**

SPECIAL EDUCATION

THE JOHN DAY COMPANY   NEW YORK

The John Day Company, 257 Park Avenue South, New York N.Y. 10010

an **Intext** publisher

Published on the same day in Canada by Longman Canada Limited.

Library of Congress Catalogue Card Number: 72-132949
Printed in the United States of America

## ACKNOWLEDGMENTS

The present writing evolved from an attempt to devise an outline for a university course whose goal was to prepare teachers to work with the moderately retarded. When pertinent work was reviewed major contributors included persons who have co-authored this book; therefore it is indeed a product of group collaboration. The authors' thoughts have been clarified by the suggestions and editorial criticisms of David W. Anderson and Gary W. Moore; their work is appreciated. There is hope that the topics to which attention is directed will stimulate others to continue to seek new methods for meeting the challenge of training those who are developmentally young.

B.S.

# CONTENTS

# PREFACE

Special education's coming of age has resulted in a critical analysis of its past, in an effort to project the pedagogic and administrative changes required to assure its confident maturity. As this analysis proceeds, the special class that came into being because of failure of the regular class to meet a child's specific need may well be dissolved. Instead, many pupils may return to regular classes and a master teacher may supervise teaching assistants in a resource room designed to provide exceptional students with daily tutorial sessions. However, there are those exceptional children who, even with tutorial aid, cannot keep step with normal children and will require that all activities be geared to their torporific tempo. These are persons whose mental ages remain less than half of their chronological ages, whose incomplete cognitive development causes them to remain intellectually young. These are persons with IQs in the 30 or 35 to 50 or 55 range, who are classified as the trainable or moderately retarded, and who in adulthood will have a mental age of five to eight. To understand these persons, both in terms of presently observed behavior and in terms of possible future accomplishments, it becomes necessary to locate them developmentally. Only when their levels of cognitive, motor, language, and social development are determined can appropriate curriculum be planned. In the main, past efforts have been to analyze the needs of these persons and, armed with these needs as goals, to develop a curriculum. By contrast, the present trend, represented by the articles in this volume, is to emphasize the desiderata to determine present levels of functioning in basic growth areas and, equipped with this knowledge, to formulate a curriculum that affords opportunity for progression to the next level. As the person proceeds through the developmental sequence, activities prerequisite to basic skills will be mastered. Optimum development at adulthood remains a goal as effort centers on methods and techniques that are applicable to the halting, minute step by minute step of sequential progression that leads up the developmental scales. The present volume is not a curriculum guide, nor is it a potpourri of activities to be tried in a school setting; rather, it sets forth ways of assessing development and presents a rationale for program planning in the areas of cognitive, language, motor, and social development.

Although the chapters that follow are written for teachers of the moderately retarded, the portions that discuss assessment and programming are appropriate for all who teach children who are developmentally young, whether these children are gifted, normal, or retarded. By way of introduction, the reader is presented with a description of the trainable retardate and his potential. Following this, discussion is divided into three sections: (1) developmental appraisal (cognitive, motor, language, and social) (2) areas of training (perceptual-motor, speech and language, self-help and independence, sociocivic and recreation, and vocational), and (3) methods and techniques of training (the Montessori method, behavior modification, and discrimination learning).

Temple University                                    Beth Stephens
December, 1970

CONTRIBUTORS

David W. Anderson, M.Ed., is currently a Research Assistant, Department of Special Education, Temple University. He was awarded an Office of Education Fellowship for graduate study in the area of mental retardation (1968–69) leading to the Master's degree, and is currently pursuing a Ph.D. in special education at Temple University. He is a member of the American Association on Mental Deficiency and the Division on Mental Retardation, Council for Exceptional Children. His major interests are the educational and psychological aspects of mental retardation.

Thomas J. Banta, Ph.D., is Associate Professor of Psychology, University of Cincinnati. He is a member of the American Psychological Association, the National Association for the Education of Young Children, and Sigma Xi. Banta carried out a Russell Sage postdoctoral residency at Rip Van Winkle Foundation and at Northwestern University and served on the faculty in the Department of Psychology at the University of Wisconsin and at the University of

Denver. More recently he was visiting professor of social psychology at The University of East Africa, Makerere College (Uganda). His major research interests are concerned with innovative and curiosity behavior in young children, application of the Montessori method, the development of conceptual behavior, and nurturance, attention, and distractibility.

Bernice B. Baumgartner, M.A., is Director of Education, Office of Mental Retardation, Department of Public Welfare, Harrisburg, Pennsylvania. She is experienced in virtually every role in special education. She has been teacher in all elementary grades and in high school, as well as teacher of special classes for the retarded in St. Louis. She has taught college classes for teachers of exceptional children in many universities, including Chicago, Pennsylvania, Michigan State, Penn State, New Haven State College, Marshall College, and others. She has also served as either supervisor, consultant, or education director in both private and/or public schools in Indiana, Illinois, New York, and Pennsylvania. She has served as consultant to numbers of state departments of education throughout the country and has been active as an officer at state and local levels of the Council for Exceptional Children. She is the author of the books *Administering Classes for the Retarded, Guiding the Retarded Child, Helping the Trainable Mentally Retarded Child, Reaching the Retarded through Art,* and of scores of articles and pamphlets.

Irene Blanchard, Ph.D., is Associate Professor in the Department of Speech-Drama-Dance at Chico State College, Chico, California. She formerly conducted diagnostic research on the speech development of mentally retarded children at Pacific State Hospital, Pomona, California. Her original research at the University Elementary School, University of Michigan, established the normative sequence of development of consonant sounds in the speech of children, a classic reference for speech therapists. While at Pacific, she developed a method of feeding neurologically handicapped children whereby structures needed for speaking can be organized at the vegetative level of functioning. She holds affiliation with major child development and speech organizations, local and international, and has contributed to a variety of professional journals.

Harold A. Delp, Ph.D., is Professor of Special Education and coordinator of the doctoral program in special education administration and supervision at Temple University. He began his career as a classroom teacher. Later he served as the first director of the University of Minnesota Psycho-Educational Clinic and has since been director of special education at several universities, most recently at Temple. He is a school and clinical psychologist and has been the major advisor for training programs for school psychologists and a qualified psychological examiner in New Jersey and Illinois. He was a member of the Board of Examiners, New Jersey Psychological Association, and is a certified psychologist in New Jersey, Illinois, and Pennsylvania. After serving as executive director of Little City, a private residential school for mentally retarded in Illinois, he became coordinator of clinical services at The Training School at Vineland, New Jersey. Dr. Delp is a Fellow in the American Psychological Association, in clinical school psychology divisions. He is also a Fellow in the American Association on Mental Deficiency and a member of the Council of Exceptional Children and various other professional organizations in education.

Joann Fokes, Ph.D., is Assistant Professor in Hearing and Speech Sciences at Ohio University. She is a member of the American

Speech and Hearing Association, the Ohio Speech and Hearing Association, and the Society for Research in Child Development. Her teaching and research activities include first language acquisition and pathological language patterns. Clinical interests concern the procedures for establishing language patterns for individuals with deviant or deficient language. In the summer of 1969, Dr. Fokes participated in a workshop on the Speech and Language of the Urban and Rural Poor at Ohio University.

B. L. Freeman, M.A., has served as Assistant Project Director on the Mental Retardation Development Staff at the University of Alabama Medical Center. Prior to this he was Director of Special Programs for the Hot Springs (Arkansas) Public School System. As a psychologist he has served with the Arkansas Children's Colony and in the Department of Special Education at Louisiana Polytechnic Institute. Mr. Freeman received his B.A. and M.A. degrees at Baylor University and currently is a Ph.D. candidate at Memphis State University, where he was awarded a graduate fellowship that made possible work in the area of mental retardation.

Frederic L. Girardeau, Ph.D., is currently Senior Research Associate, Department of Hearing and Speech, University of Kansas Medical School. Prior to this appointment, Dr. Girardeau was an Assistant Professor and Research Associate at George Peabody College, where he was also a NIMH Research Fellow. Following his work at Peabody he served as Research Associate and Associate Director of Research Training, University of Kansas, Bureau of Child Research. He received his B.A. degree from Emory University and his M.A. and Ph.D. degrees at George Peabody College. Dr. Girardeau's field of major concern is the experimental analysis of learning behavior of retarded children, including language behavior, preschool educational procedures for retarded and normal children, and the application of experimental methods to clinical problems. Although he presently teaches at University of Kansas Medical School, his additional duties as Coordinator of Research Training for the Kansas Center for Research in Human Development allow him to continue work in his field of major concern.

Marc W. Gold, Ph.D., is Research Assistant Professor at Children's Research Center and Assistant Professor of Special Education at the University of Illinois at Urbana-Champaign. He taught educable and trainable children in the Los Angeles City Schools. During summers, he has taught theory and methods courses for educable and trainable children at the University of Wisconsin-Milwaukee and at California State College at Los Angeles. He is presently conducting research on the use of learning theory to develop prevocational and vocational training programs for the moderately and severely retarded.

Gertrude G. Justison, Ed.D., is Coordinator of the Child Study Center, Department of Special Education, Howard County (Maryland) Public Schools. Prior to this appointment she was Associate Professor (Special Education), Graduate School, Howard University, Washington, D. C. Currently she is also a Faculty Associate of Antioch College, Columbia (Maryland), The Washington School of Psychiatry (D.C.), and the Howard University Child Development Center (Department of Pediatrics, School of Medicine). Prior to her full-time faculty assignment at Howard, she served ten years as teacher, principal, and supervisor in the Special Education Department of Montgomery County (Maryland) Public Schools. She is a member of the American Association for the Advancement of

Science, the American Psychological Association, the American Orthopsychiatric Association, the Council for Exceptional Children, the American Association of University Professors, the National Education Association, and the Maryland State and Howard County Teachers' Associations. She is currently serving at national committee level for the Council for Exceptional Children and the American Association on Mental Deficiency. Also, she has served as in-service or research consultant to local school systems, the Office of Economic Opportunity (Head Start) and the U. S. Office of Education (Title III) programs.

D. D. Kluppel, Ph.D., is Associate Professor of Communicative Disorders at the University of Wisconsin. She formerly held appointments at San Fernando Valley State College, University of California (Los Angeles), and Pomona College. She is a member of the American Psychological Association, several regional psychological associations, the American Speech and Hearing Association, and Sigma Xi. She was the recipient of a research fellowship for the Public Health Service. Her major interest is in the developmental acquisition of language and concepts in children. Methods she has used in language programs for retardates have served as topics at international conferences.

Wayne D. Lance, Ed.D., did undergraduate work at the University of Redlands and also completed the M. A. degree in education at the same university. After three years' active duty in the U.S. Navy, he taught for six years in grades four through eight and in special classes for the mentally retarded. He served as a counselor in a summer camp for the retarded prior to attending George Peabody College as a doctoral fellow in mental retardation. After graduate school, Dr. Lance was Director of the Special Education Program

at California State College at Fullerton for three years. He is now
Associate Professor of Education at the University of Oregon and
Director of the Northwest Regional Special Education Instruc-
tional Materials Center. He is immediate past President of the
Division on Mental Retardation of the Council for Exceptional
Children.

C. Jean Mundy, M.Ed., is an Assistant Professor in the School of
Education at Winthrop College, Rock Hill, South Carolina. She
formerly held joint appointments as Assistant Professor of Recreation and Special Education at Florida State University while developing and coordinating the undergraduate and graduate therapeutic recreation program. In addition she has served on the
Florida Governor's Committees for Mental Retardation and
Rehabilitation of the Handicapped. She has served as therapeutic
recreation consultant to many state agencies in the Southern Region of the United States and has conducted workshops on recreation for the mentally retarded. She is author of *The Mundy
Recreation Inventory for the Trainable Mentally Retarded* and is
presently co-authoring a book on habilitative recreation programming for the mentally retarded. Miss Mundy is completing her
work at Columbia University, Teachers College, for an Ed.D. degree.

Keith G. Scott, Ph.D., is Research Associate Professor of Psychology at the Children's Research Center, University of Illinois
(Urbana-Champaign). His experience includes elementary school
teaching and service as a school psychologist. He received his
doctoral training as a research assistant and associate at the University of Connecticut, where he worked with Drs. David Zeaman and
Betty House Zeaman on their attention research in the retarded.

His current major research interest is in short-term memory in the retarded. Presently his work is supported by a research grant and a career development award from the National Institute of Child Health and Human Development U.S.P.H.S.

Keith E. Stearns, Ed.D., began his work in special education as a member of the faculty of the Tri-Cities Special Education Department, Richland, Washington. During a four-year tenure there he served as a psychological examiner and Supervisor-Counselor of Special Education classes. While at Indiana University he served as a teacher of the trainable mentally retarded in the University Elementary School, with summer appointments as a teacher of the educable mentally retarded. His consultancies include in-service training for staff members of community centers for the mentally retarded, in-service training for various follow-through programs, and evaluation of institutional educational programs. Following completion of his doctoral work at Indiana University, Dr. Stearns served for one year on the Special Education faculty at the University of Michigan before returning to Indiana University in 1966. At Indiana University he is an Associate Professor of Education and coordinator of the mental retardation training program and directs a curriculum development project for the trainable in the Center for Educational Research and Development in Mental Retardation at Indiana University. Prior to entering special education, Dr. Stearns served as an elementary classroom teacher in Alaska and as a basic education instructor in the U. S. Army.

Beth Stephens, Ph.D., is Professor of Special Education, Temple University. Prior to her present post she served as a teacher of secondary classes for the educable retarded, as a Research Associate at the University of Texas, and as Research Assistant Professor at the Institute for Research on Exceptional Children, the University of Illinois. During a year of post-doctoral work at the University of Geneva she translated Bärbel Inhelder's *The Diagnosis of Reasoning in the Mentally Retarded*, a study that supplied the framework for an eight-year longitudinal project—The Development of Reasoning, Moral Judgment, and Moral Conduct in Normals and Retardates—which she is currently conducting at Temple University. She is a member of American Psychological Association, American Association on Mental Deficiency, American Educational Research Association, Council for Exceptional Children, Society for Research on Child Development, International Association for Scientific Study of Mental Deficiency, National Educational Association, and Eastern Psychological Association. Presently she is Chairman for Region IX American Association on Mental Deficiency and serves as consulting editor to the journal *Education and Training of the Mentally Retarded*.

# INTRODUCTION

## Wayne D. Lance

Educational programs for moderately retarded pupils have become the rule rather than the exception during recent years. This increase reflects the efforts of parents and other concerned groups in providing publicly supported schools, special classes, and sheltered workshops for children and youth who have traditionally been trained in residential institutions or in parent-sponsored schools, if at all. As education for all of the children of all of the people comes closer to being a reality in the United States, it is only axiomatic that provision will be made for the moderately retarded. The acceptance of these children by the public schools has not always been without some reluctance on the part of educators and members of school boards, many of whom felt that the schools existed only to provide a traditional academic program. These individuals argued that training in self-help skills, basic language, and other "functional" abilities was more appropriately a task to be assumed by institutions other than schools. The apparent success of classes for the mildly retarded, coupled with the pressures brought to bear by parents of the moderately retarded, has been successful in changing the minds of those responsible for making public taxes available for training these children. Little objection is now voiced against accepting them in community schools.

Accompanying the growth in the number of programs has been a corresponding growth in concern among special educators as to the objectives, the curriculum, the methods, and the materials best suited to the moderately retarded pupil. These concerns have not been completely resolved; in fact, the tempo of research and curriculum and materials development is ascending at a rapid pace. The sections of this book will discuss present knowledge, problems, and possible directions in the appraisal and training of the moderately retarded.

This introductory chapter includes material on each of the following topics: (1) definition of the moderately retarded, (2) etiological factors, (3) incidence, (4) educational provisions, (5) work with parents, (6) development of an educational program, and (7) the selection and preparation of teachers.

## Definition

The American Association on Mental Deficiency's (AAMD) definition and classification of mental retardation are widely accepted among professional groups in the United States. "Mental retardation refers to subaverage general intellectual functioning which originates during the developmental period and is associated with impairment in adaptive behavior" (Heber, 1961a). As used in this book, the term "moderately retarded" may be considered from two vantage points: as a measure of *intellectual functioning* and as a measure of *adaptive behavior.*

Moderate retardation as a measure of intellectual functioning encompasses the range "-3," *i.e.,* -3.01 to -4.00 standard deviation units below the mean on a standardized test of intelligence (Heber, 1961a, b). The IQ range is approximately 30 or 35 to 50 or 55 (Dunn, 1963). As a matter of practice, some children within the range "-4," "severe retardation of measured intelligence," are found in classes for the moderately retarded.

Of perhaps greater significance to educators in defining this population is a consideration of adaptive behavior. Utilizing Heber's definition, adaptive behavior ". . . refers primarily to the effectiveness with which the individual copes with the natural and social demands of his environment" (Heber, 1961a, p. 61). Children enrolled in public school classes for the trainable mentally retarded usually fall within Level "-III" of the adaptive behavior classification. Level -III is described as "severe negative deviation from norms and standards of adaptive behavior" (p. 62). Characteristics of children and adults functioning at Level -III are as follows:

Preschool age, 0-5, Maturation and Development: Poor motor development; speech is minimal; generally unable to profit from training in self-help; little or no communication skills.

School age, 6-21, Training and Education: Can talk or learn to communicate; can be trained in elemental health habits; cannot learn functional academic skills; profits from systematic training ("trainable").

Adult, 21, Social and Vocational Adequacy: Can contribute partially to self-support under complete supervision; can develop self-protection skills to a minimal useful level in controlled environment (Heber, 1961a, p. 63; Heber, 1961b).

As in any special program, the children enrolled will have abilities both above and below those normally attributed to the specific group being defined. Thus, there will be children in classes for the moderately retarded who are capable of profiting from some academic training and there will be adults who require less than complete supervision.

As scales are developed to measure independent functioning, personal and social responsibility, age-related behaviors, and critical behaviors for coping with the environment (Leland, 1966), special educators will be in a more favorable position to describe behavior diagnostically and to prepare an educational prescription. For example, when a teacher is able to state precisely the level at which the pupil masters the skills necessary to travel from home to sheltered workshop, he is then able to prescribe the training program necessary to achieve the next successive level of performance.

The term "trainable mentally retarded" (TMR) is frequently applied to the group of retarded defined, in this book, as moderately retarded. In the opinion of this writer, moderate retardation implies a level of expectancy that is commensurate with the progress that has been achieved in educational programs during the past decade.

## Etiology

With the number of known causes of mental retardation being in excess of two hundred (Covert, 1965), it is beyond the scope of this introduction to attempt a detailed discussion of etiological factors. Instead, the reader is referred to the *Manual on Terminology and Classification in Mental Retardation* developed by the American Association on Mental Deficiency (Heber, 1961a) for a brief but comprehensive review of categories and known causes of mental retardation. Etiologic groupings of retardation are outlined by the AAMD as:

1. Diseases due to infection: mental retardation is the result of damage from an inflammation due to an infection.
2. Diseases due to intoxication: damage results from serums, drugs, and other toxic agents.
3. Diseases due to trauma or physical agent: the brain is damaged due to an accident or from a mechanical or other physical agent.
4. Diseases due to disorder of metabolism, growth, or nutrition:

any metabolic, nutritional, or growth dysfunction is classified in this section.

5. New growths: this category includes tumors and other growths causing damage to the central nervous system.
6. Diseases due to (unknown) prenatal influences: the definite etiology is not established for this classification but it is known that the condition existed prior to birth.
7. Diseases due to unknown or uncertain cause with the structural reaction manifest: includes degenerative, infiltrative, inflammatory, proliferative, sclerotic, or reparative structural reactions with an unknown etiology.
8. Diseases due to uncertain (or presumed psychological) cause with the functional reaction alone manifest: no clinical or historical indication of pathology or disease to account for the mental retardation; psychosocial or psychogenic factors are presumed to be responsible for the retardation.

Considerable interest has been generated in the genetic aspects of mental retardation in recent years. Approximately 15 percent of retardation is now attributed to genetic or hereditary factors (Scheerenberger, 1965), including children with Down's syndrome (mongolism), a group accounting for perhaps one third of the children usually found in classes for the moderately retarded (Dunn, 1963). The rise in interest may be attributed to recent findings regarding chromosomal aberration in individuals with Down's syndrome and speculation that aberrations may be found in retarded individuals with other syndromes, and the ever-present hope that such findings may eventually lead to some forms of prevention.

Mental retardation due to infectious diseases is also of particular concern to special educators because of the incidence of multi-handicaps among children with moderate and severe retardation. Because of recent rubella epidemics there has been a significant increase in multi-handicapped retarded children. Undoubtedly, some of these children will be enrolled in classes for the moderately retarded and teachers will become aware of the necessity to modify teaching procedures to accommodate the special needs of these multiply impaired children.

## Incidence

Of the six million persons in the United States who are, or will sometime in their lifetime be classified as retarded, 6 percent are classified as moderately retarded and 3.5 percent as severely retarded (President's Committee on Mental Retardation, 1970). In a discussion of trainable mentally retarded children, Dunn (1963) uses the more conservative estimate that "for a typical community, it seems safe to expect that, for every 1,000 school-age children, one or two will be of trainable intellect and living at home, while another one will be in a residential facility" (p. 132). This latter estimate of .3 percent is probably the more accurate one when attempting to estimate the potential enrollment in school programs for the moderately retarded. It will be observed in the following section that even the two or three per thousand school-age children figure far exceeds the actual number of moderately retarded children enrolled in special classes.

## Educational Provisions for the Moderately Retarded

Historically, the education of the moderately retarded may be said to have had its genesis with the work of Jean-Marc-Gaspard Itard (Itard, 1962) and his student, Edouard O. Seguin (Talbot, 1964). Their work during the nineteenth century was the first well-documented attempt at systematically training the moderately and severely retarded in sensory-motor, social, and other skills. The influence of these men is apparent today, especially in Seguin's "physiological method," which is utilized in part by some educators. Unfortunately, this encouraging beginning was stifled as education and training gave way to simple custodial care in many residential institutions throughout the United States during the latter part of the nineteenth century and early twentieth century. Public apathy and professional misgivings about the value of training, coupled with a concern in some circles that the retarded were a menace to society, fostered this decline.

A brighter outlook regarding programs of education for the retarded was directed as much by the forces of social and political change as by the attempts of educators and physicians to train the retarded (Sloan, 1963). As the *zeitgeist* became more conducive to expecting change in the behavior of individuals through training programs, concerned individuals like Guggenbühl, DeCroly, Descoeudres, Montessori, and Binet abroad, and Howe and Fernald in the United States, made considerable progress in establishing programs for the moderately retarded.

Public school programs for these children are a relatively recent development except for isolated instances where districts or states made provision to provide special classes. A concerted effort to accept the moderately retarded as a part of the public school system began after World War II, and the increase in enrollment in special education classes has been dramatic during the past fifteen years. In 1953, 4,659 pupils were enrolled in classes for the trainable while for 1969 the figure was 109,175 (President's Committee on Mental Retardation, 1970). This figure should continue to increase at a rapid pace with the advent of federal financial assistance to school districts serving the handicapped. For example, under Title VI of the Elementary and Secondary Education Act, 44,519 mentally retarded pupils were assisted during the year 1969 at an expenditure of $8,964,000 (in addition to state and local funds), and projected figures indicated further increases (Secretary's Committee on Mental Retardation, 1969). The interest in providing classes should not be attributed to the effect of federal assistance alone, but to the effort that initiated the federal assistance, namely the concern and hard work of parents and others who encouraged legislation to provide for permissive or mandatory classes. The National Association for Retarded Children and its affiliated state and local chapters were instrumental in uniting the individuals and groups concerned for this group of children.

Current practices for educating these children are commonly organized in one of the following ways:

1. Residential programs for children and adults living in state and private institutions.
2. Public school programs for children living at home.
3. Parent-sponsored and private schools in local communities.
4. Sheltered workshops for adolescents and young adults.

Current trends in programming for these children indicate an extension of provisions to both younger and older children, summer school and camp programs, work experience education for older youth, and even semi-independent living programs for the graduates of school programs. It is evident that as greater numbers of the moderately retarded remain in the community with their parents or in foster homes rather than being institutionalized, the public schools will assume an increasing share of the responsibility for their education and training.

Although research evidence supporting the benefits of early educational programs for the moderately retarded is quite limited at this time (e.g., Lanyi, 1966), educators who have worked with younger children at the preschool and primary age level often express the opinion that systematic training begun early will result in more rapid and more lasting increases in achievement of language, sensory-motor, and self-help skills. Most "normal" children begin school at age five or six, and there appears to be little justification for delaying the admission of moderately retarded children. In fact, a delay in commencing training may further handicap the retarded child. If parents are assisted in applying principles of learning during the preschool years, most of these children can be toilet trained and can achieve the minimal language and social skills necessary for commencing school by the age of five or six years.

Early identification of the moderately retarded and subsequent parent guidance is essential for the well-being of both child and parents. As total community services (Meyen, 1967) become a reality, a comprehensive plan for diagnosis, parent counseling, and early education will become the rule rather than the exception. Such a plan may envision an umbrella agency in each community or region which coordinates the diagnostic, counseling, and educational services of medicine, psychology, social work, and education. Under this plan, the young child arrives at school not as a stranger, but as an individual well known to the teacher. An educational prescription is more easily developed when the school has been involved in the process of diagnosis and parent guidance for a sufficient period of time preceding the child's entrance.

## Working with Parents of the Moderately Retarded

Teachers of the moderately retarded probably have more frequent contact with parents of their pupils than is true of any other group of pupils. This may be attributed to the crisis that exists when a handicapped child is born into a family and the problems resulting from attempts to handle the deviance within the family (Farber and Ryckman, 1965). As the child enters school the parents express their concerns to the teacher and the teacher finds himself in the role of counselor. This is a role for which most teachers are inadequately prepared, and one they should be hesitant to assume.

Rather, the teacher should be in a position to refer the parents to counseling services and to parent organizations where the results of research in parent counseling are implemented by experienced personnel. Results of studies indicate that positive changes in attitudes can occur when various counseling techniques are employed (Milligan, 1965).

This is not to imply that teachers should hesitate to communicate with parents; to the contrary, continual dialogue is essential to insure that the school program and the home are pursuing similar goals using compatible methodology. Parental and community understanding of the retarded child, and of the educational program, are more likely to occur when the teacher communicates frequently and is also willing to listen to the parents when they speak of educational needs of their child. Parent study groups are recommended as a means for aiding in an understanding of the educational program (Baumgartner and Lynch, 1967). Teachers should be assisted in attaining insight into the problems faced by parents and this phase of preparation should not be neglected in college and university programs.

## Development of an Educational Program for the Moderately Retarded

Standing foremost among the concerns for educational programs for the moderately retarded is the development of curriculum (Lance, 1968). Daly (1966) lists three major problems relating to curriculum for these children: (a) ". . . the lack of a clear guiding purpose. . . ," (b) ". . . the lack of agreement between parents and educators regarding worthy educational objectives. . . ," and (c) ". . . lack of a systematized instructional program . . ." (pp. 117-118). These problems are to be expected when the relatively recent advent of programs is considered, yet they cannot be overlooked or excused by special educators. The deficiencies existing in curriculum goals and objectives are apparent when one views the emphasis given certain subjects in special classes as contrasted to the functional objectives usually outlined in guides and courses of study. For example, in the Hudson (1960) study of what was being taught in classes for the trainable, language development appeared to be receiving a disproportionate amount of emphasis as contrasted to self-help skills. It is apparent that a program highly academic in nature is inappropriate for the moderately retarded if other skills essential for successful functioning as an adult are overlooked (Warren, 1963).

A number of sources have outlined objectives and procedures for teaching the moderately retarded (*e.g.*, Baumgartner, 1960; Bensberg, 1965; Frankel, Happ, and Smith, 1966; Molloy, 1963; Perry, 1960; Rosenzweig and Long, 1960; Smith, 1968) and many local districts and some state departments of education have produced guidelines (*e.g.*, Cameron, 1966; Hanson, Daly, and Campbell, 1966). These sources have relied in varying degrees upon research and theory in the areas of appraisal and training of cognitive, motor, language, and social abilities, and it appears safe to conclude that further effort is required to produce a more definitive work. This is due to the advances that researchers have made in the development of a theory of learning and the findings of studies involving the moderately retarded as subjects.

Various approaches may be utilized in arriving at a suitable curriculum guide. An analysis of the adaptive behavior of the moderately retarded as a group, a careful analysis of the tasks necessary to function adequately as an adult, and an application of a typology of curriculum objectives (Gorelick, 1963) will lead to a set of guidelines and lesson plans that meet at least some of the objections being voiced to existing programs.

A model curriculum derived from a clinical teaching approach has been suggested by Evans and Apffel (1968). "Clinical" implies careful and continual diagnosis of individual children in the areas of physical, social, sensory, perceptual, and intellectual development in addition to the child's interests, experiences, and potential for learning. Following evaluation, objectives would be determined in weekly staff meetings and a team teaching approach would be utilized. Goals would vary with age and would change as weaknesses were remediated. The twenty-one areas of program content for pupils below the age of eight listed by Evans and Apffel (1968, p. 25) follow:

1. Sense training and stimulation
2. Motor development, including some rhythmics
3. Body-image development (beginning)
4. Intersensory integration exercises (beginning)
5. Attention training
6. Self-help skills (basic)
7. Perceptual training
8. Exercises in concept formation
9. Language development
10. Intersensory integration (advanced)
11. Visualization practice
12. Body image (advanced); use of rhythmics, personal appearance improvement
13. Reading
    (a) Rebus
    (b) Initial Teaching Alphabet (i.t.a.)
    (c) traditional
14. Self-help skills (advanced)
15. Writing and drawing
16. Arithmetic
17. Socialization skills (manners)
18. Speech therapy
19. Music
20. Gymnastics
21. Creative thinking ("brainstorming")

Another approach to curriculum might follow the model developed at Teachers' College, Columbia University, in the project that resulted in *An Experimental Curriculum for Young Mentally Retarded Children* (Connor and Talbot, 1966). Although the project was designed primarily for mildly mentally retarded preschool-age children, the model appears to be applicable for curriculum development with the moderately retarded. After a careful evaluation of children's growth, a detailed curriculum was developed following a sequential-developmental format. This approach is compatible with the developmental appraisal emphasized in this volume. The longitudinal aspects of this study permitted considerable observation of the children over time. The programming of the guide was explained (Connor and Talbot, 1966, p. 14) as follows:

The Curriculum Guide developed for use in the experimental classes contained one hundred and ninety items, each with a five point descriptive scale. The scales referred to details of development in intellectual, creative and imaginative, social, emotional, manipulative, motor, and self-help areas. They constituted a set of short-range goals toward which the teachers worked in the mediating preschool experiences, and which contributed in turn to the attainment of long-range objectives. For the teachers of the experimental classes, the Guide served two purposes, (a) for observing and rating the behavior of the preschool children, and (b) for program planning and evaluation.

The Teachers' College curriculum includes many realistic objectives for the moderately retarded and an adaption should be considered. In addition to the short-range goals, curriculum must be viewed in terms of the ultimate realistic goals appropriate to an adult world, be it in a dependent or semidependent environment. Training for sheltered workshop employment (Gold, 1968) and even for independent living (Katz, 1965) are a reasonable part of the curriculum for many moderately retarded adolescents and young adults.

Assessment of the current level of functioning in the areas of communication, self-help, sensory and perceptual, motor, sociocivic, and personal competency, plus measurement of progress toward the achievement of objectives in each area, is essential to a systematized instructional program. The curriculum guide itself may serve in this capacity if objectives and format are adaptable, as for example in the "Individualized Diagnostic Course of Study for Trainable Mentally Retarded" prepared by the Santa Barbara Schools of California (Cameron, 1966). Special scales may be developed by the school staff, *e.g.*, *Developmental Evaluation Scale for Mentally Retarded Children* (Harvey, Yep, and Sellin, 1966): "Each item of the scale represents manifest behaviors which can be rated quantitatively by an observer. . . ." (p. 101).

Other instruments which will be discussed later in this book have been developed especially for use with the moderately retarded, namely, *the Cain-Levine Social Competency Scale* (Cain, Levine, and Elzey, 1963), *Personal-Social and Vocational Scale for the Mentally Retarded* (Levine and Elzey, 1966), and *TMR Performance Profile for the Severely and Moderately Retarded* (DiNola, Kaminsky, and Sternfeld, 1963). Scales and tests for measurement of current functioning in areas such as language, visual and auditory perception, and motor development are available, and although usually developed for a less severely handicapped population, are quite useful in the data they provide the teacher. Further elaboration upon appropriate instruments will be made in subsequent chapters.

Perhaps methodology has undergone a more radical change than has curriculum for the moderately retarded during the past decade. The application of behavioral management techniques through operant methodology has been successful in extinguishing inappropriate behavior and in establishing desired behavior in moderately and severely retarded children and youth (Haring and Lovitt, 1967). The ramifications of this approach are yet to be felt in most public school classrooms, but with increased exposure of students in teacher preparation programs to these principles, it is only a matter of time until methodology will have been altered to a significant degree.

Another area in which considerable change is anticipated is that of instructional materials development and application (Martinson, 1967). Instructional materials, *e.g.*, Bitter and Bolanovich (1966) and Happ (1967), developed and evaluated along a conceptual framework and properly utilized, have the values recognized by Montessori (1965) and since capitalized upon by the network of Special Education Instructional Materials Centers (Olshin, 1968).

Methodology and materials, however important they are to a successful program, are secondary to the establishment of realistic objectives. A teacher must first be able to state his objectives in an operational manner (Mager, 1962) and then proceed to define the best means for implementation of those objectives.

## Selection and Preparation of Teachers

Some attention in the literature has been given to the necessity for the careful selection and preparation of teachers for the moderately retarded (Cain and Levine, 1963; Connor and Goldberg, 1960; Council for Exceptional Children, 1966; Heber, 1963; Lance, 1968; Wolinsky, 1959). Suggestions have ranged from recommendations for specific courses to types of practicum experiences appropriate to the preparation of teachers. Recommendations for screening and selection of teachers have often been less specific and research data in this respect is woefully lacking. The measurement of attitudes of prospective teachers by use of instruments such as the Minnesota Teacher Attitude Inventory has been explored (Condell and Tonn, 1965; Meisgeier, 1965), and at least one researcher has explored the variable of past experience as it relates to the selection of teachers (Johnson, 1964). One of the results of Hudson's study (1960) was the development of a tentative checklist of teaching competencies for teachers of trainable children. Additional investigation is required and modification is necessary to further validate this checklist.

Unresolved at this time is the question regarding preparation and the degree of involvement of paraprofessionals in programs for these children (Blessing, 1967). Teacher aides are employed in many programs, particularly when class size exceeds ten or twelve, or when the group of children is heterogeneous in age or other behavioral attributes. Teacher aides are undoubtedly effective when at least two conditions are met: (1) the teacher is proficient in directing their activities, and (2) the aide has had some training in how to work effectively with the teacher and pupils.

Another unresolved problem is that little evidence exists to indicate if regular class teaching experience is a necessary prerequisite to successful teaching with the retarded. The crucial variables may be related to the extent and kind of practicum experiences and to certain personal characteristics of the teachers.

## Conclusion

The growth of programs for the moderately retarded, coupled with a rising interest among behavioral scientists in conducting research in learning and adaptive behavior, is indicative of the progress that may be expected in the education and training of this segment of the population. Results of research and directions for future activities for the moderately retarded will be discussed in the following chapters.

# References

Baumgartner, B. *Helping the Trainable Mentally Retarded Child.* New York: Teachers College, Columbia University, 1960.

Baumgartner, B., and Lynch, K. D. *Administering Classes for the Retarded.* New York: John Day Co., 1967.

Bensberg, G. J., ed. *Teaching the Mentally Retarded: A Handbook for Ward Personnel.* Atlanta, Ga.: Southern Regional Education Board, 1965.

Bitter, J. A., and Bolanovich, D.J. "Job Training of Retardates Using 8mm Film Loops." *Audiovisual Instruction* 11 (1966): 731-732.

Blessing, K. R. "Use of Teacher Aides in Special Education: A Review of Possible Applications." *Exceptional Children* 34 (1967): 107-113.

Cain, L.F., and Levine, S. *Effects of Community and Institutional School Programs on Trainable Mentally Retarded Children.* CEC Research Monograph Series B, no. B-1. Washington, D.C: Council for Exceptional Children, 1963.

Cain, L.F.; Levine, S.; and Elzey, F.F. *Manual for the Cain-Levine Social Competency Scale.* Palo Alto, Calif.: Consulting Psychologists Press, 1963.

Cameron, E.C. "Individualized Diagnostic Course of Study for Trainable Mentally Retarded." Mimeographed. Santa Barbara, Calif.: Santa Barbara City Schools, 1966.

Condell, J.F., and Tonn, M.H. "A Comparison of MTAI Scores." *Mental Retardation* 3 (1965): 23-24.

Connor, F.P. and Goldberg, I. "Opinions of Some Teachers Regarding Their Work with Trainable Children: Implications for Teacher Education." *American Journal of Mental Deficiency* 64 (1960): 658-670.

Connor, F., and Talbot, M.E. *An Experimental Curriculum for Young Mentally Retarded Children.* New York: Teachers College, Columbia University, 1966.

Council for Exceptional Children. *Professional Standards for Personnel in the Education of Exceptional Children.* Washington, D.C.: Council for Exceptional Children, 1966.

Covert, C. *Mental Retardation: A Handbook for the Primary Physician.* Chicago: American Medical Association, 1965.

Daly, F.M. "The Program for Trainable Mentally Retarded Pupils in the Public Schools of California." *Education and Training of the Mentally Retarded* 1 (1966): 109-118.

DiNola, A.J.; Kaminsky, B.P.; and Sternfeld, A.E. *TMR Performance Profile for the Severely and Moderately Retarded.* Ridgefield, N.J.: Reporting Service for Exceptional Children, 1963.

Dunn, L.M. "Trainable Mentally Retarded Children." In *Exceptional Children in the Schools,* edited by L.M. Dunn. New York: Holt, Rinehart, and Winston, 1963.

Evans, J.R., and Apffel, J. *Educational Procedures for the Trainable Mentally Retarded: Past, Present, and Potential.* Institute on Mental Retardation and Intellectual Development, George Peabody College for Teachers, vol. 5, no. 1, Nashville, Tenn.: Peabody College, 1968.

Farber, B., and Ryckman, D.B. "Effects of Severely Mentally Retarded Children on Family Relationships." *Mental Retardation Abstracts* 2 (1965): 1-17.

Frankel, M.G.; Happ, F.W.; and Smith, M.D. *Functional Teaching of the Mentally Retarded.* Springfield, Ill.: Thomas, 1966.

Gold, M.W. "Classroom Techniques: Preworkshop Skills for the Trainable: A Sequential Technique." *Education and Training of the Mentally Retarded* 3 (1968): 31-37.

Gorelick, M.C. "A Typology of Curriculum Objectives for Mentally Retarded: From Ambiguity to Precision." *Mental Retardation* 1 (1963): 212-215.

Hanson, F.M.; Daly, F.M.; and Campbell, L.W. *Programs for the Trainable Mentally Retarded in California Public Schools.* Sacramento: California State Department of Education, 1966.

Happ, F.W. "Teaching Aids for the Mentally Retarded Child." *Mental Retardation* 5 (1967): 33-35.

Haring, N.G., and Lovitt, T.C. "Operant Methodology and Educational Technology in Special Education." In *Methods in Special Education,* edited by N.G. Haring and R.L. Schiefelbusch, pp. 12-48. New York: McGraw-Hill, 1967.

Harvey, A.; Yep, B.; and Sellin, D. "Developmental Achievement of Trainable Mentally Retarded Children." *Training School Bulletin* 63 (1966): 100-108.

Heber, R.F. "A Manual on Terminology and Classification in Mental Retardation." *American Journal of Mental Deficiency,* 1959, 64, Monograph Supplement.

Heber, R.F. "Modifications in the Manual on Terminology and Classification in Mental Retardation." *American Journal of Mental Deficiency* 65 (1961): 499-500 (b).

Heber, R.F. "Standards for the Preparation and Certification of Teachers of the Mentally Retarded." *Mental Retardation* 1 (1963): 35-37, 60-62.

Hudson, M. *An exploration of classroom procedures for teaching trainable mentally retarded children.* CEC Research Monograph, Series A, no. 2., Washington, D.C.: Council for Exceptional Children, 1960.

Itard, J.M. *The Wild Boy of Aveyron.* New York: Appleton-Century-Crofts, 1962.

Johnson, M.R. "An Experimental Investigation of Some Dimensions Underlying Preferences for Teaching Exceptional Children." Master's thesis, Fisk University, 1964.

Katz, E. "The Mentally Retarded Adult in the Community (San Francisco Program)." *Training School Bulletin* 62 (1965): 81-91.

Lance, W.D. "School Programs for the Trainable Mentally Retarded." *Education and Training of the Mentally Retarded* 3 (1968): 3-9.

Lanyi, A.F. *"Nachfolgeuntersuchungen bei 200 schwachsinnigen kindern"* [Follow-up examination of 200 mentally retarded children]. In *International Copenhagen Congress on the Scientific Study of Mental Retardation, Vol. 2,* edited by Jakob Oster. Proceedings of the 1964 Copenhagen Congress, Copenhagen, Denmark, *Det berlingske bogtrykkeri,* 1964, pp. 845-846. Abstract in *Mental Retardation Abstracts* 3 (1966): 909.

Leland, H. "An Overview of Adaptive Behavior as a Behavioral Classification." In *Conference on Measurement of Adaptive Behavior: II,* edited by E. Kagin, pp. 1-15. Parsons, Kans.: Parsons State Hospital and Training Center, 1966.

Levine, S., and Elzey, F.F. *Personal-Social and Vocational Scale for the Mentally Retarded.* San Francisco: San Francisco State College, 1966.

Mager, R.F. *Preparing Instructional Objectives.* Palo Alto, Calif.: Fearon Publishers, 1962.

Martinson, M.C. "IMC Network Report: Education for Trainable Children—An Opportunity." *Exceptional Children* 34 (1967): 293-297.

Meisgeier, C. "The Identification of Successful Teachers of Mentally or Physically Handicapped Children." *Exceptional Children* 32 (1965): 229-235.

Meyen, E.L. *Planning Community Services for the Mentally Retarded.* Scranton, Pa.: International Textbook Co., 1967.

Milligan, G.E. "Counseling Parents of the Mentally Retarded." *Mental Retardation Abstracts* 2 (1965): 259-264.

Molloy, J.S. *Trainable Children: Curriculum and Procedures.* New York: John Day Co., 1963.

Montessori, M. *Dr. Montessori's Own Handbook.* New York: Schocken, 1965.

Olshin, G.M. "Special Education Instructional Materials Center Program." *Exceptional Children* 34 (1968): 515-519.

Perry, N. *Teaching the Mentally Retarded Child.* New York: Columbia University Press, 1960.

President's Committee on Mental Retardation. Personal communication. Washington, D.C., 1970.

Rosenzweig, L.E., and Long, J. *Understanding and Teaching the Dependent Retarded Child.* Darien, Conn.: Educational Publishing Corp., 1960.

Scheerenberger, R.C. "Genetic Aspects of Mental Retardation." *Mental Retardation Abstracts* 2 (1965): 463-481.

Secretary's Committee on Mental Retardation. *Mental Retardation Activities of the U.S. Department of Health, Education and Welfare.* Washington, D.C.: Superintendent of Documents, 1969.

Sloan, W. "Four Score and Seven." *American Journal of Mental Deficiency* 68 (1963): 6-14

Smith, R.M. *Clinical Teaching: Methods of Instruction for the Retarded.* New York: McGraw-Hill, 1968.

Talbot, M.E. *Edouard Seguin: A Study of an Educational Approach to the Treatment of Mentally Defective Children.* New York: Teachers College, Columbia University, 1964.

Warren, S. "Academic Achievement of Trainable Pupils with Five or More Years of Schooling." *Training School Bulletin* 60 (1963): 75-88.
Wolinsky, G.F. "Theoretical and Practical Aspects of a Teacher Education Program for Teachers of the Trainable Child." *American Journal of Mental Deficiency* 63 (1959): 948-953.

# I

# Developmental Appraisal

# Introduction

Provision of developmental criteria is necessary if one is to assess motor, language, cognitive, and social growth. When a chronological framework of standard developmental sequences is provided it becomes possible not only to identify individuals who have abnormal rates of development in a particular area, but also to ascertain just how far they have proceeded in the sequence. When this information is obtained it becomes possible to plan individually appropriate programs. Awareness of the need for a developmental background of normality prompted Fokes to devise a scale of motor development and a scale of language development. Because progress in these areas can be highly irregular more than one criterion was furnished for each six-month period of growth. To secure coordinated sequences of analysis she organized the work of a variety of developmental lists into longitudinal growth scales which cover the periods from birth to seven or eight years, periods during which motor and language skills normally experience their most rapid development.

The appraisal of cognitive development by Stephens is presented within a Piagetian framework. Discussion of the four stages of cognitive development observed by the Geneva school is followed by a review of presently available methods for assessing growth during the sensory motor and preoperational stages, stages that generally encompass the lower and upper limits of cognitive development for the moderately retarded.

Analysis of selected measures which provide sequential inventories of skills related to social maturity is provided by Delp. Because Heber's (1959) definition of mental deficiency uses social competency as the criterion, the importance of determining an individual's level of development in this particular area is recognized. The reader will note that the measures reviewed in the three sections, motor, language, and social, tend to emphasize observed behavior or interaction with everyday objects rather than responses to test items. What a person does or does not do in his daily living frequently provides a more accurate appraisal than does his reply to an examiner's question.

# Reference

Heber, R. F. "A Manual on Terminology and Classification in Mental Retardation." *American Journal of Mental Deficiency,* 1959, 64, Monograph Supplement.

# 1

## THE APPRAISAL OF
## COGNITIVE DEVELOPMENT

## Beth Stephens

Efforts to determine the intellectual capabilities of mental retardates have prompted search for assessments which determine the *level* of cognitive functioning rather than measuring global intelligence. When a theoretical framework was desired which explored the *process* of development, attention was directed to the work of Jean Piaget. His work has provided a series of stages which form an invariant sequence of intellectual development. These stages have been carefully explored and documented by the Geneva school (Piaget, 1960). Although Bruner (1966) has considered the feasibility of using them as a backdrop against which to attempt to accelerate development, North Americans have remained almost oblivious to the implications for diagnosis and remediation to be derived from Piaget's work. Approximately three decades ago Inhelder (1968) extended use of the theory to the diagnosis of retardation; following this initial effort Woodward (1959) applied it to the assessment of cognitive development in the severely retarded person. Yet, it is only during the past decade that Americans have attended to these findings. As the work in Geneva and Britain is reviewed, there is increasing awareness that the behavior of retardates frequently appears inappropriate as compared to the actions of normals of equivalent chronological age; yet the seemingly inappropriate behavior becomes understandable when attention is addressed, not to the retardate's age, but to his stage of mental development (*i.e.*, for a person whose chronological age is fifteen to exhibit behavior characteristic of persons whose chronological age is four can appear incongruous, but if the fifteen-year-old is viewed not in terms of age but stage, the behavior usually is found to be appropriate for a person performing at that particular cognitive level).

## Theory

Because extensive discussion of the stage theory is presented by Piaget in *The Psychology of Intelligence* (1960), by Flavell in *The Developmental Psychology of Jean Piaget* (1963), and by Hunt in *Intelligence and Experience* (1961), only a brief outline is presented here. Cognitive development, as viewed by Piaget, comprises four stages and evolves from the child's interaction with his environment. The theory starts from the central postulate that motor activity is the source from which mental operations emerge (Tuddenham, 1966). From this interaction there occurs a gradual awareness of self (Stephens, 1966). The neonate knows not that he and the world are separate, different entities, but as intellectual development proceeds, boundaries are set up between self and surrounding objects. Intelligence is seen as beginning not with awareness of self or things per se, but with a recognition of their interaction (Flavell, 1963).

The influence of early zoological training is revealed in Piaget's emphasis on adaptation as intelligence develops from the continuous interaction between a person and his environment. The interaction is indicated in an outward adaptive coping and inward mental organization. Thus the process of adaptation and organization results in constant reorganization of the structures of the mind, reorganization which involves two complementary processes:

1. *Assimilation* which corresponds to inner organization and occurs when an organism incorporates something from his environment into his mental structures.

2. *Accommodation* or outer adaptation which serves as a complement to assimilation and occurs when environmental conditions require coping which necessitates a modification, revision, or rearrangement of existing mental structures or "schemas."

As the child proceeds through life, inwardly organizing or assimilating and outwardly coping or accommodating to environmental experience, he becomes more capable in his adaptations. Thought is elaborated and organized. Indirect learning and problem solving become possible. Such is the generation of the mind. Piaget examines this cognitive development in terms of stages which Inhelder (1962) defines by the following criteria:

1. A stage is comprised of a period of formation and initiation, and a period of attainment or organization of mental operations.

2. The attainment of one stage serves as the starting point for the next. Thus, mental development is ongoing and evolutionary.

3. The order of the stages is constant, i.e. attainment of stage one consistently precedes the formation of stage two.

4. As transition is made from an earlier to a later stage, the preceding thought structures are integrated in or become a part of the later structures. [Stephens, 1966, p. 76]

Change from a reflexive to an inventive organism is defined by four stages, with substages within each. These stages are presented in Table 1.

Table 1

## PIAGET'S STAGES OF INTELLECTUAL DEVELOPMENT

| *Stage and Approximate Age* | *Characteristic Behavior* |
|---|---|
| I. Sensory-Motor Operations | |
| 1. Reflexive (0-1 month) | Simple reflex activity; example: kicking. |
| 2. Primary Circular Reactions (1-4.5 months) | Reflexive behavior becomes elaborated and coordinated; example: eye follows hand movements. |
| 3. Secondary Circular Reactions (4.5-9 months) | Repeats chance actions to reproduce an interesting change or effect; example: kicks crib, doll shakes, so kicks crib again. |
| 4. Coordination of Secondary Schema (9-12 months) | Acts become clearly intentional; example: reaches behind cushion for ball. |
| 5. Tertiary Circular Reactions (12-18 months) | Discovers new ways to obtain desired goal; example: pulls pillow nearer in order to get toy resting on it. |
| 6. Invention of New Means through Mental Combinations (18-24 months) | Invents new ways and means; example: uses stick to reach desired object. |
| II. Preoperational | |
| 1. Preconceptual (2-4 years) | Capable of verbal expression, but speech is repetitious; frequent egocentric monologues. |
| 2. Intuitive (4-7 years) | Speech becomes socialized; reasoning is egocentric; "to the right" has one meaning—to his right. |
| III. Concrete Operations (7-11 years) | Mobile and systematic thought organizes and classifies information; is capable of concrete problem solving. |
| IV. Formal Operations (11 years upward) | Can think abstractly, formulate hypotheses, engage in deductive reasoning, and check solutions. |

## Stage I. Sensory-Motor Operations

During this period earlier reflexive actions, such as arm waving, grasping at objects which touch the palm, and sucking, become coordinated and generalized. An object's permanence is discovered. There is increasing awareness that things outside the field of vision can be returned. Relationships are established between objects that are similar and between objects that are dissimilar. The six sensory-motor substages are:

1. *Reflexive.* A shift occurs in the neonate's ready-made reflexive schemata. Active groping replaces passive release and is most noticeable in the sucking schema. *Sucking* becomes generalized and may even include the edge of the blanket. Later in the substage if sucking is not followed by swallowing, groping starts again.

2. *Primary Circular Reactions.* As new associations are formed experience begins to dictate the type of action. The first acquired adaptations are noted in the variations of reflexive actions. As hand movements become something to look at and something heard becomes something to see, reciprocal coordination appears. Hunt (1961) comments that although the eye follows what the hand does, the hand does not realize the eye sees. Interest is in the movement itself and not in the effect which that movement produces. If a chance-made action proves interesting or satisfying, it is repeated. As the infant sucks, saliva collects on his tongue; he enjoys playing with it so he lets it accumulate again and repeats the process. When these responses become repetitious they are termed circular reactions. Imitation will occur only if the model starts by imitating the child.

3. *Secondary Circular Reactions.* During this period there is a limited anticipation of effect. Chance-made movements producing an effect on an object are repeated intentionally. The infant may

shake his legs and in so doing move a bassinet; as the bassinet moves, the doll on the hood swings; the infant sees the doll swing, so the kicking action is repeated. Also, the meaning of an object becomes assimilated. A rattle is shaken, a noise results, so repeated shakes occur. Although there is awareness that the means (shaking) begets the end (noise), the differentiation between the two is not understood. Inappropriate means are frequently applied to a situation (Hunt, 1961). The child waves paper and it rattles; later he may get a spoon in his hand and wave it as he expects it to rattle also. Objects acquire permanence as limited but active search is made for things absent. A spatial field is constructed as looking becomes coordinated with grasping and arm movements become coordinated with sucking. Imitation is limited to sounds and movements which are a part of the child's repertoire and which are visually or auditorily perceptible to him.

4. *Coordination of Secondary Schemata.* Observation of a child's behavior indicates means are definitely differentiated from ends. Discovery of an independent universe is made, *i.e.*, the "me" is discriminated from the "not-me" (Hunt, 1961). Clear demarcation of adaptive behavior occurs. The child will remove an undesired object (hand) standing in the way of a desired one (bottle). Attempts are made to duplicate speech sounds and to imitate movements observed in others. New models are included in imitative actions although imitation may be inaccurate, *e.g.*, the child may open and close his mouth as he attempts to replicate another person's eye wink.

5. *Tertiary Circular Reactions.* Action is no longer merely repetitious or chance-made. Objects are of interest in themselves and are the cause of active experimentation. If things accidentally fall, the child purposefully lets them fall again in order to watch the act. Interest is not only in the object but what can happen to it; there will be active pursuit of a ball which has rolled under or behind

something. There also is a subordination of means to an end, and the constructive elements which characterize intelligence are displayed. If a toy is placed on a cushion the child will grasp the cushion and pull it toward himself in order to grasp the object. Assimilation and accommodation become clearly differentiated, and imitative behavior closely approximates the model.

6. *Invention of New Means through Mental Combinations.* Awareness of relationships is sufficiently advanced to permit deductions. Piaget's classic example concerns a child's attempt to extract a watch chain from a slightly opened matchbox. After initial trials to obtain the end of the chain, the child stops, looks attentively at the slit in the matchbox as she opens her mouth wide, wider, then still wider; following this she slowly enlarges the drawer opening—wider, wider, and still wider—until she can put her finger in the matchbox drawer and pull out the chain (Piaget, 1960). Deferred imitation (imitation of absent persons, etc.) presages symbolism at this period.

Origins of intelligence lie in the sensory-motor period, which Hunt likens to a slow-motion film in which pictures are viewed in succession, but without the continuous vision necessary for understanding the whole. Although sensory-motor intelligence is intelligence in action, it is not reflective. Three essential conditions for transition from sensory-motor to the reflective level are:

1. Increase in speed which allows knowledge of successive phases of an action to be integrated into a simultaneous whole.

2. An awareness of the actual mechanisms of an action; thus awareness of the nature of a problem aids in obtaining a solution.

3. Increase in conceptual distances which permit actions to go beyond the limits of near space and time.

Throughout life the perceptions and practical sets of sensory-motor intelligence lie at the source of thought.

## Stage II. Preoperational

1. *Preconceptual.* Following initial symbolic functioning which makes language acquisition possible, a period starts in which symbolic and preconceptual thought develops. The child becomes capable of educing a signifier, a word or image, which serves as a symbol for the significate, some perceptually absent object or event. Through use of symbols it becomes possible for thought to consider the interplay or grouping of separate past, present, and future events. Also, at this stage the child initiates imitative play. Piaget views imitation as a form of accommodation. As the child becomes more adept at imitation it is possible for him to engage in internal as well as external imitations. A mental image, which is internal imitation, constitutes the signifier or word. At this stage the child who earlier opened her mouth wider and wider in imitation of the possible widening of the matchbox drawer would reduce this imitation to a schematized image from which use of the signifier or word would arise. Through symbol or language usage thought becomes socialized, and from socialization a necessity arises to justify egocentric reasoning. The child attempts to think about his own thinking (Flavell, 1963). As a child, at this stage of development, views an object or event he tends to center major regard on one outstanding feature to the neglect of others. The weight of two balls of clay may be compared and found equal, yet when the child sees one of the balls rolled into a long sausage shape he tends to say the long object weighs more. He fails to decenter, to consider width as well as length. Stable equilibrium between assimilation and accommodation has not been achieved.

The type of primitive reasoning characteristic of the preconceptual child is termed transductive; it is neither inductive nor deductive, but proceeds from particular to particular. A child at this age may attempt to smoke a white piece of chalk because it resembles a cigarette. Regard is addressed only to the physical appearance of the object to the neglect of classifying one as a writing instrument, the other as something to smoke. Another characteristic of this period is the inability to distinguish play and reality as different realms which possess different rules.

2. *Intuitive Thinking.* A gradual coordination of relations leads the child from a preconceptual or symbol acquisition stage to one in which these symbols or words may be manipulated in operational thought. Although processes are often rapid, the intelligence remains prelogical. Reasoning is intuitive. Even though the child observes two small glasses, A and B, identical in size and shape and each filled with an equal number of beads, and in turn observes as the beads from glass A are emptied into another glass $A_1$ which is taller and narrower, he tends to conclude that the quantity of beads has changed. $A_1$ contains more than B because "it is higher." Concomitant to this statement may be the admission that no beads have been added or removed.

Error is perceptual in nature. Thinking is influenced by what is seen at that given moment. Attention is centered on height relations and width is ignored. However, if the beads from B are emptied into another glass $B_1$, then into another $B_2$, the two being successively taller and thinner, a point will be reached when the child will reply "there are fewer because it is too narrow." The ability to "decenter," address regard to two aspects, height and width, rather than centering on height alone, becomes possible only when reasoning gives simultaneous respect to both relations. [Stephens, 1966, p. 78]

## Stage III. Concrete Operations

From infancy onward objects or events are classified, compared for similarities or differences, located in space or time, evaluated or counted. These cognitive classifications, seriations, or systems of explanation are termed "groupings," and they last throughout a person's life. As reality is assimilated to intelligence, equilibrium of the assimilatory framework is maintained by grouping.

The integrated, intellectual system achieved through grouping is used by the child in organizing and manipulating the surrounding world. The thought structure makes possible such intellectual operations as addition, subtraction, multiplication, division, comparing classes and relations of objects and events, measurement of time and space, as well as operations which involve systems of values and interpersonal interaction. The distinguishing characteristic of the mobile equilibrium which promotes grouping is that thought is no longer centered on a particular state of an object, but can follow successive changes through various types of detours and reversals.

Grouping also permits reversibility, *i.e.*, if $B = B_1$ and $B_1 = B_2$, then $B_2 = B$, or if $4 + 5 = 9$, then $9 - 5 = 4$. In addition to these logico-arithmetical operations, there are groupings which generate time and space. Also, operational groupings require social life. Without cooperation and interchange of thoughts with others, operations could never be grouped into a coherent whole.

Because the operations involved at this stage are constantly tied to action, they are concrete, not formal, operations. Children at this stage may be incapable of these processes if there is no manipulation of concrete objects, *i.e.*, if reasoning involves only verbal propositions.

## Stage IV. Formal Operations

Achieved in most children around their eleventh year, formal operations are comprised of a stage of intellectual equilibrium which has been evolving since infancy. As this transition is completed, observation no longer directs thought, as it did in the concrete period; instead, thought directs observation. With abstract thought the adolescent extends consideration beyond the present and forms theories. He becomes capable of hypotheses and reasons deductively. Reasoning with reality involves concrete groupings.

Formal thought invokes reflection on these groupings and is, therefore, operating on operations. [Stephens, 1966, pp. 78, 79]

## Application

Inhelder's (1968) previously noted study was the first to utilize Piaget's developmental theory of intelligence to measure observed reasoning in retardates. When she chose a method of assessment purely verbal, tests were bypassed in favor of tasks which permitted the detection of precise mental sturctures which serve as markers in the development of reasoning. Analysis of the protocols for the 150 subjects indicated that stages observed in the development of reasoning in normals were also observed with regularity in retarded and slow-learning subjects. Findings also indicated that the severely retarded never outgrew the sensory-motor compositions previous to language. The trainable were capable of intuitive thought characterized by egocentrism and irreversibility, but not by operations. The educable arrived at the level of concrete operations but were not capable of formal operations which passed beyond concrete operations. A follow-up study indicated that retardates were fixated at a level of reasoning which was only transitory to normals. Although the retardate followed the same evolutive process as the normal, he did it more slowly and was arrested sooner or later at an intermediate stage. When normal subjects passed from one level of reasoning to a higher one, and later to a still higher one, the progress became more and more rapid, but in retardates the opposite was observed. In the retardates, progress from one level to a higher and then to a still higher level became slower and slower. These findings suggested that the static notion of IQ could be replaced by speed of development, tempo, and mobility. In addition, traces of a previous level persisted much longer in retardates than in normal subjects (Stephens, 1968).

Through additional use of the clinical method of questioning, Inhelder found that a young child can be quite impermeable to experience if it involves a form of reasoning he has not yet attained. Knowledge of this impermeability has been utilized in subsequent studies of learning. Notions of operatory structures cannot be acquired from the environment if they are encountered prior to the child's readiness to receive them (Stephens, 1966).

Application by Woodward to research on retardates at the sensory-motor level extends verification of Piaget's theory to this lower stage of intellectual development (Woodward, 1959). While working with the severely retarded at Fountain Hospital in London, Woodward noticed these subjects appeared engrossed in observing their hand movements, an activity which occurs during the primary circular reaction substage of the sensory-motor level. Resulting interest and additional research by Woodward extended verification of Piaget's theory at this lower stage to the intellectual development of the severely retarded. Findings indicated that performance at a more advanced substage of sensory-motor operations occurred only after successful behavior was evidenced at genetically earlier substages. Also, the subject's development in specific areas tended to be at the same substage as that for his general development. For example, if a subject's general behavior was classified at the substage termed tertiary circular reactions, his comprehension of signs probably was at this level also. [Stephens, 1966, p. 83]

# Assessment of Trainable Retardates' Performance at the Sensory-Motor and Preoperational Levels

Pursuant to findings (Inhelder, 1968) which indicate that the adult trainable retardate possesses cognitive processes characterized by the egocentrism and irreversibility of preoperational thought, attention is addressed to assessment measures derived from Piaget's theory which measure cognitive development during the sensory-motor and preoperational stages, the two stages generally achieved by a trainable retardate during his life span. Until Uzgiris and Hunt's *Instrument for Assessing Infant Psychological Development* (1966) was made available there was no scale derived from Piaget's developmental sequence of qualitatively different levels of cognitive functioning to register developmental changes as they occur or fail to occur during stages that normally are achieved from birth to two years, the same stages that generally occur in the trainable retardate from birth to approximately five to eight years. For criteria, Uzgiris and Hunt (1966) chose situations which are reasonably elicitable, which are described by Piaget in his writings on the sensory-motor period, and which can be reliably observed by different people. The six series of behavioral schemata which comprise the instrument are:

## Series I. Visual Pursuit and Permanence of Objects

This series begins with the ready-made schema of looking. The first accommodations of this schemata are manifest in the pursuit of slowly moving objects held at a constant distance from the infant's eye. This is followed by "lingers with glance on the point where a slowly moving object disappeared." Later the infant "obtains a partially hidden object"; still later he may obtain an object hidden under one or two screens (or layers of material or paper).

## Series II. Development of Means for Achieving Desired Environmental Events.

The second series begins with commonly observed "hand-watching behavior." Piaget described the development of hand watching as an assimilation of the manual schema by the visual schema. With coordination comes the ability to grasp. The development of intention comes out of the feeling of effort in reaching for desired objects. From this development, the series proceeds to clearer evidence of intention in the differentiation of means and ends. The series starts with observed hand-watching behavior and proceeds to "grasps objects when both hand and object are in view," to "grasps without hand being in view," on through a series of accomplishments to such actions as "uses string as means to obtain object (pull toy) after demonstration," and later "without demonstration," and on to "uses stick to reach object."

## Series III. Development of Schemas in Relation to Objects.

The series begins with the appearance of coordinations between the schema ready-made at birth, such as sucking, to coordination between the manual schema and sucking (hand-mouth coordination or thumb sucking) to the schema of bringing objects in front of the eyes in order to look at them. Later such schemas as hitting, patting, shaking, etc., develop. Attending to objects leads to examination of them, which provokes interest in novelty; then social interaction is observed as the schema of showing becomes evident. Later there is recognition of objects expressed in naming.

## Series IV. The Development of Causality.

Development begins with the infant's attempts to hold on to desired inputs and may be viewed as branching from Series II, Development of Means for Achieving Desired Environmental Events. Initially, hand-watching behavior is observed; later the infant keeps an object active by means of secondary circular reactions; several steps later he seeks to continue an interesting performance by touching the performing agent"; still later he "recognizes another person as an independent causal agent by giving back an object to have it activated again," *e.g.*, a musical top; and at an even later stage he "activates a mechanically operated object after demonstration."

## Series V. The Construction of the Object in Space.

As the infant coordinates the schemata of looking and listening, he begins to localize sounds and their sources; things heard become things one can find and look at. Later he begins to reconstruct the trajectory of objects. Items on the scale include "localizes the source of sound," "follows the trajectory of a rapidly moving object," "recognizes the reverse side of objects," "understanding of gravity shown by permitting an object to roll down an incline," "makes detours in order to retrieve objects from behind obstacles."

## Series VI. Development of Imitation.

The series consists of two sections, one pertaining to vocal and the other to gestural imitation. The vocal series begins with the ready-made schemata of vocalizing. With the developing interest in novelty, the infant also starts to imitate unfamiliar sound patterns, at first by gradual approximation and later by direct imitation. The infant progresses to imitate words which are within his vocabulary and systematically repeats practically all new words.

The gestural series follows a similar progression. The infant begins to imitate simple gestures (hand waving), and later progresses to the imitation of unfamiliar gestures which he can watch himself perform (stretching his leg out straight) and to gestures which he cannot watch himself perform, *i.e.*, facial gestures such as winking his eye.

Films demonstrating assessment with the Uzgiris-Hunt scale are available. Use of the measure in a project concerned with the intellectual stimulation of culturally disadvantaged infants (Stephens, Kirk, and Painter, 1966) ages eight months to two years revealed differences in the cognitive development of motor-impaired infants that were not revealed by performance on the Cattell Infant Intelligence Scale. Because younger trainable retardates frequently are found "unmeasurable" on standard tests of intelligence the provision of a scale which measures cognitive development starting at initial levels—*i.e.*, from birth onward—is of particular value for this group. When a child is located on a developmental continuum, the next step in his development is suggested.

The preoperational stage, which in normals occupies the period from approximately two to seven years, is viewed as one of prime importance; during this time language normally is acquired and prelogical thought is evidenced. Workers in the field of retardation are interested in assessment of this stage because trainable retardates generally do not develop beyond this point. Although work of the Geneva school has set forth a hierarchical sequence in which the preoperational period is described in terms of two substages, the preconceptual and the intuitive, as yet there is no series of subscales which measure the development of this period as it is measured by Uzgiris and Hunt for the sensory-motor period. Currently, however, Educational Testing Service has announced the development of procedures—*Cognitive Growth in Preschool Children* (Melton, Charlesworth, Tanaka, Rothenberg, Busis, Pike, and Gollin, 1968) —which measure areas previously identified by Genevan research as prime contributors to the intellectual development of the preoperational child. Although there is presently no reported effort to extend use of these procedures to retardates, they were devised to measure preoperational functioning, a level of functioning achieved by trainable retardates. A listing of the areas and methods of assessment follows:

**1. Classification Skills** are measured by a series of tasks designed to tap preferential sorting, ability to abstract a common property of two objects, and ability to sort when presented with a verbal clue. Interest is in exploring available and preferred organizational schema using tasks of different levels of difficulty.

**2. Time** is assessed by a time sequence task which was designed to measure the young child's understanding of time as represented in a pictorial sequence. Materials consist of thirteen sets of cards with black and white and colored cartoon type drawings.

**3. Distance** understanding is assessed through use of a pegboard frame on which are taped two paths to a three-dimensional model of a schoolhouse; one path is straight, the other crooked. The child is provided with dolls and asked to predict which of the two routes involves more traveling. The task is made up of a series of such problems. Responses are evaluated in terms of (1) prediction, (2) reason or explanation, and (3) descriptions.

**4. Number Conservation** A set of objects is placed in a row before the child (A). Then an equivalent parallel row is constructed (B). Each element of set A is directly in line with the corresponding element of B. The child is then asked if there are as many objects in row B as in row A. Next the visual cues to the one-to-one correspondence of elements are destroyed by either compressing or expanding one of the rows. The child is again questioned on the numerical equivalence of the sets.

**5. Basic Language Structure** is measured by two tasks. In one, the Language Comprehension Task (LCT), there are twenty cards containing pairs of stimulus pictures, but they depict different relationships between the elements. The child's job is to distinguish which relationship a particular word implies and then point to the corresponding picture. The other measure is termed the Verbal Instructions Task (VIT), a task which requires the child to indicate his understanding of verbal symbols by manipulating various materials. To measure understanding of the word *between*, for example, the child is asked to place a toy ladder *between* two boxes (Melton, et al., 1968).

During the preconceptual stage, the first of the two substages of the preoperational period, the child broadens and proliferates his emerging representational skill. There is ability to name, to question, to command, and to understand others. Thought, however, is egocentric, and frequently is animistic. Both play and imitation have major roles; "in play the primary concern is to adapt reality to the self (assimilation); in imitation the paramount object is to adapt the self to reality (accommodation)" (Flavell, 1963, p. 66). The intuitive, or second substage of the preoperational period generally represents the ultimate developmental level for the trainable retarded. At this level the static rigidity which characterizes preoperational thought gradually is superseded by less egocentric and more flexible thought structures.

## Preschool Cognitive Assessment

Although not based on Piaget's developmental stages per se, an instrument designed by Haeussermann (1958) is available as an inventory of developmental levels in the two- to six-year-old. The instrument affords a description of the level and pattern of functioning. Haeussermann's goal was to determine potentials for develop-

ment through circumvention of certain assessment obstacles—
visual, auditory, or motor impairment—which may be present. For
example, in assessing a child with auditory impairment effort is
made to determine if he has learned to use visual clues and to
determine if his memory has served to compensate for the insuffi-
ciency of his auditory perception. Effort is made to sample the
child's intactness as the nature and extent of the impairment are
determined. Areas included in the assessment are:

1. Recognition of concrete familiar life-size objects.
2. Recall of missing picture from memory.
3. Orientation in time.
4. Recognition of symbols and forms.
5. Color discrimination.
6. Form discrimination.
7. Multiple-choice color-form sorting.
8. Manipulative ability.
9. Amount recognition.
10. Eye motion and gross vision.

Since Haeussermann's evaluation was based on tasks which are
sequential in development the child's performance level indicates
what is to be accomplished next; programming efforts center on
methods which provide the necessary experiences. Because the
moderately retarded frequently are multiply handicapped, Haeussermann's techniques are particularly appropriate in their assessments (Stephens, 1968).

As emphasis on the early diagnosis of abilities or disabilities has
increased, there has been demand for measures which identify motor, perceptual, or cognitive deficits and which can be quickly and
easily administered, preferably by the classroom teacher. Valett
Developmental Survey of Basic Learning Abilities (Valett, 1966)
for use with children two to seven years old was designed to meet
these needs.

The survey, which is concerned with the developmental tasks prerequisite to more formal learning, was compiled through the selection or adaptation of items formerly used by Baker and Leland, Bender, Binet, Doll, Frostig, Gesell, Haeussermann, Hiskey, Jastak, Wechler, and Valett. Areas which are measured include: motor integration and physical development, tactile discrimination, auditory discrimination, visual discrimination, visual motor coordination, language development and verbal fluency, and conceptual development. Users of the test should remember, however, that when the number of items measuring a specific area is decreased the reliability of the test is lowered. Studies of the reliability of the Valett Developmental Survey are needed. Until these are furnished its adequacy for individual assessment is problematic. [Stephens, 1968, p. 185]

## Remedial Programs

Efforts to provide remediation for the trainable should proceed only after the individual's level of functioning has been determined. Generally, activities should be sufficiently in advance of the child's present level of functioning to be interesting and motivating, but not so advanced that they are frustrating. Because of the belief that cognitive development occurs as the child interacts with his environment the Geneva school emphasizes the need to *prepare the environment* for learning, rather than to attempt to accelerate cognitive development. That correctly planned programs can be beneficial is recognized.

A program for children in the final substages of the sensory-motor and early portion of the preoperational period was designed by Stephens, Kirk, and Painter (1966). Although the subjects were culturally deprived rather than retarded the training involved areas of learning common to children performing at the sensory-motor and preconceptual levels regardless of the presence, absence, or type of handicap. While essentially sensory-motor, the initial phase of the remedial program emphasized eight areas of cognitive development: (1) language, (2) symbolic representation, (3) space, (4) number, (5) classification, (6) time, (7) reasoning, and (8) imitation. Detailed description of the program is provided by Painter (1967). The organizational plan for the tutorial sessions took the following form: During an initial period of three to four weeks the one-hour tutorial sessions were spent in nonstructured activities; this was done in order to establish rapport and to confirm observed developmental levels. The child was provided toys which required both gross and fine motor activity.

As a more structured program was incorporated the child sat still and worked for increasingly longer periods of time. A "Baby-Tenda" (a canvas seat surrounded on the four sides by a work area) served as a desk for the younger children; a small table and chair were used for the older ones. At the onset a dozen or more tasks were required to maintain interest during the one-hour session. Later, primarily because activities were structured to maximize fun, success, and satisfaction for the child, each child would sit and work for the full hour on no more than five to seven tasks. The basic tutorial approach for the eight cognitive areas consisted of: (1) locating the child developmentally in a particular area, (2) devising methods which would aid transition from one developmental level to the next, and (3) dividing the training task into a sequence of activities. Soundness of the approach is demonstrated by the positive findings which have accrued from its use. Need for its implementation is demonstrated in the functional inadequacies of exceptional children two years of age and under (Stephens, 1968).

In summary, more intensive study of the moderately retarded is urged. Such study should provide a developmental diagnosis followed by an observation period in which learning opportunities are furnished to the subject. During this extended observation period, assessment can be made of the person's tempo of development as well as his basic level of functioning. Provided with this information it then is possible to afford the moderately retarded programs designed to promote optimum cognitive development.

# References

Bruner, J. S. *Toward a Theory of Instruction.* Cambridge, Mass.: Harvard University Press, 1966.

Flavell, J. H. *The Developmental Psychology of Jean Piaget.* Princeton, N. J.: D. Van Nostrand Co., 1963.

Haeussermann, E. *The Developmental Potential of Preschool Children.* New York: Grune and Stratton, 1958.

Hunt, J. Mc V. *Intelligence and Experience.* New York: Roland Press, 1961.

Inhelder, B. "Some Aspects of Piaget's Genetic Approach to Cognition." *Monograph of Society for Research in Child Development* 82 (1962): 19-34.

Inhelder, B. *The Diagnosis of Reasoning in the Mentally Retarded.* New York: John Day Co., 1968.

Melton, R. S.; Charlesworth, R.; Tanaka, M. N.; Rothenberg, B. B.; Busis, A. M.; Pike, L.; and Gollin, E. S. *Cognitive Growth in Preschool Children.* Princeton, N. J.: Educational Testing Service, 1968.

Painter, G. "The Effect of a Tutorial Program on the Intellectual Development of Disadvantaged Infants." Ph.D. dissertation, University of Illinois, 1967.

Piaget, J. *The Psychology of Intelligence.* Patterson, N. J.: Littlefield, Adams and Co., 1960.

Stephens, W. B. "Piaget and Inhelder—Application of Theory and Diagnostic Techniques to the Area of Mental Retardation." *Education and Training of Mentally Retarded* 1 (1966): 75-87.

Stephens, W. B.; Kirk, S. A.; and Painter, G. "Intellectual Stimulation of Culturally Disadvantaged Children Ages Eight Months to Two Years." Progress Report. U. S. Office of Education Projects 5-1181, Department of Health, Education and Welfare, 1966.

Stephens. W. B. "Provisions for the Young Mentally Retarded." *Education and Training of the Mentally Retarded* 3 (1968): 180-188.

Tuddenham, R. D. "Jean Piaget and the World of the Child." *American Psychologist* 21 (1966): 207-217.

Uzgiris, I., and Hunt, J. McV. *Instrument for Assessing Infant Psychological Development.* Urbana, Ill.: The University of Illinois, 1966.

Valett, R. E. *Valett Developmental Survey of Basic Learning Abilities.* Palo Alto, Calif.: Consulting Psychologists Press, 1966.

Woodward, M. "The Behavior of Idiots Interpreted by Piaget's Theory of Sensory-Motor Development." *British Journal of Educational Psychology* 29 (1959): 60-71.

# INTRODUCTION: USE OF MOTOR AND LANGUAGE DEVELOPMENT SCALES

## Joann Fokes

The developmental scale is one of many devices that may be used in the assessment of behavior. The concern of the two succeeding chapters is a method in which scales from two areas of proficiency, motoric skill and language, can be applied for the evaluation of the mentally retarded. The reason for employing a measurement device is to bring about more effective handling of the mentally retarded or dependent child. From scales, a record of achievement may be obtained which is indicative of a child's level of operation motorically and linguistically. This information aids in the decision of educational placement as well as in day-to-day handling.

The value of a scale lies in its ease of administration during a period of life when other devices may be unusable. Standardized tests of psychological measurement require cooperation and some sophistication on the part of the subject—something that the infant, young child, or retardate is unable to give with any degree of satisfaction. Attempts at testing are often frustrating in that the child is unable to follow instructions or respond according to the formal structure of the test. The evaluator, in such instances, must

*Portions of this introduction were presented at the Annual Meeting of the Council for Exceptional Children, Chicago, 1970.

rely on his powers of observation in forming judgments on the capabilities of the child. In this instance, developmental scales may be the best device available. In fact, some specialized testing situations may be reduced to the use of scales in order to obtain a description of behavior. This does not, by any means, indicate that scales are not useful adjuncts in the instances where complete evaluations can be conducted. Scales may offer valuable supplemental information in addition to standardized test scores and frequently are included as part of a battery of tests.

## Construction of Scales

Developmental scales are, in a sense, a summary of observed behavior at different age levels. Observed behavior may be made under different conditions. Some types of behavior may be noticed incidentally, *e.g.* an observer may make note of a child's manner of grasping while he is at play. A more structured condition exists when observation is carried out under preplanned situations. For instance, if grasping is of focal interest, a child would be carefully observed as he manipulated a preset arrangement of articles. His performance would be recorded on the basis of a prepared checklist. For any item to be significant, it must be repeated a sufficient number of times by the same child as well as other subjects within a relevant age span or developmental stage. If the behavior is prominent, it is recorded as characteristic of that age level. For the item to be differential in nature, it should be common to a particular period as compared to an earlier period when it was either absent or emerging. Once a particular skill such as grasping is acquired, it may be refined at later stages. Upon refinement, skill in grasping would be retained throughout later stages. Other acquired skills may be dropped at later stages of development. Crawling is an obvious example. Infants learn to crawl, are able to crawl at advanced stages of development, but give it up in preference to walking. Thus, a particular item of behavior common to a period may be refined at a later stage or discarded for another mode of behavior.

The behavioral data gathered have been surprisingly similar in placing certain acquisitions within a span of age limits for normal children. Findings have been consistent in denoting particular traits and activities as specific to an age span. Deviations, even among normals, especially when one child is compared against the norms for a group, are not rare, however. When acquisitions are scaled, or placed in a time sequence, variability is not uncommon, particularly in the area of language. The outstanding feature, however, is the sequential appearance of skills—whether linguistic or motoric. Thus, an acquisition appearing on a scale not only implies that certain specified stages of development have occurred previously but also predicts future expectations.

Scales, then, supply information about expected levels of behavior at different ages. Again, judgments are made on the basis of typical behavior of children.

A critical factor to be considered is the observational powers of the investigator. Any behavior is interpreted in the eyes of the observer. The construction of a reliable and valid scale is dependent upon the investigator's capacity as a skilled observer as well as his knowledge of child development. Obviously, he must know what to look for and how to look for it. He must be able to realize the subtlety of behavior in varying situations and to discriminate the relevant from the irrelevant. The most reliable judgments are made when the same behavior is noted by more than one investigator.

The validity of developmental scales is dependent upon the knowledge and skill of the observers plus the mode and coverage of the area of investigation. Some of the scales that have been evolved have served as guidelines in watching growth and development. Most notable is the expansive work of Gesell and his associates who charted the behavioral characteristics of infancy, early childhood, school-age children, and adolescence. The prefaces of their publications usually state that information relative to age levels is designed to serve as a guideline of expectations rather than to set any standard of behavior for a particular age.

Scales have also been designed to be utilized as standardized measuring instruments of behavior as well. A prominent device of this type is the Vineland Social Maturity Scale, which samples many areas of behavior. This scale, when administered according to instructions, will yield a social quotient and a social age. Another example is the Valett Developmental Survey of Basic Learning Abilities. Items on this instrument were drawn from various sources and compiled to form a comprehensive type of device for evaluating children's competence. A composite such as this includes items from other scales or tests. The selection of items from other sources allows the tester to look at the reliability of many entries. In summary, scales have been constructed to serve as guidelines or instruments for the evaluation of behavior. Items are selected on the basis of their validity in representing typical behavior at specific age levels. Again, scales are of value as part of a test battery or in the instance where no standardized testing is possible.

## Use of Motor Scales

Infancy is the period of life when an investigator is restricted in the use of measurements. The prominent characteristics of the period are rapid growth and the acquisition of sensory-motor skills. The early research of Mary Shirley and Nancy Bayley on motor performance during infancy and early childhood provided needed evaluative methods. When scales are applied, the state of development of the child gives an indication of the integrity of his biological system. Any mother watches for the advent of a new skill whether it is sitting up or handling a spoon. In much the same manner, the teacher or specialist can make observations on the basis of scaled behavior to estimate the level of operation of a particular child.

The Bayley and Shirley scales, or a composite, such as the Developmental Scale of Motor Abilities, provide the teacher or specialist with a checklist of expected behavior. Anyone can use a scale, but its validity depends on the teacher's or the specialist's capabilities in observing particular forms of behavior. This capability stems from knowledge of child development and simple experience in observing children. The best way to gain experience is to indulge in child watching. Watch children, at school, on the playground, or wherever you come across them. Watch what they do and precisely how they do what they do.

The intelligent use of a motor scale also requires that the user have knowledge of the basic pattern of growth and development. Growth occurs in a cephalocaudal direction, that is, from head to toe. One just does not see a child with control of the trunk and extremities of the body before he has established control of the head and neck muscles. This is obvious in the case of cerebral palsied children. One does not expect to teach a child to sit up or to work with a pattern for sitting up until he has gained head and neck control.

It takes both experience and instruction for a teacher to be able to differentiate between the grasp reflex of early infancy, the palmar grasp used during the second six months of life, and the refined grasp that children eventually acquire. The infant at twelve months may be adept in picking up objects, while close observation reveals his release to be difficult—or a voluntary kind of dropping action. The two skills are developed under different mechanisms and are not acquired simultaneously.

Intelligent use of scales can aid in determining a child's "motor age." More important, however, is the fact that scales provide information about previously acquired skills and indicate the directions that development will follow in the future.

Children who may be slow in other aspects may attain a degree of motor proficiency. Although slower rates of development or fixations in some stages may be noted among retardates, these children generally achieve motor skills unless physical handicaps, such as cerebral palsy, accompany the condition of retardation. In the case of deviate development the tester should note both the level of operation and the rate of growth through the stages.

A child's level of operation motorically does not necessarily imply a comparable level of development in other areas. Adaptive, social, or language development may follow their own courses. However, there are relationships among these areas. As the organism grows, motor functions and adaptive skills, for instance, interact for more elaborate accomplishments. Cutting with scissors is an example. The user of scales must be able to discriminate purposeful cutting from the more primitive motoric activity of simple straight-line cutting.

In summary, it should be remembered that motor control is the important characteristic of infancy and early childhood and that its progress occurs in sequential fashion. The relation of motor capabilities to other forms of behavior is not direct.

## Use of Language Scales

Scales of language development, such as the composite Developmental Scale of Language Acquisition, will be discussed in Chapter 3. There are tests for language on the market, but these usually miss the subtleties found in spontaneous speech because of the difficulties encountered in constructing devices for testing productive speech. Scaled language behavior as observed in subjects provides the user with guidelines for what to expect at certain age levels.

Again, children show considerable variability in the time at which they acquire language, but the milestones of acquisition or sequence of occurrence of speech behavior are the same from child to child. The user must be familiar with the theory and research of language development before application of any scale. The outstanding works of Brown (1965) and his associates, of McNeill (1966), of Lenneberg (1965), and others should be familiar.

The neurological mechanisms in the emergence of language are not obvious from the use of scales. Observations of child linguistic behavior reveal that most children go through various stages of babbling during the first year of life. Whether or not this type of vocal activity is necessary for the appearance of language is debatable. What is obvious, however, is that most children do travel through a "prelinguistic" stage of vocal play that is typically characteristic of infantile behavior.

One basic requirement for language, the breath group, is established during early infancy. Investigators have found that the infant's cry has a pressure waveform similar to that of adult utterance. The infant cry, very early in life, is produced within the rudimentary limits of adult phrasing of speech. This basic feature is lacking in the so-called cat cries of severely demented individuals.

Interest in prelinguistic activity during the first year also stems from the diagnosis of the hard of hearing and of the deaf. These children cease babbling during infancy, if they babble at all. Scales designate the age of six months as the time when the hard of hearing become quiet infants or discontinue vocal play. Such observations should lead to further evaluation of the hearing function.

Parents are generally aware that their year-old infants "understand" certain aspects of speech before they produce them. They also "hear" their year-old use words meaningfully. Scales generally record the advent of first words between the twelfth and eighteenth months. The use of the scale alone cannot determine if the infant's use of words is holophrastic. The observer must note if the child's intonation pattern, in the situation in which the word is used, brings about an appropriate change in meaning. This is the first essential of a grammatical system.

Scales predict not the actual words used by a child but the patterns of acquisition. After the single-word stage—for the precocious child as early as eighteen months—he may begin to construct two- or three-word phrases. At this time, he is operating on the basis of a set of linguistic rules. These are not the rules of English grammar, of course, but structured from his own primitive grammar, which will ultimately evolve into the adult language. The user of the scale who observes the young child producing word sequences must determine if the phrase is one created by the child or is simply an imitated utterance. This point is crucial in evaluating the mental retardate's speech, for his responses may be imitative or learned responses rather than creative language.

Children work on all levels of speech at once. The phonological system subdivides and expands while the transformational rules of grammar are acquired. A two-and-one-half-year-old child may be difficult to understand because of his limited speech sound repertoire and the sentence structure he uses at this stage. A four-year-old who may be using the grammar appropriate to his age but the phonological system of a three-year-old will be more difficult to understand by virtue of the increased complexity of his language. A mentally retarded child who may be using the phonological system of a four-year-old but the grammatical system of a three-year-old may be more easily understood but is capable of doing less with his expressive language. Also, scales generally report the number of words per utterance as a language measure. This item gives little linguistic information on what the child is actually doing with his language.

"Errors" typically reveal a child's level of acquisition. The utterance of *man's* for *men* or *catched* for *caught* is characteristic of four-year-old children. Such errors tell the observer that the child knows the rules for plurality and tense and is simply applying his rules to all cases. Some slowly developing children may be unaware of the aspects of plurality or tense or may persist in regularizing rules for a prolonged period of time.

In summary, the use of scales gives information about particular areas of development as well as contributing to the overall characteristics of behavior. The relation among language, motor proficiency, and intelligence is not clear. One is not dependent upon another directly but certainly there are some basic connections. For instance, some minimal intelligence must be present before language can be acquired. Some slow learners may superficially have more language than the more intellectually endowed child. In such instances, the quality or creativity of language should be considered. Or a possibility is that the endowed child may indeed have a language deficit. If little variability is observed in the depressed scores of several measures, then the slow child is probably operating at his appropriate level linguistically.

Motor ability should not be confused with problems in language unless the child has a motor problem in the production of the sounds of speech. Another interaction at the gross level is indicated by the fact that it is a rarity to observe speech in one who has not developed head control. This lack of control is indicative of gross damage.

If progress is lacking in one particular area, steps may be taken to teach the child the next acquisition to be expected. In severe cases, physical therapy upon medical recommendation may be appropriate for the motorically or physically handicapped. For the less involved, suggested activites—for example, those in *Understanding and Teaching the Dependent Retarded Child* by Rosenzweig and Long (1960)—may be carried out. For the linguistically delayed child, a program of speech and language therapy should be organized.

# References

Brown, Roger. *Social Psychology.* New York: The Free Press, 1965.

Doll, E. A. *Vineland Social Maturity Scale.* Beverly Hills, Calif.: Western Psychological Services, 1965.

Lenneberg, E. *The Biological Foundations of Language.* New York: John Wiley and Sons, 1965.

McNeill, D. "Developmental Psycholinguistics." In *The Genesis of Language,* G. Miller and F. Smith, eds. Cambridge, Mass.: MIT Press, 1966.

Rosenzweig, L.E., and Long, J. *Understanding and Teaching the Dependent Retarded Child.* Darien, Conn.: The Educational Publishing Corp., 1960.

Valett, R. *Valett Developmental Survey of Basic Learning Abilities.* Palo Alto, Calif.: Consulting Psychologists Press, 1966.

# 2

## DEVELOPMENTAL SCALE OF MOTOR ABILITIES

## Joann Fokes

Defective muscular coordination is one of the commonest abnormalities of the mentally retarded (Tredgold, 1937). Yet the area of physical development, both motor and muscular, frequently is neglected by parents and teachers of the moderately retarded although it is possible to base training programs on evaluation achieved through use of currently available motor development scales. Justification for inclusion of this area in remedial efforts is found in the fact that a major area of child development is growth in motor ability. The first years of life are concerned with the elaboration of movement and motor skills which are based on native reactions of an intact organism. This elaboration is dependent upon the neuromuscular level of development and maturation of the biological system. The rate of improvement may be dependent upon the organism's capacity to cope with or anticipate the demands of his environment as well as his internal needs. Perhaps the element of practice may be added to the development of motor proficiency.

The infant enters the world with a certain amount of motor endowment. Reflexive behavior, which is also seen in the fetal period, is dominant in the neonate. Common reflex activity includes swallowing, sucking, coughing, vomiting, the Babinski,

Moro, and pupil-contraction reflexes. The newborn also makes generalized responses to internal and external stimuli, such as arm and leg flexion and extension, trunk movements, shuddering, shivering, trembling, and body jerks.

After their initiation at a primitive level, skills and precise movements are acquired. Overall developmental trends in motor ability can be traced in a systematic and sequential fashion, although progress, particularly in the moderately retarded, is not always smooth and orderly. Growth is observed to be unidirectional, or in the cephalocaudal direction. This directionality can be seen dramatically in the young infant; head control is attained before trunk control is established and the use of upper extremities is gained before that of the lower extremities. In another sense, motor responses develop in a proximodistal direction. That is, growth occurs from a central to a distal segment. Thus, the very young child can be seen trying to catch a ball by using his arms while his superior in age will manipulate his hands and arms to grasp the ball. Initially, movements are awkward and miss their target. While early responses are of a gross nature and involve excessive bodily movements, practice and maturation lead to precision until only the appropriate muscles are involved. Skills may be of a static or dynamic nature.

Progress leads to more mature behavior and more complex interconnections. Skills which develop concurrently may require adjustments from different parts of the organism to carry out the activity. Some skills may remain constant while others mature. A child may revert to an earlier form of behavior without having lost any of his previous skill. At each age level, certain progressions occur through a spiral effect, but they are always based upon previous development.

Considerable research and observation have been directed toward discovering motor behavior characteristic of children at different age levels. The findings indicate the average age at which certain activities were found to occur and thus may be used to project the expected age of mastery. Because children vary a great deal in their motor accomplishments and still remain within the limits of normal development, it is sometimes dangerous to specify an age for a particular motor acquisition. With the understanding that children do follow certain developmental trends, a scale of motor development is useful in providing a guide in the study of child behavior. Such a scale also gives evidence of the directionality of development and of the interweaving of movements and skills as more mature activities are acquired. It is within this framework that the following scale of motor development is presented.

## Birth to Six Weeks

Height: 20 in.
Weight: 7½ lbs.

I. Characteristics of the Period
  A. Behavior at a physiological level
    1. Reflexive behavior dominant—sucking, swallowing, coughing, grasp, Babinski, Moro, tonic neck reflex (Gesell, 1940)
    2. Period of disequilibrium
      a. Little muscle control—fluctuant tonus
      b. Irregular breathing and heart rate
      c. Period of stabilization of body temperature
  B. Generalized response to internal and external stimuli (Ilg and Ames, 1960)
II. Head and Trunk Posture
  A. Lifting of head and chin when prone (Jersild, 1954; and Shirley, 1933)
  B. Head erect but with bobbing motion when held in a sitting position (Covert, 1964)
  C. Head turned to preferred side (Gesell, 1940)

   D. Uniformly rounded back (Gesell, 1940)

   E. Squirming, twisting, and arching of back (Gesell, 1954)

III. Upper Extremities

   A. Reflexive grasping (Gesell, 1940)

   B. Ring retained when placed in hand (Halverson, 1933)

   C. Fisted hands (Watson and Lowrey, 1952)

   D. Flexion and extension of arms (Gesell, 1954)

IV. Lower Extremities

   A. Reflexive creeping motions (Gesell, 1954)

   B. Extension of legs (Gesell, 1954)

   C. Unilateral flexion of knee (Gesell, 1954)

   D. Leg thrusts at play (Shirley, 1933)

V. Perceptual-Motor Development

   A. Ocular pursuit (Gesell, 1954; Shirley, 1933)

   B. Brief glance at mother (Gesell, 1940)

   C. Control of oculomotor muscles (Bayley, 1935; Gesell, 1940)

## Six Weeks to Three Months

Height: 22 in.
Weight: 10 lbs.

  I. Characteristics of the Period

   A. Continued period of disequilibrium

   B. Less fluctuant muscle tonus

   C. Regular breathing and heart rate (Ilg and Ames, 1960)

 II. Head and Trunk Posture

   A. Head erect (Ilg and Ames, 1960)

   B. Chest held up when in prone position (Jersild, 1954)

   C. Turns from side to side (Van Riper, 1963)

   D. Preferred position maintained (Ilg and Ames, 1960)

III. Upper Extremities

A. Disappearance of tonic neck reflex for symmetry (Gesell, 1954)
B. Vertical arm thrusts in random play when lying in dorsal position (Jersild, 1954)
C. First directed arm movements in response to objects (Gesell, 1940)
  1. Reaches for dangling objects in awkward fashion
  2. Reaches and touches from lying or sitting position (Ilg and Ames, 1960)
D. Plays with hands (Shirley, 1933)
E. Pulls at other's clothing (Gesell, 1940)
IV. Lower Extremities
A. Extended legs and alternate kicking (Gesell, 1954)
B. Crawling-like movements when prone (Van Riper, 1963)
C. Supports a fraction of his weight when held erect (Gesell, 1954)
V. Perceptual-Motor Development
A. Eye fixation (Ilg and Ames, 1960)
  1. Holds rattle and glances at it (Gesell, 1940)
  2. Changes activity and makes mouthing movements when presented with bottle (Covert, 1964)
B. Ocular pursuit for as much as 180 degrees (Shirley, 1933)
C. Hand to mouth (Gesell, 1940)

## Three Months to Six Months

Height: 24 in.
Weight: 14 lbs.

I. Characteristics of the Period
A. Improves in motor coordination (Ilg and Ames, 1960)
B. Likes to be held or propped up to view world (Ilg and Ames, 1960)
C. Is more alert and playful (Ilg and Ames, 1960)

II. Head and Trunk Posture
  A. Complete head control (Shirley, 1933)
    1. Rotates head (Gesell, 1940)
    2. Holds head erect when in sitting position (Ilg and Ames, 1960)
    3. Holds head erect as he leans over when supported (Gesell, 1940)
  B. Curvature of back restricted to lumbar region (Gesell, 1940)
    1. Sits with minimal support (Bayley, 1935)
    2. Lifts abdomen from floor (Ilg and Ames, 1960)
    3. Rolls from supine to side or to prone position (Bayley, 1935; Shirley, 1933)
    4. Tenses for lifting, when on back (Ilg and Ames, 1960)
III. Upper Extremities
  A. Increased arm activity (Gesell, 1954)
    1. Both bilateral and unilateral reaching for dangling objects (Gesell, 1954)
    2. Stretching of arms
      a. Slow and awkward
      b. Involvement of elbow and shoulder action (Halverson, 1933)
    3. Elevation of self by arms when prone (Shirley, 1933)
    4. Supports self on extended arms (Gesell, 1940)
    5. Extends arms to mother (Watson and Lowrey, 1952)
  B. Ability to grasp through crude palming movement (Gesell, 1940)
    1. Grasp reflex disappears (Shirley, 1933)
    2. Simultaneous flexion and thumb opposition (Shirley, 1933)
    3. Retains object when lying (Shirley, 1933)
    4. Touches and squeezes with firm hold (Halverson, 1933)
  C. Releases against resistance or drops (Jersild, 1954)

IV. Lower extremities
- A. Momentarily supports large part of weight (Gesell, 1940)
  1. Holds knees straight (Gesell, 1940)
  2. Lifts legs an inch or two (Gesell, 1940)
  3. Makes dancing and bouncing movements when head is in upright position (Gesell, 1940)
- B. Extends and lifts legs symmetrically when in supine position (Gesell, 1954)
- C. Arms and legs flex symmetrically when abdomen is lifted (Gesell, 1954)

V. Perceptual-Motor Development
- A. Ocular pursuit in a sitting position (Covert, 1964)
- B. Reaching for dangling objects (Shirley, 1933)
- C. Place object in mouth and chew (Shirley, 1933)

## Six Months to Nine Months

Height: 26 in.
Weight: 17 lbs.

I. Characteristics of the Period
- A. Maturity in previous activities
- B. Period of learning new skills (Ilg and Ames, 1960)

II. Head and Trunk Posture
- A. Sits alone without support (Ilg and Ames, 1960)
- B. Leans forward from a sitting position without losing balance (Ilg and Ames, 1960)
- C. Rights self when leaning forward (Gesell, 1940)
- D. Maintains balance when turning from side to side (Gesell, 1940)
- E. Sits ten minutes or more (Gesell, 1940)

III. Upper Extremities
- A. Props self up on one arm flexed, when in prone position (Gesell, 1940)

B. Has independent use of hands
1. May hold object in one hand and reach with another (Gesell, 1940)
2. May move arms in unison (Gesell, 1940)
3. May reach unilaterally (Jersild, 1954)
C. Grasps objects crudely (Jersild, 1954)
1. Radial palmar grasp (Jersild, 1954)
2. Complete thumb opposition (Jersild, 1954)
3. Partial finger prehension (Jersild, 1954)
4. Forearm and hand extended in straight line (Jersild, 1954)
5. Fingers object (Ilg and Ames, 1960)
6. Pats object (Gesell, 1940)
7. Transfers object from hand to hand (Shirley, 1933)
8. Picks up object if dropped (Bayley, 1935)
D. Rotates wrist in manipulation of object (Jersild, 1954)
E. Plays with toes (Shirley, 1933)
F. Drops for release (Gesell, 1940)
IV. Lower Extremities
A. Stands with support (Shirley, 1933)
1. Stepping movements when held upright (Bayley, 1935)
2. Bouncing movements when held in standing position (Ilg and Ames, 1960)
3. Stiffening of knees and extension of legs at hips for standing (Gesell, 1940)
4. Pulls to knees for standing position (Gesell, 1940)
B. Begins to crawl (Gesell, 1954)
1. Creeps on stomach (Gesell, 1940)
2. Knee push and swim (Jersild, 1954)
3. Draws up knees into crawling position (Gesell, 1940)
4. Makes rocking motion
5. Pivots by alternately flexing and extending arms and legs (Gesell, 1940)
6. Creeps backward (Gesell, 1940)

V. Perceptual-Motor Development
   A. Manipulates string of dangling rings (Gesell, 1940)
   B. Holds bottle to drink (Gesell, 1940)

## Nine Months to Twelve Months

Height: 27 in.
Weight: 19 lbs.

I. Characteristics of the Period
   A. Equilibrium in posture (Ilg and Ames, 1960)
   B. More aware of world about him (Ilg and Ames, 1960)
II. Head and Trunk Posture
   A. Sits indefinitely (Gesell, 1940)
   B. Changes from sitting to prone position (Ilg and Ames, 1960)
   C. Does not tolerate the supine position (Gesell, 1941)
III. Upper Extremities
   A. Continuous bilateral reaching (Gesell, 1940)
      1. Little spatial error (Gesell, 1940)
      2. Accompanying digression of trunk (Gesell, 1940)
      3. Extended forearm and hand in straight line (Gesell, 1940)
      4. Reach for more than one object (Gesell, 1940)
   B. More refined grasping (Ilg and Ames, 1960)
      1. Extends index finger and makes radial oblique approach to object and brings pad of thumb to index finger (Gesell, 1940)
      2. Fine prehension with pellet (Jersild, 1954)
      3. Takes tape out of wooden box (Shirley, 1933)
      4. Turns leaves of a magazine (Shirley, 1933)
      5. Holds cup with assistance (Gesell, 1940)

C. Releasing
  1. Difficult (Gesell, 1940)
  2. Drops voluntarily (Gesell, 1940)
D. Precise poking with extended forefinger (Ilg and Ames, 1960)
E. Plays pat-a-cake (Shirley, 1933)
F. Retains ball and attempts to throw or roll it (Gesell, 1940)
IV. Lower Extremities
  A. Crawling
    1. Synchronous movement of arms and legs (Gesell, 1954)
    2. Alternate flexion and extension when arm and leg on opposite sides of the body move (Gesell, 1954)
    3. Approaches bipedal walking (Gesell, 1940)
  B. Stands with support and takes steps (Shirley, 1933)
    1. Pulls up to hands and knees (Gesell, 1940)
    2. Walks when led (Jersild, 1954)
    3. Supports entire weight on sole of foot (Gesell, 1940)
    4. Lowers self from standing to sitting position while holding on for support (Gesell, 1940)
V. Perceptual-Motor Development
  A. Little spatial error in reaching (Gesell, 1940)
  B. Precise poking behavior (Ilg and Ames, 1960)
  C. Manipulation of objects (Gesell, 1940)

## Twelve Months to Eighteen Months

Height: 28 in.
Weight: 20 lbs.

I. Characteristics of the Period
  A. Extremely active with little or no inhibition (Ilg and Ames, 1960)

B. Mobile but unstable (Ilg and Ames, 1960)
C. New scope to daily activities with newfound locomotor activities (Ilg and Ames, 1960)

II. Head and Trunk Posture
   A. Good control (Gesell, 1940)
   B. Good sitting balance (Gesell, 1940)
   C. Instability compensated by elevation of arms (Gesell, 1940)

III. Upper Extremities
   A. Reaching smooth and continuous (Gesell, 1940)
      1. Little or no error in securing object (Gesell, 1940)
      2. Hand ulnar-wardly flexed at wrist (Gesell, 1940)
   B. Grasping with wide open hand (Gesell, 1940)
      1. Grasps and manipulates long, slender object with fingers (Bayley, 1935)
      2. Opens wooden slide box and places tape inside (Shirley, 1933)
   C. Attempts to feed self
      1. Handles spoon (Bayley, 1935)
      2. Uses cup (Ilg and Ames, 1960)
   D. Marks with pencil (Shirley, 1933); rather bang than write (Gesell, 1940)
   E. Throwing—favorite pastime (Ilg and Ames, 1960)
      1. Hurls ball in various manners (Ilg and Ames, 1960)
      2. Poor aim (Ilg and Ames, 1960)
   F. Releasing difficult
      1. Poor aim (Gesell, 1940)
      2. Poor timing (Gesell, 1940)

IV. Lower Extremities
   A. Agile on flat surface (Ilg and Ames, 1960)
      1. Toddles (Gesell, 1940)
      2. Walks without support (Gesell, 1940)

    3. Walks sideways or backwards (Jersild, 1954)
    4. Walks and pulls toy (Covert, 1964)
    5. Pushes chair while walking (Gesell, 1940)
    6. Cannot turn easily (Gesell, 1940)
    7. Moves from sitting to walking (Gesell, 1940)
  B. Begins to climb (Ames, 1940); can climb and seat self in chair (Gesell, 1940)
V. Perceptual-Motor
  A. Unscrews jar lid (Shirley, 1933)
  B. Places tape in box (Shirley, 1933)
  C. Stacks two blocks (Covert, 1964)
  D. Throws (Gesell, 1940)
  E. Feeds self (Ilg and Ames, 1960)

## Eighteen Months to Twenty-Four Months

Height: 31 in.
Weight: 26 lbs.

  I. Characteristics of the Period
  A. Motor activity dominant (Strang, 1959)
  B. Unmastered activities demanding of child's attention and interest (Ilg and Ames, 1960)
  C. Unstable balance (Ilg and Ames, 1960)
  D. Needs outlet for boundless energy (Ilg and Ames, 1960)
 II. Head and Trunk Posture—good balance (Gesell, 1940)
III. Upper Extremities
  A. Reaching automatized (Gesell, 1940)
    1. Still awkward and immature (Gesell, 1940)
    2. Use of other hand for balance when reaching (Gesell, 1940)

   B. Grasping with wide-open hand—primitive (Shirley, 1933)
      1. Grasping a chief concern and interest (Gesell, 1940)
      2. Picking up pellets (Gesell, 1940)
      3. Turning key in lock (Shirley, 1933)
      4. Difficulty with small objects (Gesell, 1940)
   C. Exaggerated finger extension in throwing (Gesell, 1940)
      1. Inadequate timing (Gesell, 1940)
      2. Walking before and after casting (Gesell, 1940)
   D. Primitive grasp in writing (Shirley, 1933)
      1. Use of butt end of crayon (Gesell, 1940)
      2. Use of shoulder movement (Gesell, 1940)
      3. Spontaneous activity (Gesell, 1940)
   E. Poor but improved release (Gesell, 1940)
      1. Inadequate timing (Gesell, 1940)
      2. Drops rather than releases (Gesell, 1940)
IV. Lower Extremities
   A. Secure in walking (Gesell, 1940)
      1. Stands with heels together (Gesell, 1940)
      2. Stands on one foot with help (Jersild, 1954)
      3. Walks backward (Jersild, 1954)
      4. Steps before and after throwing (Gesell, 1954)
      5. Walks a 4 cm. board for twelve inches (Gesell, 1954)
      6. Begins to run (Gesell, 1954)
   B. Climbing
      1. Climbs and stands on chair (Gesell, 1954)
      2. Descends from stool ten inches high (Gesell, 1954)
      3. Creeps up flight of six steps (Gesell, 1954)
         a. Descends by creeping or sitting bumps (Gesell, 1954)
         b. Ascends stairs by marking time (Gesell, 1954)
   C. Jumps a distance of twelve inches (Gesell, 1954)
   D. Attempts to kick ball (Gesell, 1954)

V. Perceptual-Motor Development
   A. Builds five-block tower (Shirley, 1933)
   B. Picks up object from floor (Gesell, 1954)
   C. Inserts key in lock (Gesell, 1954)
   D. Puts pellets in bottle (Gesell, 1954)
   E. Nests four boxes (Shirley, 1933)
   F. Marks with pencil (Shirley, 1933)

## Two Years to Three Years

Height: 32 in.
Weight: 28 lbs.

I. Characteristics of the Period
   A. Behavior becoming more mental than motor (Ilg and Ames, 1960)
   B. Enjoyment of activity itself (Strang, 1959)
   C. Perseverative in activity (Ilg and Ames, 1960)
   D. Behavior better organized (Ilg and Ames, 1960)
   E. More confident of self and can turn attention to other things (Ilg and Ames, 1960)
   F. Engages in rhythmic activities (Strang, 1959)
II. Head and trunk posture—secure in balance and movement (Ilg and Ames, 1960)
III. Upper Extremities
   A. Reaching
      1. Without supporting arm (Gesell, 1940)
      2. Without exaggerated twisting of trunk and arm movements (Gesell, 1940)
   B. Grasping
      1. Holds spoon by thumb and radial fingers
      2. Palm upward (Gesell, 1940)

C. Manipulation
 1. Folds paper (Gesell, 1940)
 2. Turns pages (Gesell, 1940)
 3. Pulls off socks (Gesell, 1940)
 4. Finds armholes (Gesell, 1940)
 5. Strings beads (Gesell, 1940)
 6. Turns doorknob (Gesell, 1940)
 7. Holds glass with one hand (Gesell, 1940)
 8. Builds block tower
     a. Six-block tower (Gesell, 1940)
     b. Vision obscured by hand (Gesell, 1940)
D. Throwing—steps and rotates body (Gesell, 1940)
E. Writing
 1. Palmar grip gives way (Gesell, 1940)
 2. Holds crayon with fingers (Gesell and Armatruda, 1941)
 3. Awkward extension of radial fingers to point of writing tool (Gesell, 1940)
 4. Variable pressure (Gesell, 1940)
 5. Circular or vertical strokes (Gesell, 1940)
IV. Lower Extremities
 A. Walking
     1. Stands alone on either foot (Jersild, 1954)
     2. Stands on walking board with both feet (Jersild, 1954)
     3. Stands with heels together when shown (Gesell, 1940)
     4. Walks in the direction of a line (Jersild, 1954)
     5. Walks between parallel lines (Gesell, 1940)
     6. Carries large object while walking (Gesell, 1940)
     7. Walks on tiptoe (Gesell, 1940)
     8. Turns more easily (Gesell, 1940)
     9. Walks backwards three meters (Bayley, 1935)
     10. Runs on toes (Gesell, 1940)

    B. Kicks a ball
    C. Jump
       1. Distance of twelve inches with one foot leading (Gesell, 1940)
       2. Jumps from ground with both feet (Gesell, 1940)
    D. Climbing
       1. Ascends a few steps on alternating feet (Gesell, 1940)
       2. Ascends and descends steps by marking time (Jersild, 1954)
V. Perceptual-Motor Development
    A. Unwraps paper from candy (Gesell, 1940)
    B. Strings beads with needle (Gesell, 1940)
    C. Folds paper when shown (Gesell, 1940)
    D. Turns pages in a book (Gesell, 1940)
    E. Builds a six-block tower (Gesell and Armatruda, 1941)
    F. Draws vertical and circular strokes (Gesell, 1940)
    G. Imitates simple actions of others (Gesell, 1940)

## *Three Years to Four Years*

Height: 38 in.
Weight: 33 lbs.

I. Characteristics of the Period
    A. Increased motor ability
       1. Accomplishes tasks with minimum difficulty (Ilg and Ames, 1960)
       2. Carries through with activities (Ilg and Ames, 1960)
    B. Period of incoordination at three and one half
       1. Stumbling (Ilg and Ames, 1960)
       2. Falling (Ilg and Ames, 1960)
       3. Fear of heights (Ilg and Ames, 1960)

II. Head and Trunk Posture
    A. Shoulders erect (Gesell, 1940)
    B. Abdomen less protruding (Gesell, 1940)
III. Upper Extremities
    A. Reaching
        1. Leans as reaching (Gesell, 1940)
        2. Extends arms (Gesell, 1940)
        3. Twists trunk (Gesell, 1940)
    B. Grasping
        1. Aligns fingers without touching the tabletop (Gesell, 1940)
        2. Picks up small objects (Gesell, 1940)
    C. Manipulation
        1. Unbuttons but cannot button clothing (Gesell, 1940)
        2. Forces and pats form into formboard (Gesell, 1940)
        3. Drives nails, pegs (Strang, 1959)
        4. Uses both hands to steady block tower (Gesell, 1940)
        5. Begins to use scissors (Strang, 1959)
    D. Throwing
        1. Uses shoulders and elbows (Gesell, 1940)
        2. Guides course of ball with fingers (Gesell, 1940)
    E. Writing
        1. Rests shaft at juncture of thumb and index finger (Gesell, 1940)
        2. Extends medius on shaft (Gesell, 1940)
    F. Releasing—free and easy (Gesell, 1940)
IV. Lower Extremities
    A. Uniform walking (Jersild, 1954)
        1. Heel to toe progression (Jersild, 1954)
        2. Walks backward a long distance (Gesell, 1940)
        3. Walks 6 to 8 cm. on walking board in 15 seconds with three errors (Gesell, 1940)

      4. Walks in circular path 4½ feet in diameter (Jersild, 1954)

      5. Tiptoes 3 meters (Jersild, 1954)

      6. Runs easily and smoothly with moderate speed (Gesell, 1940)

   B. Hops up to 7 steps on one foot (Gesell, 1940)

   C. Skips on one foot (Jersild, 1954)

   D. Uses alternate feet in ascending up to three steps (Jersild, 1954)

   E. Erects self from a squatting position (Jersild, 1954)

   F. Rides tricycle (Gesell, 1940)

V. Perceptual-Motor Development

   A. Holds pen between thumb and index finger (Gesell, 1954)

      1. Copies circle (Covert, 1964)

      2. Traces a square (Gesell, 1940)

   B. Uses blunt scissors (Strang, 1959)

   C. Builds tower with 9 to 10 one-inch blocks (Gesell, 1940)

   D. Drives nails into wood (Strang, 1959)

   E. Catches a large ball with arms fully extended (Gesell, 1940)

   F. Pours from a pitcher without spilling (Gesell, 1940)

   G. Care of self

      1. Feeds self without spilling food (Gesell, 1940)

      2. Laces shoes (Gesell, 1940)

      3. Removes clothing (Gesell, 1940)

## *Four Years to Five Years*

Height: 42 in.
Weight: 39 lbs.

I. Characteristics of the Period

   A. Peak of motor activity stage (Strang, 1959)

      1. Motor stunts (Strang, 1959)
      2. Strength (Strang, 1959)
      3. Facility (Gesell, 1940)
      4. Rhythmic activity (Strang, 1959)
   B. "Out of bounds" in nature
      1. Runs, kicks (Gesell, 1940)
      2. Throws things (Gesell, 1940)
      3. Breaks things (Gesell, 1940)
   C. Better control at four and one half (Ilg and Ames, 1960)
      1. Calmer play (Ilg and Ames, 1960)
      2. Perfecting skills (Ilg and Ames, 1960)
      3. Fine motor control (Ilg and Ames, 1960)
      4. A "catching-up" period for some children (Ilg and Ames, 1960)
  II. Head and Trunk Posture—balanced and steady (Gesell, 1940)
 III. Upper Extremities
   A. Reaching
      1. Lacks poise (Gesell, 1940)
      2. Uses arms rather than hands (Gesell, 1940)
   B. Grasping—picks up small objects with thumb and index finger (Gesell, 1940)
   C. Manipulation
      1. Helps mother
         a. Puts toys away (Strang, 1959)
         b. Brushes teeth (Gesell, 1940)
         c. Washes face and hands (Strang, 1959)
         d. Undresses with assistance (Gesell, 1940)
      2. Uses preferred hand in throwing (Gesell, 1940)
         a. Throws forward without regard for height (Gesell, 1940)
         b. Throws overhand (Gesell, 1940)
      3. Catches a large ball, one in three trials (Gesell, 1940)

D. Release
   1. Precision and timing good (Gesell, 1954)
   2. Releases without pressure (Gesell, 1954)
   3. Sufficient opening of hand to allow withdrawal (Gesell, 1954)

IV. Lower Extremities
   A. Walk—steady gait (Gesell, 1940)
      1. Walks and runs long distances (Strang, 1959)
      2. Walks and rotates head (Gesell, 1940)
      3. Walks between parallel lines (Gesell, 1940)
      4. Walks on haunches (Gesell, 1940)
      5. Stops and goes quickly in running (Gesell, 1940)
   B. Balances on toes (Gesell, 1940)
   C. Hops
      1. On toes with both feet off ground seven or eight times (Gesell, 1940)
      2. On one foot seven to nine times (Gesell, 1940)
   D. Descends stairs on alternate feet (Jersild, 1954)
   E. Jumps skillfully (Strang, 1959)
   F. Shifts weight in throwing (Gesell, 1940)
   G. Rides tricycle easily (Gutteridge, 1939)
   H. Slides (Gutteridge, 1939)

V. Perceptual-Motor Development
   A. Small cramped writing (Gesell, 1940)
      1. Finger flexion (Gesell, 1940)
      2. Wrist movement (Gesell, 1940)
      3. Paper held taut with nondominant hand (Gesell, 1940)
      4. Copies circle and square (Gesell, 1940)
      5. Difficulty with diamond (Gesell, 1940)
   B. Folds and creases paper three times when shown (Gesell, 1940)
   C. Laces shoes with difficulty (Gesell, 1940)

D. Begins to button clothing (Gesell, 1940)
E. Touches end of nose with forefinger (Gesell, 1940)
F. Carries water without spilling (Gesell, 1940)

## Five Years to Six Years

Height: 43½ in.
Weight: 42½ lbs.

I. Characteristics of the Period
   A. Peak of motor urge (Strang, 1959)
     1. Dependent upon environment (Strang, 1959)
     2. Purposeful activity (Strang, 1959)
   B. Economy of movement (Gesell, 1940)
     1. Decrease in generalized movement (Strang, 1959)
     2. Facility (Gesell, 1940)
II. Upper Extremities
   A. Continuous movement in reaching and grasping (Gesell, 1940)
   B. Manipulation
     1. Precision in use of tools (Gesell, 1940)
     2. Makes ball of tissue paper (Gesell, 1940)
     3. Puts matches in box (Gesell, 1940)
     4. Throws skillfully at shoulder level (Gesell, 1940)
     5. Catches ball with hands (Gesell, 1940)
   C. Precise release (Gesell, 1940)
III. Lower Extremities
   A. Walks long distance on tiptoe (Gesell, 1940)
   B. Balances on toes for several seconds (Gesell, 1940)
   C. Stands on one foot indefinitely (Gesell, 1940)
   D. Hops more than ten steps on one foot (Bayley, 1935)
   E. Skips on alternating feet (Gutteridge, 1939) to music (Strang, 1959)

   F. Climbs easily (Gutteridge, 1939)

   G. Descends long staircase with alternate feet (Gesell, 1940)

   H. Roller skates and rides bicycle (Strang, 1959)

   I. Kicks ball 8 to 10 feet (Gesell, 1940)

   J. Broad jumps 28 to 30 inches (Gesell, 1940)

IV. Perceptual-Motor Development

   A. Marks with crayon precisely (Gesell, 1940)

      1. Copies circle, square, triangle (Gesell, 1940)

      2. Traces diamond and cross (Gesell, 1940)

      3. Draws within a small area (Gesell, 1940)

   B. Builds block structures (Jersild, 1954)

      1. Uses each hand singly to place blocks (Gesell, 1940)

      2. Aligns blocks (Gesell, 1940)

      3. Does not block vision with hand (Gesell, 1940)

      4. Places two at a time sometimes (Gesell, 1940)

   C. Ties bow knot (Gesell, 1940)

   D. Buttons (Gesell, 1940)

   E. Laces shoes easily (Gesell, 1940)

## Six Years to Seven Years

Height: 46 in.
Weight: 48 lbs.

I. Characteristics of the Period

   A. Expansive age (Ilg and Ames, 1960)

      1. Vigorous and energetic (Ilg and Ames, 1960)

      2. Strong, steady, and speedy (Ilg and Ames, 1960)

   B. Purposeful activity (Strang, 1959)

II. Upper Extremities

   A. Improved in all areas (Strang, 1959)

   B. Makes crude models (Strang, 1959)

    C. Throwing
       1. Uses elbows and wrists (Gesell and Armatruda, 1941)
       2. Guides path of the ball (Gesell and Armatruda, 1941)
    D. Catches tossed ball chest high from a distance of one meter two out of three trials (Gesell and Armatruda, 1941)
III. Lower Extremities
    A. Uses walk, run, jump in strenuous activities (Gesell and Armatruda, 1941)
    B. Stands on each foot alternately with eyes closed (Gesell and Armatruda, 1941)
    C. Hops 50 feet in nine seconds (Gesell and Armatruda, 1941)
    D. Jumping
       1. Jumps up 12 inches and lands on toes (Gesell and Armatruda, 1941)
       2. High jump of 8 inches (Gesell and Armatruda, 1941)
       3. Broad jump of 8 inches (Gesell and Armatruda, 1941)
    E. Kicks soccer ball for 10 to 18 feet (Gesell and Armatruda, 1941)
IV. Perceptual-Motor Development
    A. Writing
       1. Slow and labored
       2. Left-to-right progression
       3. Recognizable figures drawn, but out of proportion (house, tree, man) (Strang, 1959)
    B. Folds square piece of paper three times in 80 seconds (Gesell and Armatruda, 1941)

# References

Ames, L. "The Constancy of Psycho-Motor Tempo in Individual Infants." *Journal of Genetic Psychology*, 1940, pp. 445-450.

Bayley, N. "The Development of Motor Abilities During the First Three Years." *Monograph of Society for Research in Child Development*, 1 (1935): 1-26.

Covert, C. *Mental Retardation*. Chicago: American Medical Association, 1965, pp. 101-103.

Gesell, A. "The Ontogenesis of Infant Behavior." In *Manual of Child Psychology*, edited by L. Carmichael, pp. 335-373. New York: John Wiley and Sons, 1954.

Gesell, A. *The First Five Years of Life*. New York: Harper and Bros., 1940.

Gesell, A., and Armatruda, C. *Developmental Diagnosis*. New York: Harper and Bros., 1941.

Gutteridge, M. "A Study of Motor Achievements in Young Children." *Archives of Psychology* 244 (1939): 5-178.

Halverson, H. M. "The Acquisition of Skill in Infancy." *Journal of Genetic Psychology* 43 (1933): 3-48.

Ilg, F., and Ames, L. *Child Behavior*. New York: Dell Publishing Co., 1960.

Jersild, A. *Child Psychology*. New York: Prentice-Hall, 1954, pp. 147-176.

Shirley, M. "The First Two Years: A Study of 25 Babies." *Institute of Child Welfare Monograph*, Series 7, 2 (1933): 47-72.

Strang, R. *An Introduction to Child Study*. New York: Macmillan Co., 1959, pp. 139-141, 271-274.

Tredgold, A. F. *A Test Book of Mental Deficiency*. 6th ed. Baltimore: William Wood, 1937.

Van Riper, C. *Speech Correction*. Englewood Cliffs, N. J.: Prentice-Hall, 1963.

Watson, E. H., and Lowrey, G. H. *Growth and Development of Children*. Chicago: Year Book Co., 1952, pp. 90-95.

# 3

## DEVELOPMENTAL SCALE OF LANGUAGE ACQUISITION

## Joann Fokes

When the acquisition of language is viewed as a developmental sequence, the monosyllabic utterances which frequently characterize the speech attempts of the school-age moderately retarded will be viewed with understanding rather than dismay. When there is an awareness of the stages of language development through which children progress, the speech attempts of these moderately retarded children generally are found to be appropriate to their level of speech development. If speech training efforts center on progression to the next level rather than trying to effect immediate change from monosyllables to phrases or sentences, then growth may be achieved. To provide appropriate training requires knowledge of the stages that occur in the development of language. With this need in mind a sequence has been devised which draws from a wide variety of studies in language acquisition to provide a sequential scale.

Most children begin to develop language during early childhood and leave this period of life as competent speakers of their particular speech community. Their parents observe them with pride or dismay, depending upon their progress. Parents show that they are cognizant of the characteristic levels of achievement by expecting that their children attain mastery of certain language skills by specified times. Most parents look for signs of progress, but they rarely attempt to teach language in any systematic fashion. Yet normal children do a rather efficient job of acquiring their mother tongue in a relatively short period without special tutoring. One would expect that the human infant is endowed with the ability to make use of certain acoustic signals he hears in his speech environment.

Besides parental observation, empirical studies have provided examples of types of language behavior characteristic of children at different ages. Some denote the advent of specific achievements while others point out patterns of development. These findings make it possible to project the time when most children will attain a certain level of performance. These levels can be ordered to produce a scale of language development. Besides the overview or picture of the pattern of acquisition which it provides the scale might designate expected behavior at certain ages. With this scale of normal language development it becomes possible to determine if an individual's language acquisition is accelerated, normal, or retarded, that is, to locate his language performance and to plan training appropriate for that level.

The initial picture presented is one in which the infant is preoccupied with sound making. Many of his waking hours are spent in this activity. By the fourth quarter of the first year of life, he seems to be experimenting with sound combinations. Some sequences of sound come to specify things in the child's environment. His sound utterance may vary from time to time, but his mother can usually tell what it is that her child is saying. At this point, he has developed a basic phonological system which he uses to utter meaningful words. He continues to indulge in a great deal of practice in which he seeks to imitate adult utterances.

For a time, single-word utterances serve him. These give way to two-word phrases which seem to be fragmented forms bound by the limits of memory span. Inspection of the phrases reveals that they

are not randomly produced but are constructed by the child's design. Through his own discovery, he seems to be operating on the
basis of a set of rules. Oddly, his childlike errors of adult grammar
expose his knowledge of his language.

Structure allows language to take on more meaning. It allows for
concept formation and the development of the semantic system.
This aspect of language is the last to be developed and the least well
understood.

Children vary in their language development timetables. Work
by Brown and Fraser (1964) found one child, "Eve," who was
precocious in her development while another, "Adam," traveled
through similar stages at a later age, and still another, "Sarah,"
(Bellugi, 1965) at yet an older age. Thus, it would be dangerous to
place strict time scales on the emergence of particular happenings.
However, with the realization that language development is systematic, expected behavior can be tentatively scaled by age.

## *Birth to Six Weeks*

I. Characteristics of the Period
   A. Reflexive vocalization
      1. Sounds produced from a column of air expelled from
         lungs and passed through tensed vocal bands (Berry
         and Eisenson, 1956)
      2. Primary purpose of speech mechanism for breathing
         and eating (McCarthy, 1954)
      3. Undifferentiated vocalization—first three weeks
         a. No intent, awareness, meaning or purpose
         b. Total bodily expression in response to stimulus
            (1) No distinguishable response to cold, hunger,
                pain, etc.
            (2) Variety in intensity (Berry and Eisenson, 1956)

(3) Total emotional response (Anderson, 1953)
4. Differentiated vocalization—second three weeks
   a. Vocalization related to stimulus
   b. Muscle pattern sets for different cries (Berry and Eisenson, 1956)

II. Sound Making
  A. Grunts, sighs, gurgles, glottal catch
    1. Similar to swallowing movements
    2. Present in whimpering rather than in crying (Van Riper, 1963)
  B. No sex difference (Irwin, 1952)
  C. Nasalization (Van Riper, 1963)
  D. Average of seven phoneme-like sounds (Irwin, 1952)
    1. Monosyllabic cries
    2. Predominantly front vowel-like sounds
      a. Average of 4.5 distinguishable sounds (Irwin, 1948)
      b. /ae/ most predominant sound (Berry and Eisenson, 1956)
      c. Other sounds: / ɪ ɛ ʌ ʊ / (Irwin, 1948)
    3. Predominantly glottal and velar consonant-like sounds
      a. Average of 2.7 sounds
      b. Predominantly plosive and fricative /h/ sounds (Irwin, 1947)
      c. Other sounds: /k g h / (Irwin, 1947)

III. Intonation
  A. Variety in intensity (Berry and Eisenson, 1956)
  B. Fundamental frequency of infant cry: 556 Hz.* (Fairbanks, 1942)

IV. Meaning
  A. Beginning of crude vocabulary (Berry and Eisenson, 1956)

*Hz.-cycles per second

B. Response to other's voice (McCarthy, 1954)
C. Response of crying when other babies cry (Lewis, 1963)

## *Six Weeks to Three Months*

I. Characteristics of the Period
  A. Beginning of babbling period (Berry and Eisenson, 1956)
    1. Sounds made "for their own sake"
      a. Satisfaction from utterance
      b. Different from comfort sounds
      c. Play with sounds (Lewis, 1963)
    2. Spontaneous production of sounds
      a. Encompass more sounds than spoken by parents
      b. Indicate pleasurable mood (Anderson, 1953)
      c. Self-initiated vocal play (Berry and Eisenson, 1956)
      d. Random production of sounds
        (1) /a/ produced at length
        (2) Most sounds not repeated (Berry and Eisenson, 1956)
      e. Predominantly noncrying sounds (Berry and Eisenson, 1956)
      f. Self-enjoyment from sound making (Berry and Eisenson, 1956)
  B. Sound making still essentially reflexive (Berry and Eisenson, 1956)
II. Sound Making
  A. Coos, gurgles, squeals, sighs of contentment (Berry and Eisenson, 1956)
  B. Monosyllabic utterances (Shirley, 1933)
    1. Combination of consonant- and vowel-like sounds (McCarthy, 1954)
    2. Little repetition (Berry and Eisenson, 1956)

   3. Nasalization of sounds
    a. Vowel-like sounds—displeasure
    b. Consonant-like sounds—pleasure (Berry and Eisenson, 1956)
   C. Average of thirteen to fourteen different sound types (Irwin, 1952)
III. Intonation
  A. Variation in pitch
  B. Variation in loudness (Berry and Eisenson, 1956)
IV. Meaning
  A. Vocalizes for pleasure or displeasure (McCarthy, 1954)
  B. Reacts to sounds made (Berry and Eisenson, 1956)
  C. Smiles at mother's voice (Lewis, 1963)

## *Three Months to Six Months*

I. Characteristics of the Period
  A. Continuation of the babbling period
   1. Associated with pleasure, contentment
   2. Autistic enjoyment (Mowrer, 1952)
   3. Self-imitation
    a. Occurs when child is alone
    b. Disappears when distracted by someone else (Templin, 1957)
   4. No longer reflexive
    a. Source from internal stimulation
    b. Hearing not important (Berry and Eisenson, 1956)
II. Sound Making
  A. Some control over oral region (Irwin, 1952)
  B. Disyllabic utterances (Shirley, 1933)
   1. Consonant-like plus vowel-like sounds (Irwin, 1952)

   2. Average of seventeen different sound types (Irwin,
      1952)
      a. Predominantly vowel-like sounds
         (1) More frequent front and mid sounds
         (2) A few back sounds
         (3) Distinguishable sounds: / ɪ ɛ ʌ ʊ u /
             (Irwin, 1948)
      b. Consonant-like sounds
         (1) Predominantly glottal /h/ and velar sounds
         (2) Appearance of labial sounds (Irwin, 1947 b)
         (3) Appearance of nasals, plosive, and glide types
             (Irwin, 1947 a)
III. Intonation—infant cry of similar pressure waveform much as
     the expiratory form of adult utterances (Lieberman, 1967)
IV. Meaning
    A. Babbling—speech without content (Bullowa, 1967)
       1. Dental and labial sounds expressive of contentment
       2. Velar sounds expressive of distress (Lewis, 1963)
    B. Noises—rudiments of the vocal response (Lewis, 1963)
    C. Systematic response to specific stimuli (Lewis, 1963)
    D. Awareness of human speech (Shirley, 1933)


## Six Months to Nine Months

I. Characteristics of the Period
   A. Lalling stage—repetition of vocal play
      1. Expression of self
      2. Association of hearing with sound production
         a. Ear reflex—circular response involving hearing and
            sound production

  b. Repetition of selected heard sounds

  c. Imitation as incentive for repetition (Berry and Eisenson, 1956)

 B. Accompanying motor responses to vocalizations

  1. Particular sounds accompany motor response (Berry
and Eisenson, 1956)

  2. Arm movements more meaningful than mouth movements (Van Riper, 1963)

 C. Language problems evident at this age through lack of
lalling behavior; the deaf, retarded, aphasic, emotionally
deprived (McCarthy, 1954)

II. Sound Making

 A. Frequent change in syllable repetition (Van Riper, 1963)

 B. Consonant-vowel type combinations reduplicated (Weir,
1966)

 C. Predominantly vowel-like sounds

  1. Front sound 92 percent of the time (Irwin, 1948)

  2. Some back vowels: / v u o / (Weir, 1966)

III. Intonation

 A. Pattern of intonation heard over a number of syllables

 B. Little pitch variation within a single syllable (Weir, 1966)

 C. Expressive intonation

  1. Dominating factor

  2. Discrimination among different patterns of expression
(Lewis, 1963)

   a. Questions or commands

   b. Elicit surprise (Van Riper, 1963)

 D. Use of rhythm in vocal play (Van Riper, 1963)

IV. Meaning

 A. Application of vocalization

  1. For getting attention

  2. For socialization

      a. Support rejections
      b. Express demands (Van Riper, 1963)
    3. Re-creation of sound to replace or recall a pleasurable situation or object (Mowrer, 1952)
  B. Response to human speech by smiling or vocalizing
  C. Distinction between angry and pleasant sounds
  D. Beginning of imitation of parental utterances (Van Riper, 1963)

## Nine Months to Twelve Months

I. Characteristics of the Period
  A. Echolalic stage
    1. Repetition of sounds made by others
      a. Sounds confined to those of native language (Berry and Eisenson, 1956)
      b. Awareness of sound patterns of native language
      c. Fixation of these sounds in vocalization (Anderson, 1953)
    2. Sounds devoid of meaning (Berry and Eisenson, 1956)
    3. Vocally fluent (Lewis, 1963)
  B. Imitation
    1. Perpetuation of sounds that interest him (Weir, 1966)
    2. Rudimentary imitation—speaks on hearing someone else speak (Lewis, 1963)
    3. Regularity in response to particular sounds (Lewis, 1963)
  C. Vocal play
    1. Production of vegetative sounds without demand
    2. Vocalization while playing (Weir, 1966)

II. Sound Making
  A. Consonant-like sounds beginning to exceed vowel-like sounds
    1. Front and mid vowel-like sounds less frequent
      a. Most frequent types: / ɪ ɛ ʌ /
      b. Back sounds appearing (Irwin, 1948)
    2. Glottal and velar sounds frequent
      a. Appearance of postdental and labial types (Irwin, 1947b)
      b. Additional semivowel and fricative types (Irwin, 1947a)
III. Intonation
  A. Discrimination among different patterns of expression (Lewis, 1963)
  B. Development of stress/unstress pattern (Weir, 1966)
  C. Fundamental frequency
    1. 340 Hz. when with father
    2. 390 Hz. when with mother
    3. Higher frequency when crying (Lieberman, 1967)
IV. Meaning
  A. Beginning of single-word stage
    1. First word a crude approximation (McCarthy, 1954)
    2. Babblings shortened into words (Irwin, 1952)
    3. Manipulation of others through sound making (Lewis, 1963)
  B. Understanding of a few words and gestures (Myklebust, 1957)
    1. Listens with selective interest (McCarthy, 1954)
    2. Responds discriminatingly to adult verbalizations (Van Riper, 1963)

## *Twelve Months to Eighteen Months*

I. Characteristics of the Period—true speech
  A. Period of silence between babbling and true speech (Jakobson and Halle, 1956)
  B. Intentional use of speech
    1. First word—accident of vocal play (Berry and Eisenson, 1956)
    2. Approximation of sound through echolalia (Lewis, 1963)
    3. Strengthening of word through repetition (Berry and Eisenson, 1956)
  C. Accompanying motor activity or gestures to aid in understanding and stabilizing speech (Van Riper, 1963)
II. Sound Making—developing of phonological system
  A. Acquisition built on system of contrasts
    1. /pa/ universal syllable (Jakobson and Halle, 1956)
    2. Consonants more frequent than vowels (Irwin, 1952)
      a. Nasal/oral distinction made (Jakobson and Halle, 1956)
      b. Labial/nonlabial contrast (Leopold, 1953-54)
      c. Consonant used in initial position most frequently rather than medial or final (Irwin, 1952)
    3. Vowel system
      1. High/low contrast
      2. Front/back contrast (Weir, 1966)
  B. Monosyllabic or disyllabic words—some onomatopoeic in character *(bow-wow)* (Irwin, 1952)
  C. Girls' achievement greater than that of boys (Irwin, 1952)
III. Intonation
  A. Intonation and pitch dominating over phonetic form (Lewis, 1963)

   B. Marking of sentence boundaries by intonation contours (Weir, 1966)
     1. Referential breath groups as phonetic markers of complete sentences (Lieberman, 1967)
     2. Juncture evident in utterances (Weir, 1963)
   C. Stress pattern: stress/unstress (Weir, 1963)
IV. Grammar
   A. Holophrastic utterances
     1. Single-word utterances
     2. Ambiguous in meaning—broad and diffuse (McNeill, 1966)
     3. Meaning derived from the situation (Berry and Eisenson, 1956)
   B. Parts of speech (adult grammar)
     1. Nouns most common
     2. A few verbs and adjectives (McNeill, 1966)
V. Meaning
   A. Development of vocabulary
     1. One to three words (*bye-bye, no,* etc.) (Lewis, 1963)
     2. Adaptation of child's primary experience to adult form of word (Lewis, 1963)
     3. Words learned through associated actions (Lewis, 1963)
     4. Names objects (Bayley, 1935)
     5. Performative utterance—names what he is doing at the time (Bullowa, 1967)
     6. Begins to apply words to categories (Brown, 1965)
   B. Verbal understanding greater than production (McCarthy, 1954)
     1. Responds to commands (McCarthy, 1954)
     2. No understanding of questions
       a. At times no response (Bellugi, 1965)

b. At times imitation or repetition of question (Bellugi, 1965)

## Eighteen Months to Twenty-four Months

I. Characteristics of the Period
   A. Acquisition of new words
      1. Perception of new experiences
      2. Manipulation of object or activity
      3. Introduction of word by adult (Van Riper, 1963)
   B. Use of echolalia
      1. Used in private (Van Riper, 1963); monologue-type speech (Weir, 1963)
      2. Prolongs sounds
      3. Occurs instantly and unconsciously (Van Riper, 1963)
   C. Use of jargon
      1. Purposeful to child
      2. Provides for fluency (Van Riper, 1963)
   D. Beginning of primitive grammatical system (McNeill, 1966)
   E. Motor activity
      1. Much activity with speech
      2. Overflow in lips, jaw, tongue, eyes, head (Metreaux, 1950)
II. Phonological system
   A. Many variants in child's system
      1. Vowels most changeable (Metreaux, 1950); more front vowels than back (Irwin, 1952)
      2. Instability of voicing feature (Weir, 1963)
      3. Rare use of medial and final consonants (Metreaux, 1950; Irwin, 1947a)

    B. Articulation change under pressure of adult responses (Lewis, 1963)

    C. Periods of practice in perfecting sounds (Weir, 1963)

III. Intonation

    A. Earliest feature acquired (Weir, 1963)

    B. Indication of contrastive elements of stress (Weir, 1966)

        1. Inconsistent use

        2. Overuse of stress on syllables other than correct one (Weir, 1966)

    C. Pitch rise at end of sentence (Metreaux, 1950)

    D. Voice control—unstable

        1. Variation from good modulation to straining

        2. Much experimentation (Metreaux, 1950)

    E. Fluency—frequent repetition of words and syllables—unforced and easily terminated (Metreaux, 1950)

IV. Grammar

    A. Beginning of structure

        1. Two-word sentences—words in juxtaposition (McNeill, 1966)

        2. Telegraphic utterances

            a. Result of limited memory span

            b. Inclusion of informational content of message

            c. Omission of auxiliaries, prepositions, articles, verbs, and inflections (Brown and Fraser, 1964)

        3. Use of nouns, a few verbs, adjectives, and some pronouns of adult categories (McCarthy, 1954)

    B. Average of 1.7 words per utterance (McCarthy, 1954)

V. Meaning

    A. Twenty- to 100-word vocabulary (Irwin, 1952)

        1. Prominence of meaningful words (McCarthy, 1954)

        2. General referents (*cookie* refers to anything similar) (Van Riper, 1963)

3. One fourth of utterances understood by others (Van Riper, 1963)
4. Beginning of substitution of words for physical acts (Lewis, 1963)
    a. Extension of use of words (*pay* for anything that flies)
    b. Rudiment of generalization (*tee* for *cat* as well as *dog*) (Lewis, 1963)
5. Naming of objects in books (Shirley, 1933)
B. Reportive utterances—description of things in environment without accompanying action (Bullowa, 1967)
C. Lower boundary for beginning of semantic system (McNeill, 1966)

## *Two Years to Three Years*

I. Characteristics of the Period
A. Period of preoccupation with sound (Weir, 1966)
B. Rapid increase in language growth
    1. Use of speech for self-assertion, self-awareness, and as safety valve (Van Riper, 1963)
    2. Growth in grammatical capacity
C. Demand of response from others
    1. Demand from adults
    2. Kicks and screams with peers (Metreaux, 1950)
D. Motor activity
    1. Able to speak before he acts
    2. Acts in relation to task at hand (Metreaux, 1950)
II. Phonological system
A. Mastery of two thirds of adult speech sounds (Irwin, 1952)
    1. Vowels—90 percent correct (Irwin, 1948)
    2. Specific pronunciation for most consonants

a. Most correct—plosives
b. Slighting of medial consonants (Irwin, 1952)
c. Overpronunciation of some words—*flonwer* for *flower* (Metreaux, 1950)
B. Distinctive features in production and recall
1. Voicing and nasality best maintained
2. Continuancy and stridency least maintained
3. Sounds differing in one feature (especially continuancy) most difficult (d for ð)
4. Nonperipheral sounds more difficult than peripheral (Menyuk, 1968)

III. Intonation
A. Intonational pattern becoming subordinated to phonetic (Lewis, 1963)
B. Voice—unstable pattern
1. Range from high to low
2. Presence of nasality
3. Straining and forcing (Metreaux, 1950)
C. Fluency—broken rhythm
1. Repetition of sounds, words, phrases
2. Use of starters
3. Echoic of others (Metreaux, 1950)

IV. Grammar
A. Two-word utterances—primitive grammar
1. Selection not random
2. Patterned arrangements in sequential order
3. Missing elements
a. Auxiliaries, articles, determiners, pronouns, prepositions, inflections
b. Small-sized categorical classes
c. Words predictable from context
d. Intermediate words in adult constructions (Brown and Fraser, 1964)

4. Elements retained in imitation of adult
   a. Initial and final words
   b. Reference-making forms
   c. Nonpredictable forms
   d. Words with heavier stress
   e. Expandable classes (Brown, 1964)
5. Development of word classes based on privilege of occurrence (Brown, 1964)
   a. Class distinction into pivot and open word classes
      (1) Pivot—distinct category similar to function words (McNeill, 1966)
          (a) Few members
          (b) Frequent use
          (c) Heterogeneous selection on basis of adult grammar (articles, greetings, adjectives, verbs)
      (2) Open class—similar to nounlike categories
          (a) Many members
          (b) Less frequent use of each member (Brown and Fraser, 1964)
   b. Predictable structure of utterance
      (1) Pivot plus open *(pretty shoe, see mommy)*
      (2) Open plus open *(daddy shoe)*—similar to adult possessive form (McNeill, 1966)

B. Later constructions
   1. Mean word length per utterance is 3.5 words (McCarthy, 1954)
   2. Original pivot class reduced by subdivision
   3. Treatment of demonstrative pronouns and adjectives as unique classes to yield *a that horsie*
   4. Development of hierarchial structure
      a. Structure of noun phrase
      b. Structure of verb phrase

    c. Ultimate combination of noun phrase and verb phrase to form adultlike grammar (McNeill, 1966)

C. Transformations
  1. Stages of negative structure development
    a. *No* or *not* plus primitive structure *(No wash)*
    b. Addition of *can't* and *don't* as vocabulary items contained in primitive structure
    c. Indication of adult rule
      (1) Use of auxiliary in affirmative *(I can see it)*
      (2) Use of auxiliary with *n't (I can't see it)*
    d. Copular *be* optional *(I not big enough)*
    e. Appearance of double negatives *(He never made no trip)* (Bellugi, 1964)
  2. Stages of interrogative structure development
    a. No use of questions or comprehension of question
      (1) No response or inappropriate response
      (2) Imitation of question
    b. Intonational question *(See doggie?)*
    c. Use of interrogative words—*who, what, where*
      (1) Initial word *(How you do it?)*
      (2) *Why not* a single vocabulary item
      (3) Better comprehension of adult questions
    d. Approaching of adult form
      (1) Use of auxiliaries
      (2) Use of interrogative words as replacement for missing element in sentence (Bellugi, 1965)

D. Inflections—latter part of second year
  1. Use of present progressive
  2. Use of present indicative (Miller and Ervin, 1964)

V. Meaning
A. Two-hundred-and-fifty-word vocabulary (Irwin, 1952)
  1. Words still general in content (Metreaux, 1950)

2. Assignment of each referent to a category (McNeill, 1966)
3. Categories learned from actions rather than names of words (Brown, 1965)
4. Children's definitions of words in terms of action
5. Order of learning adverbs—locative, temporal, manner (Miller and Ervin, 1964)
B. Period of compiling a word dictionary in building of semantic system (McNeill, 1966)

## Three Years to Four Years

I. Characteristics of the Period
A. Becomes linguistic adult
1. Acquires adult syntax
2. Is versatile in use of language (McNeill, 1966)
a. To express emotions
b. To manipulate associates
c. To express relations
d. To satisfy needs
e. To seek verification *(What's this?)*
f. To express dependency
g. To entertain self (Templin, 1957)
h. Verbalizes as he acts (Lewis, 1963)
B. Can be controlled by language (Metreaux, 1950)
C. Learns to whisper (Metreaux, 1950)
D. Squeals, sputters, laughs, sighs (Metreaux, 1950)
E. Accompanies speech with tongue protrusion, lip smacking, tongue clicks (Metreaux, 1950)
F. Continues to use echolalia
a. When speech becomes difficult
b. To assimilate associations (Myklebust, 1957)

II. Phonological system
   A. 90 percent of vowels and diphthongs mastered (Templin, 1957)
   B. 60 percent of consonants mastered (Templin, 1957)
      1. By manner of articulation
         a. Nasals—92.5 percent
         b. Plosives—79.1 percent
         c. Fricatives—41.0 percent
      2. By position
         a. Initial sound—70 percent
         b. Medial sound—68 percent
         c. Final sound—52 percent (Templin, 1957)
      3. By mastery of specific sounds—/ p b m w h/ (Poole, 1934)
      4. Inconsistent production (Metreaux, 1950)
   C. Greatest change in articulatory ability
      1. Between 3 to 3.5 years for girls
      2. Between 3.5 to 4 years for boys (Templin, 1957)
III. Intonation
   A. Well patterned (Van Riper, 1963)
   B. Normal loudness and tone
   C. Breathiness
   D. Nasality with soft voice
   E. Faster rate
   F. Fluency
      1. Recurrence of compulsive repetitions
         a. Tonic blocks on initial syllables
         b. Grimacing, puffing
      2. Use of starters (Metreaux, 1950)
IV. Grammar
   A. Mean word length per utterance: four words (Templin, 1957)
   B. Mean number of different words per fifty utterances

      1. 92.5 at three years
      2. 104.8 at three and one half years (Templin, 1957)
  C. Acquisition of adult grammar
      1. Well-formed utterances but not always grammatical (Brown and Fraser, 1964)
      2. 48 percent of utterances grammatically correct (Templin, 1957)
      3. Copular *be* optional (Brown and Fraser, 1964)
      4. Incorporation of rules of grammar
         a. Understand and produce sentences
         b. Has difficulty in repetition because of structure complexity and not because of sentence length (Menyuk, 1963)
  D. Inflectional rules
      1. Use of past tense
         a. Omission (*push* for *pushed*)
         b. Redundancy (*pushted* for *pushed*) (Menyuk, 1963)
      2. Use of present progressive (Bellugi, 1964)
      3. Use of present indicative (Bellugi, 1964)
V. Meaning
  A. 900-word vocabulary (Berry and Eisenson, 1956)
  B. Use of linguistic symbols in dealing with situations (Lewis, 1963)
  C. Use of language in imaginative play (Lewis, 1963)
  D. Self-centered explanations
      a. Egocentric speech
      b. No apprehension of information requirement of others (Piaget, 1960)
  E. Few semantic markers for words (McNeill, 1966)

## Four Years to Five Years

I. Characteristics of the Period

    A. Language a facile tool
      1. Commands giving way to spontaneous speech
      2. Questions other's activity (Metreaux, 1950)
    B. Girls exceed boys in linguistic ability at four and one half years (Templin, 1957)
    C. Motor activity
      1. Tension at a minimum
      2. Overflow in gross activity
      3. Less verbalization with activity (Metreaux, 1950)

II. Phonological system
    A. Consonant production 90 percent correct by four and one half years (Templin, 1957)
      1. Percent of correct scores by manner of articulation
        a. Nasals—95 percent
        b. Plosives—90 percent
        c. Semivowels—85 percent
        d. Fricatives and combinations—60 percent (Templin, 1957)
      2. Percent of correct scores by position
        a. Initial—88 percent
        b. Medial—86 percent
        c. Final—74 percent (Templin, 1957)
      3. Substitution of /w/ for /l/ and /r/ (Metreaux, 1950); example of hierarchical development of distinctive features (Menyuk, 1968)
      4. Additional mastered sounds—/d t n g k ŋ j/ (Poole, 1934) (Templin, [tʃ] 1957)
    B. Production more stable (Metreaux, 1950)

III. Intonation
    A. Imitation of parents' intonation pattern (Metreaux, 1950)
    B. Voice—well modulated and firm (Metreaux, 1950)

  1. Subdued at times

  2. Whining at times (Metreaux, 1950)

 C. Rate—186 words per minute (Metreaux, 1950)

 D. Fewer repetitions

  1. For emphasis at times

  2. Continued blocking and grimacing (Metreaux, 1950)

IV. Grammar

 A. Mean number of words per utterance: 5½ (Templin, 1957)

 B. Mean number of different words per utterance: 2½ (Templin, 1957)

 C. Mean number of different words per fifty utterances:

  1. 120.4 at 4 years

  2. 127.0 at 4½ years (Templin, 1957)

 D. More complicated sentence structure (Anderson, 1953)

 E. Use of rules for forming simple plural, present progressive, and possession when expanded to new words never heard before

  1. Unable to expand /ed/ to new words when final sound is /t/ or /d/ for past tense

  2. Operate on rule: "A voiceless sibilant after a voiced consonant and a voiced sibilant after all other sounds makes a word plural." (Berko, 1958)

  3. Use plural for counting nouns (Bellugi, 1964)

 F. No awareness of separate elements of compound words (Berko, 1958)

V. Meaning

 A. Rapid increase in vocabulary (Berry and Eisenson, 1956)

 B. Speech egocentric in nature (Piaget, 1960)

 C. Use of descriptive types of explanations in word definitions (Feifel, 1950)

 D. Word association studies

  1. Multiple-word responses

2. Excessive number of syntactic responses
3. Excessive number of noun responses (Entwisle, et al., 1964)

## Five Years to Six Years

I. Characteristics of the Period
  A. More sophisticated use of language
  B. More use of language
  C. More comprehensible
  D. Increased speech in social interaction
  E. Less repetition of adults (Brown, 1965)
II. Phonological system
  A. 98 percent of vowel production correct (Templin, 1957)
  B. 88 percent of consonant production correct (Templin, 1957)
    1. Percent of correct production by manner of articulation
      a. Nasals—95 percent
      b. Plosives and semivowels—85 percent
      c. Fricatives—68 percent
      d. Combinations—60 percent (Templin, 1957)
    2. Percent of correct production by position
      a. Initial—90 percent
      b. Medial—84 percent
      c. Final—80 percent (Templin, 1957)
    3. Additional sounds mastered: /f v s z/ (Poole, 1934)
  C. Occasional reversals of sounds (Van Riper, 1963)
III. Intonation
  A. Continued improvement in fluency and phonation
  B. Hesitations, pauses, and slower rate evident in speech requiring explanation rather than description (Levin, 1967)

IV. Grammar
    A. Mean number of words per utterance: 5.7 (Templin, 1957)
    B. Mean number of different words per fifty utterances: 132.4
       (Templin, 1957)
    C. Improved syntax (Van Riper, 1963)
    D. Perfecting of rules for forming inflections
       a. Use of possessive
       b. Use of third person singular (Berko, 1958)
    E. Production and recall of nongrammatical material not different from grammatical (Menyuk, 1965)
V. Meaning
    A. Vocabulary of 2,000 words (McCarthy, 1954)
    B. Word association studies
       1. Percentage of noun responses decreases
       2. More paradigmatic responses to verbs and adjectives (Entwisle, et al., 1964)
       3. Children less able to take advantage of semantic consistency in sentences when shadowing speech than an eight-year-old group (McNeill, 1965)

## *Six Years to Seven and Beyond*

I. Characteristics of the Period
    A. Language more socially oriented (Piaget, 1960)
    B. Language as instrument for growth of individual personality (Lewis, 1963)
    C. Different languages
       1. Of elders
       2. Of peers
       3. Of reading and writing (Lewis, 1963)
II. Phonological System

A. Boys' requirement of additional year for mastery of sounds (Poole, 1934)
B. Six-year-old status
   1. Correct production by manner of articulation
      a. Nasals and plosives—98 percent
      b. Semivowels—92 percent
      c. Fricatives—75 percent
      d. Combinations—65 percent
   2. Correct production by position
      a. Initial—92 percent
      b. Medial—91 percent
      c. Final—90 percent
   3. Additional sounds mastered: /vð ʒ ʃ l/; loss of /s z/ (Poole, 1934)
C. Seven-year-old status
   1. Correct production by manner of articulation
      a. Nasals—99 percent
      b. Plosives—98 percent
      c. Semivowels—95 percent
      d. Fricatives—88 percent
      e. Combinations—70 percent (Templin, 1957)
   2. Correct production by position
      a. Initial—100 percent
      b. Medial—98 percent
      c. Final—100 percent (Templin, 1957)
   3. Additional sounds mastered: /r θ hw/ with recurrence of /s z/ (Poole, 1934); /d/ (Templin, 1957)
D. Eight-year-old status
   1. Correct production by manner of articulation
      a. Nasals—100 percent
      b. Plosives—98 percent
      c. Semivowels—98 percent

           d. Fricatives—98 percent

           e. Combinations—75 percent

      2. Little difference in percentage of correct production by position with the exception of difficulty with fricatives in final position (Templin, 1957)

III. Intonation

    A. Fundamental frequency for seven-year-old boys: 294 Hz; for eight-year-old boys: 297 Hz.

    B. Fundamental frequency for seven-year-old girls: 281 Hz; for eight-year-old girls: 288 Hz.

    C. Upward and downward voice breaks common to all groups (Fairbanks, 1950)

IV. Grammar

    A. Mean number of words per utterance

      1. 6.4 words for six years

      2. 7 words for seven years

      3. 7.7 words for eight years

    B. Mean number of different words per fifty utterances

      1. 147 at six years

      2. 157.7 at seven years

      3. 166.5 at eight years

    C. Grammatical system well established (Slobin, 1966)

      1. Evaluation of passive, negative, and negative passive sentences by six-year-olds

      2. More time required for evaluation of complex structure (Slobin, 1966)

      3. Percentage of correct grammatical utterances

        a. 73.7 by six-year-olds

        b. 76.1 by eight-year-olds (Templin, 1957)

      4. Learning tasks and recall easier with grammatical material than with nongrammatical material (Menyuk, 1965)

  V. Meaning

A. Basic estimated vocabulary
  1. 13,000 words (2,000 spoken) at six years
  2. 21,600 words at seven years
  3. 28,300 words at eight years (Templin, 1957)
B. More discriminate use of vocabulary (Lewis, 1963)
C. Definitions of words
  1. By use or description below six or seven years
  2. By synonym at eight to eleven years
  3. By categorical description or explanation above eleven years (Feifel, 1950)
D. Language taking on idiosyncrasies (Lewis, 1963)
E. Word association studies
  1. Primarily syntagmatic responses at six years (McNeill, 1965)
  2. Decrease in percentage of noun responses from six to eight years (Entwisle, et al., 1964)
  3. Increase in percentage of paradigmatic responses for verbs
F. Continuation in developing of semantic markers in child's word dictionary (McNeill, 1966)

# References

Anderson, V. *Improving the Child's Speech.* New York: Oxford Press, 1953.

Bayley, N. "The Development of Motor Abilities During the First Three Years." *Monograph Society for Research in Child Development* 1 (1935): 1-26.

Bellugi, U. "The Development of Interrogative Structures in Children's Speech." Paper prepared for the First Symposium on the Development of Language Functions. Ann Arbor, Mich., October, 1965.

Bellugi, U. "The Emergence of Inflections and Negation Systems in the

Speech of Two Children." Paper read at The New England Psycholog-
ical Association Conference. Chicopee, Mass., November, 1964.
Berko, J. "The Child's Learning of English Morphology." *Word* 1 (1958):
150-177.
Berry, M., and Eisenson, J. *Speech Disorders.* New York: Appleton-Cen-
tury-Crofts, 1956.
Brown, R., *Social Psychology.* New York: The Free Press, 1965.
Brown, R., and Fraser, C. "The Acquisition of Syntax." *Monograph of
Society for Research in Child Development* 29 (1964): 43-79.
Bullowa, M. "The Onset of Speech." Paper presented at Society for Re-
search in Child Development, March 1967.
Bullowa, M. "The Start of the Language Process." Paper presented at the
Tenth International Congress of Linguists, Bucharest, September,
1967.
Entwisle, D.; Forsyth, D.; and Muuss, R. "The Syntactic-Paradigmatic
Shift in Children's Word Association." *Journal of Verbal Learning
and Verbal Behavior* 3 (1964): 19-29.
Fairbanks, G. "An Acoustical Comparison of Vocal Pitch in Seven- and
Eight-Year-Old Children." *Child Development* 21 (1950): 121-129.
Fairbanks, G. "An Acoustical Study of the Pitch of Infant Hunger Wails."
*Child Development* 13 (1942): 227-232.
Feifel, H., and Lorge, I. "Qualitative Differences in the Vocabulary Re-
sponses of Children." *Journal of Educational Psychology* 41 (1950):
1-18.
Fry, D. "The Development of the Phonological System in the Normal and
the Deaf Child." In *The Genesis of Speech*, edited by F. Smith and G.
Miller, pp. 187-206. Cambridge, Mass.: The M.I.T. Press, 1966.
Irwin, O. "Infant Speech: Consonant Sounds According to Manner of
Articulation." *Journal of Speech Disorders* 12 (1947): 402-404.
Irwin, O. "Infant Speech: Consonant Sounds According to Place of Articu-
lation." *Journal of Speech Disorders* 12 (1947): 397-401.
Irwin, O. "Infant Speech: Development of Vowel Sounds." *Journal of
Speech and Hearing Disorders* 13 (1948): 31-34.
Irwin, O. "Speech Development in the Young Child: II. Some Factors
Related to Speech Development of the Infant and Young Child."
*Journal of Speech and Hearing Disorders* 17 (1952): 269-279.

Jakobson, R., and Halle, M. *Fundamentals of Language.* Gravenhage: Mouton & Co., 1956.

Leopold, W. "Patterning in Children's Language Learning." *Language Learning* 5 (1953-54): 1-14.

Levin, H., Silverman, I., and Ford, B. "Hesitations in Children's Speech During Explanation and Description." *Journal of Verbal Learning and Verbal Behavior* 6 (1967): 560-564.

Lewis, M. *Language, Thought, and Personality in Infancy and Childhood.* London: G.G. Harrap, 1963.

Lieberman, P. *Intonation, Perception, and Language.* Research Monograph No. 38. Cambridge, Mass.: The M.I.T. Press, 1967.

McCarthy, D. "Language Development in Children." In *Manual of Child Psychology,* edited by L. Carmicheal, pp. 492-630. New York: John Wiley & Sons, 1954.

McNeill, D. "Development of the Semantic System." Paper prepared at Center for Cognitive Studies, 1965, at Harvard University.

McNeill, D. "Developmental Psycholinguistics." In *The Genesis of Language,* edited by F. Smith and G. Miller, pp. 15-84. Cambridge, Mass.: The M.I.T. Press, 1966.

Menyuk, P. "A Preliminary Evaluation of Grammatical Capacity in Children." *Journal of Verbal Learning and Verbal Behavior* 2 (1963): 429-439.

Menyuk, P. "Children's Learning and Recall of Grammatical and Nongrammatical Nonsense Syllables." *M.I.T. Quarterly Progress Report* 80 (1965).

Menyuk, P. "The Role of Distinctive Features in Children's Acquisition of Phonology." *Journal of Speech and Hearing Research* 11 (1968): 138-146.

Metreaux, R. "Speech Profiles of the Preschool Child—18 to 54 Months." *Journal of Speech and Hearing Disorders* 15 (1950): 35-53.

Miller, W., and Ervin, S. "The Development of Grammar in Child Language." *Monograph of Society for Research in Child Development* 29 (1964): 9-34.

Mowrer, H. "Speech Development in the Young Child: I. The Autism Theory of Speech Development and Some Clinical Applications." *Journal of Speech and Hearing Disorders* 17 (1952): 263-268.

Myklebust, H. "Babbling and Echolalia in Language Theory." *Journal of Speech and Hearing Disorders* 22 (1957): 356-360.

Piaget, J. *Language and Thought in the Child.* New York: Meridian Books, 1960.

Poole, I. "Genetic Development of Articulation of Consonant Sounds in Speech." *Elementary English Review* 2 (1934): 159-161.

Shirley, M. "The First Two Years: A Study of 25 Babies." *Institute of Child Welfare Monographs,* Series #7, Vol. 2, 1933, pp. 139-141.

Slobin, D. "Grammatical Transformations and Sentence Comprehension in Childhood and Adulthood." *Journal of Verbal Learning and Verbal Behavior* 5 (1966): 219-227.

Templin, M. *Certain Language Skills in Children.* Minneapolis, Minn.: University of Minnesota Press, 1957.

Van Riper, C. *Speech Correction: Principles and Practices.* Englewood, N.J.: Prentice-Hall, 1963.

Weir, R. *Language in the Crib.* The Hague: Mouton and Co., 1963.

Weir, R. "Some Questions on the Child's Learning of Phonology." In *The Genesis of Language,* edited by F. Smith and G. Miller, pp. 153-168. Cambridge, Mass.: The M.I.T. Press, 1966.

# 4

## SOCIAL DEVELOPMENT OF
## THE MENTALLY RETARDED

## Harold A. Delp

Social behavior is a description of the physical and psychological interactions between two or more persons (Thompson, 1962). A generally accepted concept is that *all behavior of individuals is learned.* No matter what our heredity or predispositions to behavior, every act we perform has been learned through interaction with our environment and the persons in it. *Behavior is complex.* Each time a person learns from an experience, it is combined with all past learning into a new type of potential behavior. Social behavior, like all other types of behavior, is the result of learning through interaction with other persons. This behavior at any one time is spoken of as the social maturity level of the person and is indicative of the relative behavior of this person compared to a general population.

Socialization is the process by which a person learns the ways of a given society or social group so that he can function within it (Millard, 1951). Every new baby is born into an environment of ideas, feelings, and beliefs, and related patterns of activities. It is a social-cultural environment (Baller and Charles, 1968). However, at birth the child has no social concerns. His interests and needs are related only to himself and are based on physical factors.

As his physical needs are met by people, he begins to learn social responses. The child's early training changes him from a self-centered to a socially centered being. Thus, for good or bad, the total environment is involved in the social development of each individual.

Mental, physical, and emotional development of the child are closely related to his social development (Crow and Crow, 1962). His mental level influences the interpretations he places on the behavior of others and on their reactions to his behavior. His physical development controls his movement and opportunities for social development. His emotional development controls his responses to others and their responses to him. While there is not an absolute relationship, evidence does indicate a positive correlation between social maturity and the other areas of development, with the highest relationship between mental and social development.

Social development progresses only to the extent to which the child has opportunity to relate with an increasing number of various types of people. That the majority of a child's problems and maladjustments are in the social area is understandable when the variations and complexities of behavior of the persons around the child are observed.

A mentally retarded child may show social competence or incompetence disproportionate to his IQ. Because of their lack of appreciation of subtleties, some children respond inappropriately to communication, consequently finding interpersonal relationships difficult. Others develop little social competence because they remain isolated from normal society; little opportunity is provided to improve their social skills (Covert, 1965). Handicaps in speech or language lead to difficulties in a child's relationships with others; they impede his ability to be tested, to learn, and to communicate.

Doll's (1942) classic definition of mental deficiency places social competence as the first criterion. However, as early as 1917, Doll considered changes in society and its effects on the mentally retarded as he wrote that "a serious limitation of the social criterion is its variability in time and place and to the relative complexity of the social structure" (Doll, 1917). Thus, an individual's social development is dependent on the present social structure and on acquired social learning, skill which enables him to live adequately in that social environment.

Farber (1968) has developed a new philosophy of the social context and consequences of mental retardation, that of social surplus. According to Farber, "in any society there are always persons who cannot be used to fill slots in tables of organization. Frequently, this inability to fill an organizational slot results from the incompetence of the individual" (p. 10). Thus a surplus population is engendered as the mentally retarded join others incapable of filling slots in social organization. Farber regards the mentally retarded as constituting a segment of this surplus population by being labeled as deviants and by their incompetence. As deviants, they are stigmatized and treated differently from others; as incompetents, they generally fail to perform roles adequately in the basic institutions of society.

Various studies (Delp and Lorenz, 1953; Saenger, 1957) have shown that an educational program emphasizing social development adjusted to the needs and levels of trainable retarded children can be effective in improving the performance of these individuals whether in the community or in an institution. Delp (1957) found that social development and adjustment training offer added possibilities for vocational training and for future success in a sheltered workshop or, if possible, in competition employment. Social adjustment, including acceptance of supervision, was found to be critical to performance on almost any job regardless of its location.

The President's Committee on Mental Retardation (1968) indicates that present trends of day care centers are toward more professional programs and away from babysitting. For the preschool programs early diagnosis and education are emphasized. "Preschool classes aim to give the retarded child a running start when his potential for learning is highest. Another goal is to prevent functional retardation. Programs should teach concepts of language and systemic thinking to preschool children who have language difficulties. The aim is to overcome retardation caused by social deprivation" (p. 5).

Social development appears to be a critical element in defining mental retardation, whether one uses the definition of social incompetency directly or whether one subscribes to Farber's social surplus philosophy. In all cases the assessment of the present level of social development of a child is primary in understanding his present status as well as in planning his educational program and in predicting his future place in society. Several scales and devices exist for the assessment of social maturity; eight of these devices and techniques are described below.

## 1. Vineland Social Maturity Scale (VSMS)

Doll developed the VSMS at The Training School at Vineland, New Jersey, as a means of comparing the social development and maturity level of mentally retarded children with others of their own mental level (see Doll, 1947). Intelligence testing had progressed, but Doll felt that an important area of development was omitted. His approach was to devise a scale of social maturity using an organization somewhat similar to Terman's Stanford-Binet; the use of age levels resulted in a Social Age (SA) and a computed Social Quotient (SQ). The VSMS has been criticized because it was standardized on a relatively small number of normal children from one geographic area. Since its original publication, however, it has been used with at least moderate success throughout the country. The scale has been translated into several foreign languages, but these translations are questionable since acceptable social behavior differs radically from one culture to another. Awareness of these cultural differences has prompted several foreign adaptations.

Like most techniques for evaluating social maturity, the VSMS obtains an estimate of the child's social behavior through an interview of a parent or individual in daily contact with the child. Basically, the 117 items of the scale are grouped into age levels from birth to thirty years. A total point system is used to determine the Social Age. The items are grouped into six categories of development: self-help, self-direction, communication, socialization, locomotion, and occupation. The category of self-help has three subdivisions: general, eating, and dressing. A profile for graphing responses was developed and, although not published for distribution, it is used to advantage by many psychologists (See Figure 1).

The VSMS attempts to report overall habitual behavior rather than to give scores based on immediate responses. Scoring procedures indicate positive success or failure and allow half credit for items in transition, as well as provide an evaluation of items for which the child has had "no opportunity" to perform because of special restraint or lack of environmental opportunity. Provision for the "no opportunity" items serves to acknowledge that the mentally retarded child, whether in the home or in an institution, often is in a situation where "normal" development is virtually impossible. A common error in administering the VSMS is to ask a direct question when information on a specific item is sought. In this case the respondent's tendency is to tailor answers favorable to himself. The desired approach is to ask more general questions concerning the social area being evaluated, following up with detailed questions where items are not answered in sufficient detail to permit scoring. The scale is not a rating scale and scores should not be based on mere opinion. The informant is expected to give factual data concerning the child's usual behavior of a particular kind.

Advantages of the VSMS include the use of SA and SQ, terms generally accepted by psychologists and others concerned with children's behavior. Comparisons between MA and SQ have be-

Figure 1
## THE TRAINING SCHOOL AT VINELAND, NEW JERSEY
### DEPARTMENT OF RESEARCH
### PROFILE: VINELAND SOCIAL MATURITY SCALE

Name                Res          Age          SA          SQ          Date

                    Adm          Born         MA          IQ          Exmr

Diagnosis                        Etiology

| Years | SELF-HELP General | Dressing | Eating | Self-Direction | Communi-cation | Social-ization | Loco-motion | Occu-pation |
|---|---|---|---|---|---|---|---|---|
| 25 plus | | | | 112 | | 115-117 109-10 | | 116 111-13-1 106-7-8 |
| 25 to 20 | | | | 102, 105 | | 103-4 | | |
| 20 to 18 | | | | 100-1 97, 99 | | | 96 | 98 |
| 18 to 15 | | | | 93, 94, 95 | 90, 91 | | 92 | |
| 15 to 12 | | 86 | | 87 | | 85, 88 | | 89 |
| 12 to 11 | | | | 83 | 84 | | | 82 |
| 11 to 10 | | | | 81 78, 79 | | | | 80 |

| rs | SELF-HELP | | | Self-Direction | Communi-cation | Social-ization | Loco-motion | Occu-pation |
|----|-----------|---------|--------|----------------|----------------|----------------|-------------|-------------|
|    | General | Dressing | Eating | | | | | |
|    |         |          | 75 | 76 | | 77 | | |
|    |         | 74 |      |    | 73 | | | 71, 72 |
|    | 66 | 70 | 67 | | | 68, 69 | | |
|    |    | 64, 65 | 62 | | 63 | | | |
|    |    |    |    | 60 | 58 | 59 | 61 | 57 |
|    | 51 | 52, 54 | | | | 56 | 53 | 55 |
|    |    | 47, 50 | | | | 46, 49 | 45 | 48 |
|    | 35, 41 | 37, 40, 42 | 38, 39 | | 44 | | | 36, 43 |
|    | 23, 26 | 21 | 30, 33 20, 25, 28 | | 31, 34 | 27 | 18, 29, 32 | 19, 22, 24 |
|    | 15 8, 9, 13 2, 3, 5, 6 | | 11, 16 | | 1, 10, 17 | 4, 14 | 12 | 7 |

BLUE—PASSED                    RED—FAILED

come standard. As with all psychological material, there are those users who place undue statistical meaning on almost any data, and care should be exercised in planning the life of a child on mathematical scores alone.

## 2. Preschool Attainment Record (PAR) (Research Edition)

The Preschool Attainment Record (Doll, 1966) is a refinement and an extension of the VSMS for the first seven years of life. The research edition is organized into three major areas, each with separate categories:

| *Physical* | *Social* | *Intellectual* |
|---|---|---|
| Ambulation | Rapport | Information |
| Manipulation | Communication | Ideation |
| | Responsibility | Creativity |

The rationale was to develop an omnibus type of total evaluation of the child, rather than concentrating on the more limited areas reflected in intelligence tests, the VSMS, and other tests in general use. This technique would permit more adequate evaluation of the child, in spite of clinical handicaps often found in children who were in need of such evaluation. Early deprivations, physical handicaps, or emotional limitations become involved in any evaluation of children and must be recognized as well as included in a total description of the child's ability to respond to his environment.

Like the VSMS, assessment by the PAR is obtained by means of interview and observation. Different from the VSMS, the PAR has one item for each subcategory at each half-year level from 0–.5 to 6.5–7.0 years. This grouping of items modifies the scoring procedure in that each item carries an equivalent age value. Items are presented according to subcategories and a rough age value can be estimated for each. Total raw score is converted into Attainment Age in years by dividing the score by 16 (the number of items at each year level).

The PAR is a standardized omnibus type evaluation useful for children with a variety of handicaps because it measures a child's behavior in given areas. Doll suggests that the PAR be administered and correlated with the VSMS, the VSMS giving gross social maturity data and the PAR being a more intensive and extensive inventory of specific attainments. Because PAR has not been fully standardized as yet, the author suggests its use as a developmental inventory "which is speculatively developmental but not statistically verified." Nonetheless, the PAR, used with discretion, should add information to the assessment of social adjustment and maturity of the mentally retarded.

## 3. Cain-Levine Social Competency Scale

The Cain-Levine Social Competency Scale (Cain, Levine, and Elzey, 1963) is specifically intended to measure the social competency of trainable mentally retarded children. The scale uses the interview method in the assessment of social competence of trainable mentally retarded children. This specific coverage was used since the growth of facilities for trainable retarded children indicated much greater need for instruments which would be useful in school programs, diagnostic services, and habilitation centers for these children.

The Cain-Levine Scale consists of forty-four items divided into four subscales: self-help, initiative, social skills, and communication. Most items are scored on a four-point basis (six items are scored on five points) with level one representing the least independent performance and level four (or five) representing the most independent level. Descriptive behavior for each level of each item is given in the manual as a guide to scoring. For boys, the self-help category requires a score adjustment based on age. Norms were developed from a population of 716 trainable mentally retarded children, ages five through thirteen years. Norm tables cover two-year spans. Tables which provide percentile ranks for each subscale and for the total permit comparison of the child with his age group of trainable mentally retarded children.

Statistically, the scale is limited in that only trainable mentally retarded children from California were used in the standardization. Today, as discussion and practice tend to emphasize early (pre-school) recognition of children with problems, the limited age range also is a disadvantage. Percentile norms, while comfortable for many persons, have the usual weakness inherent in such norms— unequal differences in various parts of the distribution. Particular advantages of the Cain-Levine would seem to include (1) comparisons between subscales for the child, (2) relative variations of sub-scale scores with the child's total score, and (3) an objective measure of changes in behavior over time and between different environments for the same child.

# 4. Social Competence Inventory for Adults

The Social Competence Inventory for Adults (Banham, 1960) has been developed to aid in the assessment of social behavior of adults. Federal and state programs for the mentally retarded involve an evaluation of permanent and total disability of adults in order for them to participate in the advantages of the laws. In other situations involving the necessity of long-range planning for adults, the question of their relative social competence is paramount. The VSMS has been found lacking when used to estimate social maturity in adults and Banham felt the need for a new device.

The inventory is essentially a standardized interview. It consists of fifty-five items divided into four categories: motor skills and control, perception and memory, self-care and self-help, and social relationships and emotional control. These items consist of descriptive statements of behavior or habits of action which may be considered characteristic of a particular adult. Only those items have been included which are essential to some aspect of social competence and self-maintenance.

The author cautions the user that "a rating scale of this kind could never be considered an exact measuring device." Instead, it is intended merely as a means of general classification. Scores are grouped into tentatively meaningful classes, e.g., "50–55 indicates adequate social competence for normal community living," "40–50 indicates fairly adequate social competence," whereas "below 15 may be considered permanent and total disability."

Little is mentioned concerning the standardization; hence, such data cannot be evaluated. However, the State of North Carolina has found value in the use of the inventory for adults. If used in the nonstatistical evaluation of individual adults for relative social competency, the inventory should provide pertinent information.

# 5. Verbal Language Development Scale (VLDS)

Since communication and language are considered essential elements in social maturity measures, such devices as the Verbal Language Development Scale (Mecham, 1958) and Fokes' Developmental Scale of Language Acquisition, presented in Chapter 3, should add to the total information on individual children. The VLDS consists of fifty items of progressive difficulty based on material from the VSMS, the Stanford-Binet, Gesell and Armatruda's Developmental Diagnosis, as well as material from discussions and empirical clinical observations. Four categories of language development are included: listening, speaking, reading, and writing. The scale uses a point system for converting total score to equivalent Language Age. For an estimate of language development of children independent of other social measures, the VLDS or others may at times be useful to the teacher or clinician.

## 6. T.M.R. and Y.E.M.R. Performance Profiles

The T.M.R. Performance Profile for the Severely and Moderately Retarded and the Y.E.M.R. Performance Profile for the Young Moderately and Mildly Retarded (DiNola, Kaminsky, and Sternfeld, 1963, and DiNola, *et al.*, 1967) were developed by classroom teachers to assist them in obtaining information about the behavior of retarded children in the classroom. Although the profiles include certain elements beyond general social development, for the most part they are primarily socially oriented. Even with these added areas they become techniques used by classroom teachers of trainable and young educable retarded children in evaluating each child's present status, areas of strengths and weaknesses, and directions for training emphasis. Both performance profiles were designed to enable the teacher to

1. record observations
2. view these scores in graphic form
3. identify the areas of need and competence
4. adapt curriculum, methods, and materials
5. review periodic changes and developments
6. maintain a cumulative record

Each profile is an evaluation scale based on teacher observation and is intended to identify performance levels of the pupil in a wide variety of daily tasks in the curriculum. They were also designed, not for classification purposes, but for evaluation which should lead to training and retraining programs. Hence, no norms are involved in the profile technique. The child is assessed on each item on the basis of his actual level of performance rather than on an age comparison. The item score range on the T.M.R. is from 0 to 4 while it is 0 to 6 on the Y.E.M.R. In each profile a score of 0 indicates no performance on the item, an intermediate score (3 on the T.M.R. and 4 on the Y.E.M.R.) indicates acceptable performance on the item, while the top scores on each scale indicate highly desirable performance above the expected goal.

While both profiles are similar in construction, some variations were made in the development of the Y.E.M.R. based on experience with the first profile, the T.M.R. The T.M.R. Profile is organized on the "six major areas most frequently referred to in curriculum guides for the severely and moderately retarded":

1. Social Behavior
   A. Self-control
   B. Personality
   C. Group participation
   D. Social amenities
3. Communication
   A. Modes of communication
   B. Listening
   C. Language activities
   D. Language skills
5. Practical Skills
   A. Tools
   B. Household items
   C. Family chores
   D. Vocational readiness

2. Self-Care
   A. Bathroom and grooming
   B. Dealing with food
   C. Clothing
   D. Safety
4. Basic Knowledge
   A. Information
   B. Numbers
   C. Awareness
   D. Social studies
6. Body Usage
   A. Coordination
   B. Health habits
   C. Fitness
   D. Eye-hand coordination

Each of the lettered subdivisions has ten specific items to be scored. Descriptions of sample behavior for each score (0–4) are presented in the manual. Two types of profiles are obtained: (1) the profiles of each major area based on its four subdivisions, and (2) the profile of overall performance level based on the six major area totals.

The Y.E.M.R. Profile was modified so that there are ten major areas "based on the developmental abilities necessary for growth and adjustment of the young mentally retarded child to his social and intellectual environment before and after he enters the public school program." The major areas are:

1. Social Behavior
2. Self-Help
3. Safety
4. Communication
5. Motor Skills
6. Manipulative Skills
7. Perceptual & Intellectual Development
8. Academics
9. Imagination & Creative Expression
10. Emotional Behavior

Each of the ten major areas is subdivided into ten related topics, each in turn scored on a 0–6 basis. With the increase of the major areas from six to ten, the Y.E.M.R. gives only one profile, the total based on the major area divisions.

While the profiles do not have norms in the usual sense, each child is scored on an "expected" score basis. This permits a comparison of the child's performance on each item with the level of acceptable behavior for that item, as well as on the total score. Strong and weak areas are immediately noticed on the profiles. An additional score is available, the Habile Index. This score is merely another method of comparing the child's total score with the general acceptable goal level in an index form.

The T.M.R. and Y.E.M.R. are not intended as measures of social maturity but, rather, as means of comparing the child's behavior in various areas, including those involving social development, with an acceptable criterion for each item. As such, the profiles offer the teacher a means of adjusting social development training so that one can improve the competence of each child to participate more adequately in everyday life both now and in the future. Areas of weakness in social behavior, as well as in the other areas of the profiles, should prompt the modification of curricular experiences to accomplish improvement in these areas. Areas of strengths might be used as a basis for assistance in the weak areas.

## 7. Progress Assessment Charts (P-A-C)

The Progress Assessment Charts by Gunzburg (1964) were developed in England as a method to be used by teachers for regular assessment of trainable retarded children. There are two forms: Form I for the junior stages in the education and training of the trainable child, and Form II for the senior stages. The charts involve social education, to differentiate from the academic education of normal children. Social education is defined as "helping the mentally handicapped to develop those skills and to obtain that knowledge which will help him to live as happily and as socially competently as possible as a child and later on as an adult."

The social education approach places a premium on activities which contribute significantly to improved social functioning. The P-A-C ignores subjects or areas not related to social education. The inventory of the P-A-C consists of one hundred items, each of which is contained in one or another well-known and standardized psychometric assessment procedures. These procedures include the VSMS, the Stanford-Binet, and the Oseretsky Motor Development scales.

The primary purpose of the inventory is to draw attention to particular weak and underdeveloped social skills. Therefore, no attempt is made in the P-A-C to score and add items or to derive total scores, ages, or quotients.

The visual summary of the P-A-C charts is a system of concentric circles with lower-level items toward the center and the most advanced items in the outer circle. The circles are also divided into four quadrants for the major areas of activites: self-help, communication, socialization, and occupation.

As is obvious, the P-A-C is not a test or measure of social maturity or social development per se. Rather, the charts appear to be most useful for the purpose for which they were designed: to assess the child's situation and to check the effect of remedial measures taken in social education.

## 8. Ottawa School Behavior Check List (OSBCL)

The Ottawa School Behavior Check List (Pimm and McClure, 1963) was developed as a teacher observation method of screening children with behavior problems. Since behavior of children is usually considered in a social context, this checklist is also included. It may prove valuable in the social assessment of mentally retarded children, many of whom have behavior problems.

The OSBCL has two purposes: "(a) to provide an objective, reliable, and economic method of studying school behavior in large populations and (b) to function as a screening device for children with potential school behavior problems." Because of its screening function this checklist is suggested. The list consists of one hundred items designed empirically from teachers' descriptions of a child with behavior problems. Each of the items of behavior listed is considered inappropriate or unacceptable behavior. Factor analytic studies have shown four basic factors: verbal overactivity, immaturity, conduct problem, and personality. These factors would seem to have definite relationships to the elements usually considered in social behavior and should be of value to those persons, particularly teachers, interested in such behavior reports, even though the checklist has not been developed specifically for retarded children.

# References

### General Growth and Development

Baller, W. R., and Charles, D. C. *The Psychology of Human Growth and Development*. 2nd ed. New York: Holt, Rinehart, and Winston, 1968.

Crow, L. D., and Crow, Alice. *Child Development and Adjustment*. New York: Macmillan, 1962.

Millard, C. V. *Child Growth and Development in the Elementary School Years*. Boston: Heath, 1951.

Thompson, G. G. *Child Psychology*. Boston: Houghton Mifflin, 1962.


### Mental Retardation

Covert, C. *Mental Retardation*. (Monograph reprinted from *Journal of the American Medical Association*, no. 3, 18 January 1965.) Chicago: American Medical Association, 1965.

Delp, H. A. "Criteria for Vocational Training of the Mentally Retarded." *Training School Bulletin* 54 (1957): 14-20.

Delp, H. A., and Lorenz, Marcella. "Follow-up of 84 Public School Special Class Pupils with IQ's Below 50." *American Journal of Mental Deficiency* 58 (1953): 175-182.

Doll, E. A. *Clinical Studies in Feeblemindedness*. Boston: Badger, 1917.

Doll, E. A. "The Essentials of an Inclusive Concept of Mental Deficiency." *American Journal of Mental Deficiency* 47 (1942): 49-57.

Farber, B. *Mental Retardation: Its Social Context and Social Consequences*. Boston: Houghton Mifflin, 1968.

Saenger, G. *The Adjustment of Severely Retarded Adults in the Community*. Albany, N. Y.: New York Interdepartmental Health Resources Board, 1957.

The President's Committee on Mental Retardation. *MR 68: The Edge of Change*. Washington, D.C.: U. S. Government Printing Office, 1968.

Assessment of Social Behavior

Banham, Katherine. *A Social Competence Inventory for Adults.* Durham, N. C.: Family Life Publications, 1960.

Cain, L. F.; Levine, S.; and Elzey, F. F. *Cain-Levine Social Competency Scale.* Palo Alto, Calif.: Consulting Psychologists Press, 1963.

DiNola, A. J.; Kaminsky, B. P.; and Sternfeld, A. E. *T.M.R. Performance Profile for the Severely and Moderately Retarded.* Ridgefield, N. J.: Reporting Service for Exceptional Children, 1963.

DiNola, A. J.; Kaminsky, B. P.; and Sternfeld, A. E. *Y.E.M.R. Performance Profile for Young Moderately and Mildly Retarded.* Ridgefield, N. J.: Reporting Service for Exceptional Children, 1967.

Doll, E. A. *Vineland Social Maturity Scale.* Circle Pines, Minn.: American Guidance Services, 1947 (rev. manual, 1965).

Doll, E. A. *Preschool Attainment Record.* (Research edition.) Circle Pines, Minn.: American Guidance Services, 1966.

Gunzburg, H. C. "A New Method of Charting Social Skills Progress." *Mental Retardation* 2 (1964): 370-373.

Mecham, M. J. *Verbal Language Development Scale.* Circle Pines, Minn.: American Guidance Services, 1958.

Pimm, J. B., and McClure, G. *Ottawa School Behavior Checklist.* Rockcliffe Park, Ottawa, Canada: J. B. Pimm, 1963.

*Progress Assessment Charts* (P-A-C). Form I (3rd ed.) for children unsuitable for education at school; Form II (2nd ed.) for older mentally handicapped trainees. London: N.A.M.H. (39 Queen Anne St., W. 1), n. d.

# II

# Training Areas

# Introduction

Self-help skills, social skills, academic skills, and vocational skills all are prerequisites to independence, be it the limited independence that is the goal of training programs for the moderately retarded or the complete independence that is the goal of programs for the normal. Skills in each of these four areas have perceptual-motor and language development as their prerequisite. For this reason discussion in ensuing chapters gives detailed description of motor- and language-training programs. The program to promote perceptual-motor development presented by Justison derives from Getman's classification of movement patterns and from his belief that these basic movement patterns are fundamental to the acquisition of all other perceptual-motor skills. A contrasting program, also developmental in nature, but one which addresses consideration to the sequential stages of four areas of motor training—gross motor, balance, eye-hand, and finger dexterity as outlined by such workers as Cattell, Gesell, Doll, and Fokes—is discussed by Stephens. In the same vein two approaches to language training are included. In the first, Blanchard gives detailed analysis of the articulatory problems of the moderately retarded and then presents techniques for remediation. In the second, Kluppel advocates the use of operant techniques as she recognizes verbal stimulation as one of the first requisites for oral language. She also recognizes the naming activity as a method of teaching a basic vocabulary, as a way of providing meaning to these words, and ultimately as a way to combine these words or units to form discourse.

As attention focuses on efforts to promote self-help and independence, the need for optimistic but realistic goals is emphasized by Baumgartner. In her discussion of an experiential curriculum there is reminder that lessons (which point the way toward growth in needed skills) should emerge from patterns of development. A subsequent chapter by Stephens outlines a program designed to promote self-help, social, and academic skills.

In habilitative recreation, as defined by Freeman and Mundy, an activity is included in an individual's program only if it helps improve a particular skill. This presupposes a program based on evaluation as well as awareness that all activities are comprised of a number of component skills. The recreator chooses tasks which afford practice first in isolated skills and then in coordinated effort.

Habilitation efforts which have sought to prepare the moderately retarded for community or sheltered workshop employment are analyzed by Stearns. From this analysis an outline emerges which provides a continuum of service which starts with diagnostic evaluation and proceeds through training programs to community or sheltered workshop placement. Preparation also is required in order to derive optimum benefit and enjoyment from nonworking hours. To this end steps in the establishment of leisure skills are reviewed by Anderson and Stephens.

# 5

## MOTOR LEARNING

## Beth Stephens

To emphasize the importance of motor learning, Stein (1963, p. 231) wrote:

The earliest behavioral responses of the human organism are motor or muscular responses that actually begin during the prenatal period. From this relatively simple and inconspicuous beginning develop highly complex and integrated mechanisms fundamental to all activities of life. The early motor explorations of the child begin a long process of growth, development, and learning by which he finds out about himself and the world around him. Motor experimentation and motor learning become the foundation upon which the entire personality of the child rests. In early childhood mental and physical activities are closely related, and motor activities play a major role in intellectual development. To a large extent, so-called higher forms of behavior develop out of, and have their roots in, motor learning.[1]

The importance of both motor development and the rate of motor development is recognized (Dunham, 1969; Francis and

[1]Permission to use the above quote was granted by *Rehabilitation Literature*, 2023 West Ogden Avenue, Chicago, Illinois.

155

Rarick, 1959). As though to confirm that the tempo or rate of development involves various areas, Robinson and Robinson note that the ages of sitting, walking, and talking are likely to be delayed in retardates (Thompson, 1969). Because the two are aspects of the total functioning organism, Sloan (1951) posited that motor proficiency was related to intelligence, and indeed work by Distefano, Ellis, and Sloan (1958) indicated a positive relationship did exist between mental age and motor proficiency. If this is true, then one would expect differences between the motor performance of normal and retarded children of equivalent chronological age. Significant differences were found by Malpass (1960) when the performance of normals was compared with that of retardates on the Lincoln-Oseretsky Test. In reviewing the motor characteristics of retardates Tredgold (1937) noted their most pronounced deficiency was in finer hand and finger movements, but added that the grosser functions involving body balance and locomotor development usually were clumsy and ungainly (Thompson, 1969). In discussing the contribution of motor activity to learning Thompson (1969) notes that Kephart (1964) identifies four motor patterns (*i.e.*, motor acts which have a great deal of variability and possess extensive variations which are significant to education):

(1) balance and maintenance of posture, (2) locomotion— walking, jumping, etc., (3) contact—motor activities with which the child manipulates objects, and (4) receipt and pro- pulsion—skills with which the child investigates movements in space. Many children required additional help and addi- tional learning experiences to continue this motor learning until a level is reached which permits the use of movement, not only for specific purposes, but for the more generalized purpose of information gathering. Therefore, it becomes the responsibility of the school to offer this aid and to help the child expand his motor learning [p. 4].

With a realization that an improvement in gross and fine motor skills increases the young retardate's ability to interact with and therefore gain additional information from his environment, as well as to increase his ability to participate successfully in daily activities which surround him, and with the realization that repeated demonstrations, opportunities, and training are required for him to master that which is acquired incidentally by normals, Stephens, Smeets, Baumgartner, and Wolfinger (1969) formulated a motor-development program for institutionalized borderline trainable-custodial retardates, ages seven to twelve. A brief outline of the method is presented, not as something to be copied laboriously, but as suggestion of areas to be considered in devising a motor-training program for persons who are developmentally young. Initially the workers assigned to the program were provided information on motor development and were given practice in the use of the Fokes Developmental Scale of Motor Abilities (see Chapter 2) and the Lincoln-Oseretsky Motor Development Scale (Sloan 1948 and Sloan 1955) to determine a specific child's level of motor development. Proficiency in the use of these scales assured knowledge of the sequential development of motor abilities.

Individually planned programs were indicated which contained activities commensurate with the child's level of development. In organizing the training schedules consideration was given to four areas of development—gross motor, balance, arm-hand coordination, and manual dexterity.

To achieve concise, efficient measurement of these four areas, items were selected by Smeets from six different scales and arranged in the chronological sequence set forth in Table 1. If performance in any of the four areas was at the 48-month level, the Valett Motor Integration and Physical Development Sub-Scale of the Valett Developmental Survey (1966) was also used; the latter is designed to measure performance in children from two to seven years. Guidelines for the formulation of the program were furnished by

## Table 1
## SMEETS' ADAPTED MOTOR DEVELOPMENT SCALE

NAME: _____  DATE: _____  SEX: _____  C.A.: _____

|  | GROSS MOTOR | BALANCE | ARM-HAND COORDINATION | MANUAL DEXTERITY |
|---|---|---|---|---|
| 12M. | Walks, one hand held. (Gesell) | Stand alone. (Vineland) | Beats two spoons together at least 3 times. (Cattell) | Marks with pencil. Holds pencil in fist. (Cattell) |
| 18M. | Walks, seldom falls. (Gesell) | Kicks large ball without holding wall. (Gesell) | Throws ball; any definite fling. (Merill-Palmer) | Turns pages; 2-3 at once. (Gesell) |
| 24M. | Walks upstairs alone. (Vineland) | Imitates standing on one foot. Lifts foot. No support. (Merill-Palmer) | Eats with spoon. (Vineland) | Attempts to fold paper. Any fold is a plus. (Cattell, Merill-Palmer) or Turns pages singly. (Gesell) |
| 30M. | Jumps with both feet. (Gesell) | Walks on tip toe. (Gesell) | Eats with fork. (Vineland) | Holds crayon by finger. (Gesell) |
| 36M. | Walks downstairs one step per tread. (Vineland) | Stands on one foot. Real balance for a moment. (Gesell) | Pours well from pitcher. (Gesell) | Closes fist and moves thumb. (Merill-Palmer) |
| 42M. | Jumps high, distance of 1 ft. to 25 inches. (Strang) | Stands on one foot, for 2 seconds. (Gesell) | Puts on sweater. (P.M.S.) | Buttons coat or dress. (Vineland) |
| 48M. | Walks downstairs, alternating feet last few steps. (Gesell) | Stands on one foot more than 4 seconds. (Gesell) | Throws ball overhand. (Gesell) | Opposition of thumb and fingers (one successful trial out of 3). Dressing, button- |

Baumeister's *Mental Retardation* (1967), Baumgartner's *Guiding the Retarded Child* (1965), Bensberg's *Teaching the Mentally Retarded* (1965), Connor and Talbot's *An Experimental Curriculum for Young Mentally Retarded Children* (1966), Denhoff's *Cerebral Palsy, The Preschool Years* (1967), Espenschade and Eckert's *Motor Development* (1967), Frankel, Happ, and Smith's *Functional Teaching of the Mentally Retarded* (1966), Hatcher and Mullin's *More Than Words* (1967), Rosenzweig and Long's *Understanding and Teaching the Dependent Retarded Child* (1960), and Valett's *The Remediation of Learning Disabilities* (1967).

*Sample:* Twenty-four subjects (12 male, 12 female), CA 6-11, were randomly drawn from a unit which contained trainable and custodial retardates, ages seven to twelve. Six males and six females (N = 12) were randomly assigned to the experimental group and six males and six females (N = 12) were randomly assigned to the control group.

*Procedure:* Individual levels of motor development were determined through use of the Smeets' Adapted Scale and the Valett Developmental Survey, Motor Integration and Physical Development Sub-Scale. During additional observational periods more extensive knowledge of each subject's level of performance was made possible through use of Fokes Developmental Scale of Motor Abilities. Following this the experimental group was divided into two training groups, those whose performance was below the 30-month level, and those whose performance was above that level. Few pupils had equivalent performance in the four areas measured by Smeets' Adapted Scale; a subject could perform below the 30-month level in one area but above in others. Generally, membership was not in the same group for all four training activities.

An example of the irregular development that characterized the group was observed in the performance of an eight-year-old arrested hydrocephalic female (see Table 2).

Table 2

Motor Development of Eight-Year-Old Girl

---

*Gross Motor*

24 months—walks upstairs
30 months—*does not* jump
  with both feet

*Arm-Hand Coordination*

36 months—pours from pitcher
42 months—*does not* put on
  sweater

*Balance*

12 months—stands alone
18 months—*cannot* kick ball

*Manual Dexterity*

18 months—turns pages two or
  three at a time
24 months—*does not* fold paper
  or turn pages singly

---

A teacher and three tutors were assigned to work with each of the two subgroups (those performing above and those performing below the 30-month level) for one hour a day, five days a week. While it is not an exhaustive inventory of activities employed, the list presented in Table 3 illustrates the technique used in programming training.

---

Table 3

Activities for Group 1 (performance below 30-month level)
and Group 2 (performance above 30-month level)

---

## GROSS MOTOR

*Rolling*
Group 1   Demonstrate roll; manipulate a roll
Group 2   Demonstrate roll; manipulate roll; have children roll over and over outside on grass or inside on bed

*Jumping*
Group 1   Hold child's hand (or body) and jump with him; step over objects
Group 2   Jump over low object; jump to obtain object above him; jump down from box; broad jump; jump rope

*Sliding*
Group 1   Hold child's hand and his body as he goes down slight incline
Group 2   Slide down slide

*Walker and Tricycle*
Group 1   Guide child's legs through motions necessary to move walker or kiddie car
Group 2   Ride tricycle

### Dancing
Group 1   March and walk to music
Group 2   Hop, skip, and then dance to music

## BALANCE

### Walking
Group 1   Walk on mattress
Group 2   Walk on wide part of 2" x 6" board; then 2" x 4" board

### Trampoline
Group 1   Jump on mattress
Group 2   Jump on trampoline

### Balance Board
Group 1   Crawl or walk on slightly elevated balance board
Group 2   Crawl or walk on board elevated one foot or more; later while holding ball

### Tiptoe and Skipping
Group 1   Demonstrate standing on tiptoe; play game to promote ability; stand on tiptoe and run forward and backward
Group 2   Tiptoe; follow leader (pattern of circles, loops, etc.); when mastered, move to skipping; stand on tiptoe while counting to ten

### Kicking
Group 1   Kick large ball while holding on to support
Group 2   Kick ball without being supported; later, execute a running kick

## ARM-HAND COORDINATION

*Throwing*
Group 1   Roll ball on floor; throw sponge or textured ball; later, throw to other person
Group 2   Throw and catch medium-sized ball; later, ring-toss game; beanbag; bucket throw (throw into bucket); still later, bounce ball and hit ball

*Angels in the Snow*
Group 1   Simple arm extension
Group 2   Alternate arm, leg, etc.

*Rhythm*
Group 1   Tap drums
Group 2   Beat simple pattern

*Bowling*
Group 1   Bowl with big ball and pins
Group 2   Bowl with smaller ball and pins

*Pouring—Sand and Water*
Group 1   Pour into large container
Group 2   Reduce size of container; later, pour to certain level or line on container

## MANUAL DEXTERITY

*Pegboard*
Group 1   Pound pegs (large pegs)
Group 2   Make pegboard designs

*Clay*
  Group 1  Roll ball; poke, roll, squeeze, stick, make pie.
  Group 2  Put two pieces together to make shape; make spe-
           cific objects
*Puzzles*
  Group 1  Work simple two-piece puzzle
  Group 2  Work with smaller pieces; three or four or more

*Dressing*
  Group 1  Take off and put on clothes with help
  Group 2  Work buttons and simple fastening

*Pasting*
  Group 1  Paste large picture
  Group 2  Paste small objects

The experimental group contained some members who were preoccupied with self-stimulating behavior and some who evidenced little or no concern for the manipulative value of objects. Techniques were devised to elicit their interest and attention employing Bruner's (1966) three levels of representation: (1) *enactive* (the child is physically guided through motor activity), (2) *iconic* (precise demonstration precedes the subject's attempt to perform an activity), and (3) *symbolic* (verbal instructions and explanations precede the subject's attempt). Subjects who were not amenable to the symbolic approach were found to profit from teaching geared to the enactive or iconic levels. Attempts to break established habits of inattentiveness or destructive use of objects required a one-to-one or, in some instances, a two-to-one tutor-pupil ratio. For example, one subject upon entrance into the program refused to manipulate objects manually or attend to them visually. Initial training, which required two tutors, was at the enactive level; one person was responsible for seeing that the subject remained at the table while the other obtained materials and guided the subject's hands in activities which involved kneading play dough, rolling a ball, and squeezing a sponge. The immediate goal was to promote spontaneous manipulation of objects, *i.e.*, interaction with the immediate environment. Efforts, whether guided or self-initiated, were rewarded with cookies and candy. To analyze the degree of skill displayed by a subject when he was presented with activities, a scaling technique suggested by Connor and Talbot (1966) was used. For example, members of the group displayed various levels of performance when they were provided the opportunity to put on a sweater: (1) some evidenced no interest in the object, (2) others picked it up and draped it around themselves in a vague, unsuccessful way, (3) others attempted unsuccessfully to get their arms in the sleeves, (4) while others succeeded in getting at least one arm in a sleeve, although the sweater itself frequently was upside down, (5) and still others after extended effort succeeded in getting it on correctly. The immediate goal was to promote the pupil's performance from the present level to the next higher one rather than expecting an immediate progression from misuse to use, or from failure to success.

Justification is difficult for prolonged use of a two-tutors-to-one-pupil ratio; however such concentrated effort may be supplied initially if it leads to spontaneous exploration and manipulation of objects, and later to self-initiated activity. Through such highly concentrated effort the child may be prepared for a one-to-one teacher-pupil tutorial situation, and in turn the one-to-one relation may prepare him for learning in a small group.

At present, final results are not available from the study. The program is ongoing; however, at the end of three months the mean increase for the experimental group was 5.83 points versus 2.33 for the control group (one point being awarded for each item successfully performed on either the Smeets' Adapted Scale or the motor portion of the Valett Developmental Survey). Findings substantiate those of Lillie (1968), namely, that diagnostically based motor-development lessons appear to have a facilitating effect on the development of motor proficiency of preschool retardates.

# References

Baumeister, A. A. *Mental Retardation.* Chicago: Aldine Publishing Co., 1967.

Baumgartner, Bernice B. *Guiding the Retarded Child.* New York: John Day Co., 1965.

Bensberg, G. J., ed. *Teaching the Mentally Retarded.* Atlanta, Ga.: Southern Regional Education Board, 1965.

Bruner, J. S. *Toward a Theory of Instruction.* Cambridge, Mass.: Harvard University Press, 1966.

Connor, Frances P., and Talbot, Mabel. *An Experimental Curriculum for Young Mentally Retarded Children.* New York: Teachers College Press, 1966.

Denhoff, Eric. *Cerebral Palsy, The Preschool Years.* Springfield, Ill.: Charles C. Thomas, 1967.

Distefano, M. K., Jr.; Ellis, N. R.; and Sloan, W. "Motor Proficiency in Mental Defectives." *Perceptual and Motor Skills* 8 (1958): 231-234.

Dunham P. "Teaching Motor Skills to the Mentally Retarded." *Exceptional Children* 35 (1969): 739-744.

Espenschade, Anna S., and Eckert, Helen M. *Motor Development.* Columbus, Ohio: Charles E. Merrill, 1967.

Fokes, Joann. "Developmental Scale of Motor Abilities." In *Training the Developmentally Young,* edited by Beth Stephens. New York: John Day Co., 1970.

Francis, R. J., and Rarick, G. L. "Motor Characteristics of the Mentally Retarded." *American Journal of Mental Deficiency* 63 (1959): 792-811.

Frankel, Max G.; Happ, F. William; and Smith, Maurice P. *Functional Teaching of the Mentally Retarded.* Springfield, Ill.: Charles C. Thomas, 1966.

Hatcher, Caro C., and Mullin, Hilda. *More Than Words: Movement Activi-*

*ties for Children.* Pasadena, Calif.: Parents-for-Movement Publication, 1967.

Kephart, N. C. "Perceptual-Motor Aspects of Learning Disabilities." *Exceptional Children* 31 (1964): 201-206.

Lillie, David L. "The Effects of Motor Development Lessons on Mentally Retarded Children." *American Journal of Mental Deficiency* 72 (1968): 803-808.

Malpass, L. T. "Motor Proficiency in Institutionalized and Non-Institutionalized Retarded Children and Normal Children." *American Journal of Mental Deficiency* 64 (1960): 1012-1015.

Robinson, H. B., and Robinson, N. M. *The Mentally Retarded Child—A Psychological Approach.* New York: McGraw-Hill, 1965.

Rosenzweig, L. E., and Long, Julia. *Understanding and Teaching the Dependent Retarded Child.* Darien, Conn.: Educational Publishing Corp., 1960.

Sloan, W. *Lincoln Adaptation of the Oseretsky Test.* Lincoln, Ill.: The Author, 1948.

Sloan, W. "Motor Proficiency and Intelligence." *American Journal of Mental Deficiency* 55 (1951): 394-406.

Sloan, W. "The Lincoln-Oseretsky Motor Development Scale." *Genetic Phsychology Monographs* 51 (1955): 183-252.

Stein, Julian U. "Motor Function and Physical Fitness of the Mentally Retarded." *Rehabilitation Literature* 24 (1963): 230-242.

Stephens, W. B.; Smeets, Paul; Baumgartner, Bernice B.; and Wolfinger, William. Promoting Motor Development in Young Retardates (In press). Philadelphia, Temple University, 1970.

Thompson, Laura. Motor Development of the Young Retardate (Unpublished manuscript). Philadelphia, Special Education Department, Temple University, 1969.

Tredgold, A. F. *A Test Book of Mental Deficiency.* 6th ed. Baltimore, Md.: William Wood, 1937.

Valett, R. E. *Valett Developmental Survey.* Palo Alto, Calif.: Consulting Psychologists Press, 1966.

Valett, R. E. *The Remediation of Learning Disabilities.* Palo Alto, Calif.: Fearon Publishers, 1967.

# 6

## PERCEPTUAL-MOTOR TRAINING

### Gertrude Justison

Effective educational management of the mentally retarded depends largely upon the identification of patterns of neurophysiological and psychological growth and development. As previous chapters have indicated, such identification and appraisal make it possible for the teacher to recognize the child's developmental status, to anticipate his developmental needs, and to establish appropriate educational opportunities to assure his optimal progress. It is incumbent on teachers to be quite clear in stating objectives, in formulating methods, and in evaluating efforts in effecting programs which are built on sound, logical, sequential stages of human development.

For these compelling reasons, the current interest in applying Piagetian theory and techniques to the retarded is an encouraging development in special education. First, it will undoubtedly force teachers to recognize that learning is an active process beginning with each unique learner and continuing on his terms as he interacts with his environment. Secondly, it will require that teachers become skilled and proficient in the art and science of observing and analyzing both the demands of the learning task and the behavioral responses to it (casting teachers into new and expanding roles). Finally, and most importantly, by honoring the unity and integrity of the human organism as an active agent of his own development, it may well demonstrate among the retarded a potential educability as yet unchallenged.

How one conceptualizes the relationship between perception and the action systems in learning depends upon how one conceives of both perception and learning. Accordingly, it seems important to define what we mean by perceptual-motor, to identify the mechanisms of perception, and to construct a model of theoretical relationships among the modes of translation in cognitive behavior.

To begin, one can say that sensation is a precursor of perception. Sensations, as they become associated with one another and interact within the central nervous system, become interpreted and gain meaning. This reaction to sensation may be regarded as perception. As sensory experiences (sensations) accumulate, the infant or child begins to make simple associations between the sensations he experiences and their meanings to him. He perceives one experience as different from previous experiences. As these *perceptions* relate and take on general meanings (which can, in turn, be carried over to other situations in which similar objects or conditions exist), the child can then be said to have a *concept* of that object or condition. Now it is important to note that there is active or covert *movement* involved in all sensation or perception. Therefore, the movement aspect of perception as an internalized or observable neurophysiological response is characterized as the *motor* activity. In oversimplified terms, then, information comes to the individual by means of sensory impressions (sensations) which become meaningful as they are elaborated by other sensations and are interpreted in the brain (thus constituting *percepts*), which in turn become interrelated into the building blocks of *concepts.* The exact mechanisms for these neurophysiological phenomena are still little understood, though widely researched. The important generalization to be drawn from our oversimplified definition of a highly complex act is that the input and output stimulus-response nature of perception demands that we consider not isolated aspects but the *unitary* behavior of the individual in what we call perceptual-motor training or integration. Because there can be no pure sensation without a motoric component, sensorimotor training shall be referred to as a very basic developmental curricular activity for the moderately retarded, regardless of age or stage of growth.

Perceptual data as listed in Figure 1 reach us through our sense organs. We perceive by sight, hearing, smell, taste, touch, and through the proprioceptive-kinesthetic system which makes us aware of our musculoskeletal position in space. Information coming to us through the elaborate intercommunication and feedback between these input sources is coded within the central nervous system, where it is available for immediate use or stored for retrieval and use in the future. Not all such information is a part of our active, conscious awareness, but there is evidence that even those impressions recorded subconsciously are available for recall and use under appropriate conditions. The degree to which visual, auditory, gustatory, olfactory, tactile, and proprioceptor-kinesthetic senses function fully and adequately at the various stages of development is basic to the individual's power to interact with and understand the people, things, and activities of the environment. It seems clear that some senses are more actively involved in growth and development at some periods than at others. It is also obvious that the experiences of the individual would govern both the quantity and quality of information filtered through the senses and translated or integrated by the central nervous system, thus affecting behavior in significant ways. These facts have particular relevance for the retarded if we assume that biological deficits have often been compounded by ineffective opportunities for learning and/or inappropriate experiences—in terms of maturational, mental, or social development.

The "feedback" system operating between the sensory modalities and the brain in the perceptual-motor act deserves special

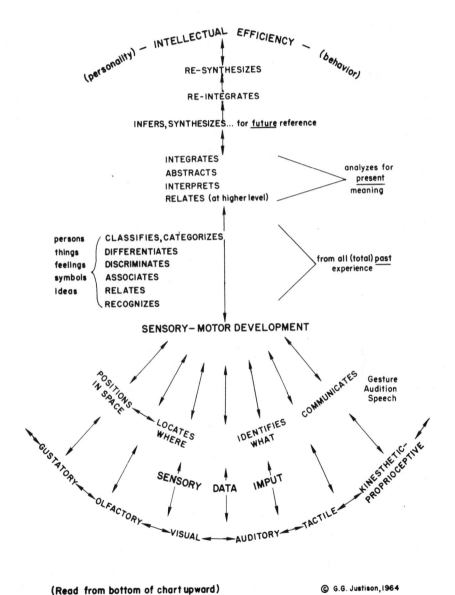

(Read from bottom of chart upward)    © G.G. Justison, 1964

Figure I

mention. It is much more than a simple stimulus-response circuit; it is rather a complex neurophysiological system which permits the individual to get the maximum information from the greatest number of possible sources and to organize and utilize this information in his own learning responses. Single senses, in fact, never act in isolation. The information we receive comes simultaneously from many sources. The multisensory teaching of Montessori and others exploits the feedback system for maximizing the amount of information and monitoring the behavioral response to it. Our own extended practice led to our most successful learning in the use of sensory modalities. Most of us continue to use a preferred mode and to capitalize on perceptual-motor learning in that primary mode. We speak of "visual learners," of "auditory" learners, and even complain about the child who "has to touch" an object to explain its operation. The modalities of sensory information, then, are interdependent and intercommunicating in their operation and dependent on experience for their development and elaboration as a source of perceptual-motor or cognitive efficiency.

It may be useful to trace a sensory impression from its initial impact on the child through the orders of ascending skills to the highest level of integration. The child's first exposure to apple may well be from a baby food jar, which has little immediate relation to the ripe fruit. For discussion purposes, however, it is assumed that our learner is about six or seven months old when he contacts, in his environment, his first apple. His responses would most likely include looking at the apple, licking, touching, rolling, trying to grasp, pat, or push the apple with both hands, one hand, or alternate hands (even feet, depending on his location and his freedom to move), listening to talk about apples, smelling the apple, etc. With accumulated "apple experiences" over time and with the development of locomotion, prehension, and control over body movements, the properties of apple take on meanings (association and relationship with all past "apple experiences") and permit our learner to recognize apples when he sees them at the supermarket or in pictures in a magazine. He ultimately sees the differences in apples (color, size) and recognizes their common qualities. With repeated and continuous apple experiences (each a new and different context), he can make more subtle and complicated discriminations (texture, odor, special form qualities)—learning to discriminate on several levels between apples—and finally to sort and categorize apples in relation to other fruit, in relation to other apples, apples pictured in the book, apples in the alphabet book, apples in the "set" in the mathematics problem, and finally the word *apple* in the primer. To that word stimulus, he then projects *to* the word his apple experiences over time, internalized and integrated as a multidimensional concept of apple in assorted contexts of meaning, including problem solving at the symbolic level.

To this point, our learner has, under the stream of direction of his own action systems (general movements, special movements), experienced apples through all of his senses, interpreted and responded to apple perceptual data, matched his perceptions to the object-time-space reality, tested and evaluated what he saw, moved, smelled, touched, tasted, threw, ate, etc., until he had less and less need to manipulate the object apple to understand apple when he heard about an apple in the absence of the object. As Getman (1965) so succinctly describes, the general movement patterns of locomotion (steered by eyes) permit exploration of the spatial world; special movement patterns permit control and manipulation of the things of the world by using the eyes and hands in combination; eye movement patterns permit the use of vision to get information about the world *without* the movements previously used for exploration and manipulation (thus *reducing* general movement); communication patterns *replace* action by establishing a visual and language relationship which permits the exchange of information through speech. This sequence from action to action reduction, to action replacement, to substitution for action, speech, and time (the development of the ability to visualize past real or vicarious experiences) has important correlates in cognitive development. It is not overdrawn to conclude that effective learners are those using their action systems at optimum efficiency with the least expenditure of movement through time and space. (Those who can hear, absorb, and remember a lecture without the action of note-taking are, in these terms, more efficient learners than those who must motorize the auditory input, translating it to its visual symbolic form to insure that the message is safely in the memory bank for retrieval at some future time.) The retarded, by virtue of inherent or imposed deficits in both perceptual-motor and cognitive sequences of development, reflect corresponding lags in both movement patterns and cognitive skills.

For curricular purposes, then, it is important to recognize the interdependence of movement and cognition in the unitary process of learning. It is equally important to remember that, while omission of exploratory experiences and practice in perceptual-motor skills can create gaps in information and understanding, appropriate opportunities, training, and supervised practice in these skills can facilitate consolidation of next steps in learning. Since, with a majority of our retarded pupils, we can assume biological deficits and delays, we can realistically expect not only omissions, but also overemphasis, or underexposure, in skill acquisition as the products of well-intended but misguided parental, institutional, or school management. It is understandably much easier and less frustrating for adults to dress a retarded child than to permit him the time and freedom to dress himself. It is understandably more economic of time, energy, and effort to do *for* him than to encourage him to do for himself. For teachers, however, there is understanding that if one does enough explaining and demonstrating (and exercises sufficient patience) the child should finally learn to do what you ask. From some source long forgotten, there is a quotation on teachers and teaching that has important implications for us: "A master teacher is one who stops mastering children and helps children to master themselves."

## Guidelines for Training

It is beyond the scope of this chapter to outline in detail a program in perceptual-motor training. Further, it would defeat our purposes in advocating individualized developmental appraisal to prescribe a common-denominator, activity-recipe program. It is important, however, that teachers have some basic guidelines both for assessing current performance and for developing interventions or strategies for providing appropriate experiences.

Two screening forms are reproduced here as suggested outlines for measuring the levels of proficiency in gross and fine motor skills and in the perceptual/cognitive tasks. They are in no way intended to replace standardized measures. However, they do provide adequate cues from which teachers can begin to build an awareness of what to look for in task performance and how to use information yielded by their own observations to provide appropriate learning experiences.

The *Gross Motor Screening Form* is an adaptation of performance measures used by Ayres to assess organically impaired children. As adapted, it omits some clinically based measures and adds other manual and eye movement items which have significance for classroom activities. (For example, item 9a—touching fingers to thumb on command—will reveal the child's skill, or lack of it, in controlling and coordinating eye-hand movements essential in manipulating objects like buttons, pencil, keys, and scissors. Likewise, the child who cannot lift the tongue or "curl" it toward the nose—item 8—may, in this attempt, be demonstrating why he cannot articulate the *l* sound in speech.)

# GROSS MOTOR SCREENING FORM
(Adapted from A. Jean Ayres by G. G. Justison)

Name: _____  Date: _____  Examiner: _____

| | Rhythmic, smooth, coordinated | Adequate: took effort | Erratic: much motor "overflow" | Could not accomplish | Made no effort |
|---|---|---|---|---|---|
| **1. Crawl** | | | | | |
| (a) Homologous (bunny) | | | | | |
| (b) Homolateral (bear) | | | | | |
| (c) Cross-pattern (baby) | | | | | |
| **2. Walk** | | | | | |
| (a) Heel-to-toe forward | | | | | |
| backward | | | | | |
| (b) On toes forward | | | | | |
| backward | | | | | |
| (c) On heels forward | | | | | |
| backward | | | | | |
| **3. Hop** | | | | | |
| (a) Both Feet forward | | | | | |
| backward | | | | | |
| (b) Spontaneous hop right _____ | | | | | |
| left _____ | | | | | |
| (c) Left foot forward | | | | | |
| backward | | | | | |
| (d) Right Foot forward | | | | | |
| backward | | | | | |
| **4. Skip** forward | | | | | |
| backward | | | | | |

| | Accomplished with ease | Accomplished with effort | Could not complete task | Made no effort |
|---|---|---|---|---|
| 5. *Sit-up* (with hands clasped behind neck) | | | | |
| (a) Legs flat | | | | |
| (b) Knees flexed | | | | |
| 6. *Laterality* | | | | |
| Hand | | Right hand higher | Left hand higher | |
| (a) Eyes closed, arms extended, hands relaxed (wrists flexed to count) | | | | |
| (b) Which is the wider thumb nail | | left | right | |
| (c) Thumb on "top" with both hands folded (fingers interlaced) | | left | right | |
| Foot | | | | |
| (a) Kick a ball | | left | right | |
| (b) "Step-out to me" (Stamp out the "fire") | | left | right | |
| Eye | | | | |
| (a) Paper tube | | left | right | |
| (b) Paper peephole | | | | |
| 7. *Eye movements* (tested with dangled bell) | Trunk Movement | Head Movement | Eye movement smooth; held on target | Eye movement jerky-spastic-erratic; could not hold on target |
| (a) Vertical | | | | |
| (b) Horizontal | | | | |
| (c) Diagonals | | | | |

| | Smooth | Erratic | Could not accomplish |
|---|---|---|---|

8. *Tongue movement*
   (a) to nose
   (b) to chin
   (c) toward left ear
   (d) toward right ear

9. *Finger movement*
   (a) Touch fingers to thumb on command, increasing speed
   Both hands
   Right hand
   Left hand
   "House-steeple"
   (b) Clasped hands, fingers interlaced, lift finger pointed to or touched
   (c) Thumb-forefinger "climb" using opposite hands
   (d) Tapping (index finger) with increasing speed
   Right
   Left
   Both

| | Able to identify, move or coordinate: | | Unable to coordinate |
|---|---|---|---|
| | right | left | |

10. *Part/Whole body responses*
   (a) *Supine* (eyes closed)
   Lift lower extremity as touched on command
   (b) Tactile orientation (eyes closed) Upper extremity and opposite lower extremity
   (c) "Angels-in-the-Snow" (prone)
   or
   "Jumping Jack" (erect)

The *Educational Evaluation Form* is an adaptation of procedures used by Petersen and described by Tannhauser (1964). While designed originally for screening and identification of young children with specific learning disabilities, it has proven useful in assessing moderately retarded pupils.

Child's Name: —————————————————————

Birth date: ———————————————————————

Examiner: ————————————————————————

Date: ———————— School: ————————————

## EDUCATIONAL EVALUATION FORM

1. Colors
   Sort one-inch cubes according to color.              ——————————
   Name the colors.                                     ——————————
   Match color words to colored pieces of paper.        ——————————
2. Sort *forms* (blocks or large beads).                ——————————
3. Copy forms below.

4. Work puzzle (4 to 8 pieces). Observations:           ——————————
5. Reproduce design with parquetry blocks.              ——————————

   Blue                              Blue

   Red

6. Reproduce peg design from pattern below to another pegboard.

   Pattern starts one row from top and one row from left side. Use one color only, 5 pegs one each side.

   Correct ——————————      Disorganized ——————————
   Draw the design on the blackboard using correct color. ——————————

7. Color a picture.                                          _____

8. Cut out a picture.                                        _____
   (Attach)

9. Write name.                                               _____
   Manuscript _____
   Cursive        _____
   (Attach)

10. Arrange 3 or 4 pictures in sequence.                     _____
    Tell story the pictures tell.

11. Tell a personal story, as in answer to the query, "What
    did you do yesterday?"                                   _____
    Logical      _____
    In sequence _____
    Has good recall _____

12. Match "like" pictures (about 5 simple, clear-cut pairs).  _____
    Match "like" words (6-8 pairs).                          _____

13. Count by rote.
    How far? _____
    Count blocks.
    How far? _____
    Select and group number of blocks asked for by examiner.
    2 _____ 4 _____ 1 _____ 3 _____ 5 _____
    Write numbers in sequence (until told to stop).
    How far? _____
    Write digits as dictated by examiner.
    6 _____ 10 _____ 3 _____ 12 _____ 8 _____
    Match numbers to domino patterns.                        _____
    Match numbers to number words.                           _____

14. Use pencil to reproduce patterns as tapped out by examiner _____
    . _____ _____ _____ . _____ . _____ . . _____ _____ . . .
    _____      _____      _____      _____


OBSERVATIONS

1. Could *listen* and follow directions.                     _____

2. Reversals _____ Rotations _____ Dissociations         _____

3. Hand preference or use.
   Right _____ Left _____

4. Distractible.                                             _____

5. Hyperactive.                                              _____

6. Perseverative.                                            _____

7. Could organize task.                                      _____
8. Fatigued quickly.                                         _____
9. Fine motor coordination, evidence of "overflow."          _____
   Mouth muscles _____
   Hand muscles _____
10. Speech.
    *Articulation*
    Distinct _____        Cluttered _____       Substitutions _____
11. Length of speech units.
    Words _____        Phrases _____       Sentences _____
12. Grammar (*i.e.* structure)
    Me for I _____                    Her for she _____
    Other _____ _____ _____ _____ _____
13. Draw picture of self. (Attach).

The key to the use of both forms is to observe very carefully and note *how* the child executed the task (if he did meet the task demand) and at what point he exhibited difficulty (if he could *not* meet the performance expectancy). For example, an item not included on the Gross Motor Screening Form, but easily observable under ordinary school conditions, is that of negotiating steps or climbing stairs. The fact that the child can somehow get up the steps alone tells us only that he has sufficient strength and balance to shift his body weight from one riser to the next until he manages to reach the top step. If we are to help him adapt to his environment by mastering the general skills of body movement, however, we need to examine his walking pattern on flat surfaces, on ramps, as he climbs stairs, as he descends, and so on. Stair-climbing abilities are revealing developmental behaviors that we can easily observe and assess. Does he advance the same foot on each step with the trailing foot brought up and placed beside the lead foot before the next step is taken? Or does he alternate the use of his feet in making the climb? Does he call on an adult or another child for support when he climbs? Or does he use the rail? Does he look at each riser as he steps up on it? Does he hesitate at each step, getting ready

for the next one? Or is his progression smooth and easy? Does his
foot contact the riser with each step, scarring his shoes? Or does
he plant his foot squarely on the tread without bumping the riser?
Do his feet "toe out"? Or toe in? Or are they in reasonably good
alignment? What is the position of head, trunk, and arms during
climbing? Is the body pitched forward with hands ready to break
an anticipated misstep? Or is the body erect with arms free? Does
the climb seem to require unusual exertion? Or does it seem easy
and almost automatic? Does the climb require so much concentration of attention that he seems not to hear your directions? Or,
when you speak to him while he is climbing, can he interrupt his
own movement to look in your direction and listen to what you
have to say? Can he carry a lunch box in one hand and a toy in the
other while he climbs without dropping one or the other? Can he
reverse his direction on the step without losing his balance? Such
questions can be answered by the observant teacher and the information obtained can be utilized to plan sequentially ordered experiences in stair climbing. Such a sequence of locomotor skills can,
indeed, be instrumental in building a more stable and secure space
world for the retarded child and helps to make him a more confident and comfortable person.

Taking another perceptual-motor task from the Educational
Evaluation Form, let us examine how to observe and assess a child's
performance on item 3—copying a square. Does he seem to "see"
the total figure in one inspectionary glance? Or does he seem to
visually examine it, line by line? Does he study it with his eyes and
immediately concentrate on his pencilwork in the copying act? Or
does he pencil a part and then look back at the model for his next
direction? Where does he start in executing the geometric figure?
At the upper left angle? Or the lower right angle? Is his pencil
performance executed in a single line without lifting the pencil from
the paper? Or does he make a series of four lines approximated at
the four corners of the square? Does he rotate the paper to accom-

modate changes in the direction of his work? (Is he drawing a *series* of vertical lines to constitute a square by moving the *paper* rather than the pencil?) Or does he negotiate vertical and horizontal lines and angles in an easy, single sweep of the pencil, without moving the paper? What about the pencil grasp? Is it natural, secure? Or is it awkward, tense? What about posture during the performance? Are head and trunk aligned for the task? Or is the head resting on the desk, eyes very close to paper with body tilted forward and feet extended behind the center of gravity? Are mouth movements obvious in the copying task? Is the tongue extended? And, if so, does it act like a "pointer" for the directionality of the pencil? These and other questions may lead the observer to discover behaviors unexamined in the usual discourse of teaching. A square copied—closely resembling the model in form, size, and the execution of angles—can too easily be accepted as adequate. And, indeed, by examining only the *end product* (and not the *process*) of copy performance, one could assume the performance as adequate. But examination of *how* the copy performance was accomplished can supply a multitude of clues on which to provide learning experiences in both general and special body movements, use of eyes and hands together on a visual-motor task, use of eyes for visual inspection of form, etc.—any and all of which help to build skills for more efficient movement and adaptation to the environment.

There are some useful guidelines to direct teachers in their observation, analysis, and training of perceptual-motor behavior. Such guidelines are those dictated by the biological integrity of the child no matter how deviant his physical or intellectual development may be. Guiding principles include the *directional* trends of human development (the cephalocaudal, or head-to-tail, flow of growth; the proximodistal, or midline-to-periphery, trend; and that from gross-to-fine or general-to-specific patterns of function); the ontogenetic *sequence* of steps or stages in development; and the *reciprocal interweaving* of the oppositional neuromuscular halves of the body. While we speak of children "growing up" we know that in fact they grow down—that control of head, trunk, and arms precedes control of the feet and legs, that head and trunk movements affect both upper and lower extremities, and that gross or whole body movements precede more specialized, refined movements like those of the hands. We recognize, too, that the acquisition of all general and special movement patterns occurs in a predictable, orderly sequence—that children learn to walk before they learn to hop, jump, or skip, and that early eye pursuits are accompanied by turning of the head and body and only over time does the teamed action of eyes occur without observable head movement. We know, too, that perceptual-motor efficiency depends on increasingly mature relationship between the neuromuscular systems and that, as in locomotion, arms and legs function in oppositional action to each other, with one arm counteracting the thrust of the leg of the other side to maintain erect posture and facilitate movement. Keeping these principles in mind, evaluation of performance programs for building perceptual-motor skills can be planned to maintain both the sequence and directional unity of growth and development.

Ayres (1961) reminds us that the ability to perform complex motor tasks is dependent on mastery of the ability to do certain basic motor planning and that acquisition of these two kinds of abilities occurs simultaneously in mutually dependent fashion. Getman (1966) stresses that the skills acquired from general (locomotion) movements include the special movements of the mobile sight system which permits the child to sight and visually steer himself through the world of space, objects, and persons. If we accept these principles, we recognize the importance of beginning the training of children deficient in perceptual-motor functions by providing extensive practice at each step and building toward fundamental competence. A majority of moderately retarded children will have learned to do specific tasks without having necessarily acquired the generalized ability which would enable them to do similar or related tasks. If the generalized ability is not evident, it could be inferred that some of the steps in perceptual-motor development were insufficiently integrated to insure next steps.

Because it is rather characteristic to find trainable retardates inefficient in general movement patterns, frequently training should begin with activities at this level, *e.g.*, rolling. Ayres (1961) describes the rolling procedure as it occurs in infancy in the neuromuscularly normal child: the eyes lead and follow with head turning to the side, with shoulders, hips, and legs moving to complete the roll from one side to another, or face-up to face-down position. She suggests that the retardate learn to roll over, initiating the motion by looking at a bright object placed at the side. Ocular control is a special movement pattern which becomes increasingly crucial in all later perceptual-motor functions. The turning of the eyes facilitates head turning; head turning facilitates ocular efficiency. Thus eyes guide total body action and total body action affects visual efficiency. This principle is fundamental in the implementation of any perceptual-motor training and particularly crucial in adapting procedures for the retarded.

Body roll with visual targeting can be developed in a variety of ways, depending on the teacher's specific objectives. Young children enjoy and profit from rolling in cardboard drums (with ends open) or in barrels. With practice and reminders on keeping the "roll" visually steered they become proficient in keeping the "body-in-tube" in good alignment while in motion. Rolling to count or in rhythm adds a dimension of controlled motion. The flexible body caterpillar (tractor) made of carpeting and snowfence as described by Frankel, Happ, and Smith (1966) can be modified for the body roll. Rolling on bare floor, carpeted floor, grass, sand, and asphalt will provide tactile differentiation of experience, feeding back into the perceptual-motor system through whole body contact. Estimating the number of complete rolls from starting position to the wall will be appropriate for some retardates. Talking about the experience, finding words to describe the experience, repeating the *words* for the directions of the movement all have a role in the training program. Once children have mastered alignment and control of motion by visual steering, the training activity can become a recreational or free-play activity. However, the activity should not be abandoned as a training procedure until the child can move easily in both directions, maintaining good body alignment with eyes steering the motion.

The next activities in programming general locomotor skills constitute the crawling sequence. While the "bunny hop" (both arms alternating with both legs in flexion-extension propelling through space) is the first pattern checked on the screening form, some physical education specialists recommend phylogenetically earlier patterns in the training sequence. Thus, the "inch worm" pattern would start from the supine position with legs extended. Progression forward (guided by a visual target or a toy to reach and grasp) would be accomplished by the use of head, both arms, and trunk with feet and legs being pulled along without actively helping the forward motion. The "seal" pattern differs only slightly in that the arms alternate in the forward propulsion in contrast to both arms working simultaneously in the "inch worm." In both patterns the arms are flexed with hands directed to the midline and elbows acting as stabilizers in controlling forward motion. Both patterns are facilitated by visual steering but require considerable strength and conscious control of the lower extremities.

The homologous crawl (bunny hop) combines the use of both arms alternating with both legs in a cooperative endeavor. Many retarded children seem quite unable to use both arms, both legs, or both eyes simultaneously in the same motion. They need many activities involving the push-pull or crawling action. Ayres (1961), Getman (1962), Hayden (1964), Frankel, Happ, and Smith (1966), and Kephart (1960) suggest many activities involving upper and lower body coordination. Most children enjoy and profit from floor activities in which crawling becomes a game. Again, it is important to keep the action visually steered. The target in this case may be gradually lifted from a tape or line on the floor in front of the child to an eye-level target on a distant wall. Boards mounted on freely moving casters can be used to provide the push-pull action of upper-lower extremities in a pleasurable yet productive way.

In the homolateral (bear) crawl the right arm and right leg are moved at the same time; one side of the body moves in coordinated fashion and in alternation with the other side. As Ayres (1961) notes, the homolateral pattern is not frequently reflected in games or sports, but teaching the pattern helps the child to motor-plan basic movements and to learn to alternate sides in coordinate fashion. The scooter board can be used in either supine or seated position to give practice in pushing alternately with right and left hands (supine) or right and left foot (seated).

Reciprocity of arm motion helps to build trunk control and to facilitate the cross-pattern crawl. In the cross-pattern (baby) crawl the right arm and left leg move forward simultaneously in alternate action with the left arm and right leg, the right and left sides of the body performing different but interdependent, coordinated movements at the same time. The cross-pattern movements are those used in walking, climbing, swimming, and many playground activities. Mastery of these basic crawling-movement patterns provides the child with the sensory awareness of his own physical self—his own body scheme. Further, it is these early basic patterns which are the foundation skills on which, later, refined and complex special movements are elaborated. By keeping activities visually steered, and by providing a variety of stimulus objects or conditions of movement, practice can be made productive and recreational at the same time.

Creative teachers who are aware of how children learn and grow can follow the guidelines reviewed in Fokes' chapter on motor development and can find many ways to incorporate the basic crawling patterns into everyday indoor and outdoor activities. For example, an obstacle course devised from existing furniture or equipment can be as constructive and enjoyable to a preschool make-believe seal as to a twelve- or thirteen-year-old make-believe Marine on combat manuevers. Both will learn that to negotiate movement of their bodies through a confined overhead space requires that knees remain stiff, that legs be held close together, that shoulders be squeezed close to the midline. Both will require repeated practice to learn the coordinate actions which allow control of movement of legs when head, arms, and trunk propel and thrust the body weight forward. With practice they will learn how to estimate distance, when to make contact, or how to avoid contact, "what" moves "next" and "how" in "front" space, "back" space, and "side" space, and in "over" and "under" space. The preschooler, whatever his current functional level of development, is learning to motor-plan purposeful whole-body movement and is integrating the information received by tactual, kinesthetic-proprioceptive feedback. The teenager, by virtue of more or different primary experiences, is learning or relearning to motor-plan through purposeful whole-body movement and probably is acting on different cues or integrating at a different level from that of the preschooler but he is receiving some of the same values in his sensory-motor exploration of space.

The point to be emphasized is that these skills of body movement and *control* of movement cannot be left to recess period, free play or a twenty-minute period called "gross-motor training." Until we bring to our programs more realistic and developmentally sequenced activities we perpetuate deficiences in performance that can be remediated and we build special skills on a shallow base, often at great cost in frustration and failure. Time spent in general movement yields dividends directly affecting the quality of performance in other aspects of the curriculum. Regular, daily practice in the routines described assists the retardate to gain full awareness of his body scheme for freedom of movement in purposeful action. In addition to the body rolls and creeping routines, modifications of the same basic patterns can be extended to other floor activities which have the values of reinforcing tactual-kinesthetic awareness of the extremities and building muscle strength and flexibility. Three such routines are:

1. *The stomach rock* starts in the face-down position with hands held out and legs lifted at the same time, the arched body is "rocked" forward and backward.

2. *The rolling sit-up* starts face-down with hands on floor (palms down) as if ready to do push-ups. On signal, the child rolls to a sitting position by using his upper body with arms steering the roll from the sitting position back to the supine position from which he started. (The regular sit-ups required in the screening procedures also constitute a good practice routine in muscular strength and flexibility. In these, the hands are clasped behind the neck with fingers interlaced. The child lies flat on his back with legs and feet together and body in good alignment. On signal, with the teacher holding the child's ankles to the floor, he should try to sit up. In the second sit-up, the legs are flexed with feet flat on floor, knees together. The teacher holds feet and, on signal, the child tries to sit up. In either case, failure may be due to lack of strength in the abdominal muscles or in the hip flexor-extensor muscles.)

3. *In the feet lift,* the child lies flat on his back, arms at sides close to body with palms down, and legs and feet together. Feet and legs are lifted to about ten inches from floor and held there to count (of one minute).

One floor activity merits special consideration as valuable for retardates of any age as a daily routine—either for building body coordination skills or in reviewing them to build precision in movement *timing*. This exercise, described in detail by Getman (1962) and cited by Kephart (1960), Barsch (1965), and others, is called Angels-in-the-Snow. The child lies flat on his back, legs stretched out straight and together, arms at sides close to body. In the first movements, arms are moved away from the body in a full arc to a position where hands touch above the head. Arms are then swept back in an arc until hands and arms are at sides of body. In the second series of movements, while arms are at the sides, the feet and legs move apart as widely as possible and then back to a heels-together position. When efficiency is established and there is synchronized bilateral movement in first the arm and then the leg movements, the movements of arms and legs are then combined. The total pattern is executed when arms move out and up at the same time that legs move apart. When arms arc back to sides, the legs move toward each other. Angels-in-the-Snow requires control, coordination of movements, and timing, which make it an appropriate activity for any age group. The more practice retardates have in learning and reviewing these bilateral movements on the floor, the more efficient the same and related movements become in erect posture. (The Jumping Jack calisthenic drill is the erect equivalent of Angels-in-the-Snow.)

All movement activities discussed thus far should be carried out in bare or stockinged feet. The same is true for those general movement patterns to follow; these are more demanding of coordination and control.

The simplest routine for building bilateral synchrony, balance, and control is the heel-toe walk on a ten- or twelve-foot "track." Generally, it is safer and more desirable to initiate these activities on the floor itself, using four-inch-wide masking tape to mark the track, rather than on a balance beam. Through information obtained on the screening form, teachers will learn that many retardates have considerable difficulty in maintaining postural balance because of their excessive preoccupation with the task of touching heel-to-toe while keeping feet on the taped track. More often than not, retardates will have to look at their feet to confirm their position on the track.

Naturally, as they do so, there is a resulting shift of the center of gravity which seriously threatens equilibrium and they lose their balance as they try to maintain erect posture under the task demand. It is useful and practical, then, to direct the child to look at a bright target placed at the far end of the track and to "feel" for his toes (instead of looking at them) as he advances one foot ahead of the other in negotiating the track. As movement in reasonable balance improves, the target (such as a colored six-inch circle on the wall) can be gradually lifted until it is at eye level for the child. When heel-to-toe movement is free and coordinate in both forward and backward direction on the taped track, a two-by-four ten- or twelve-foot wooden beam (four-inch side up) can be used. With mastery of forward and backward movement with a centered target at eye level, a next step would be to elevate the board (four-inch surface up) on wooden braces, bricks, or cinderblocks, so that the walking surface is several inches above the ground. The visual target should be used consistently, starting at the floor level of the board and raised gradually to eye level. The visual target helps the retardate to organize and direct his body movements as a reference to guide him from where he is to where he is going as it helps him to know himself in relationship to his environment.

The walking-beam routines are beneficial even for those retardates who seem to master them quickly. For them, the beam can be used on the two-inch surface and the heel-toe progression can be extended to side steps. Steering by peripheral vision (vision target placed to the left or right of the beam and on different planes) can be built by practicing forward and backward motion with eyes directed to the peripheral target. Walking the board under this additional stress demands considerable practice. For the older children who can move with reasonable efficiency, the beam may be used as an action exercise in estimating distance—that is, the number of heel-toe steps, side steps, "widest" steps, etc., it takes to walk the beam. Variations of orientation can be introduced as well as combinations of activity. For example, a directional series might be one step forward, one step sideways, one step facing backward, then a repeat of the series. Kinesthetic-proprioceptive awareness of the reciprocal interweaving of left arm with right leg may be heightened by strapping light sandbags or beanbags to one hand and the opposite foot. Postural balance may be stimulated by using a full-length mirror.

Walking activities need not be restricted to the walking beam or to a straight track. Floor areas and playground surfaces can be marked with large geometric forms for directional and orientation activities. The same areas may be used for crawling by some, walking by others, hopping by still others, depending on individual assessment and needs. The addition of rhythm, whether by count, beat, or musical background, often enhances performance.

Jumping activities often require adult assistance and rather prolonged practice. Jumping skills are not easily acquired, especially the two-footed jump which is a necessary skill for skipping. Getman (1962) describes a jumping board of three-quarter-inch plywood, about a foot wide and eight feet long, supported at each end by blocks. The child of fifty pounds or less should be able to jump in the center of the board without having the board touch the ground. Until the child has freedom and confidence it may be necessary for the teacher to hold both hands while the child jumps. As jumping movements become more controlled and coordinated, the jumping task demand may be made increasingly complex—for example, three two-footed jumps in place, then a half turn to the *left*, and so on. When the child has facility in the two-footed jump, then the one-foot hop—forward and backward—can be practiced on the taped track used for the walking sequence. When practice has assured skill and coordination on one foot, then the alternate foot is stressed. Visual targets should be used in the hopping activity in the same way they were used in the walking sequence—to help steer the movements and guide the body through space. Once retardates have mastered the creeping, walking, and jumping sequences in forward, backward, and sidewise directions, they will often show notable improvements in general posture, more refined movement patterns, and, in general, confidence and willingness to try more demanding activities. Children who hesitate to play on climbing equipment, for example, or those who cannot reverse their direction or alternate legs in ascending stairs are often those who cannot get both feet off the ground at the same time. Once they have mastered the full sequence of rolling, creeping-crawling, walking, and jumping with practiced skill at each step before advancing to the next step, they reflect notable changes in total behavior, in posture, and general appearance. For the very young, such a program prevents the distorted postures which get "structured in" over time by maladapted movement patterns. But even for those who have habitually assumed the "head-on-chest, looking-down-at-the-ground" posture of many retardates, a structured sequential-movement activities program can and will modify, if not correct, maladaptive postures and practices.

Many other activities can and should be programmed to provide practice and skill in general movement patterns. Where facilities and personnel permit the use of swimming pool and trampoline, both are highly recommended. The retardate's own buoyancy in water and the natural thrust of the trampoline supply a freedom that is basic in learning the control of movements required for bilateral coordination. When swimming pools and trampoline programs are used, trained personnel should direct and supervise activities under appropriate safety precautions.

Getman (1962), Kephart (1960), Barsch (1965), Hayden (1964), Frankel, Happ, and Smith (1966), and many standard physical education texts outline in detail other activities which can be adapted for use in the *general movements* sequence. Those specifically cited here are those found particularly useful in children with neurological handicaps. Because each activity will have different purposes and application for different children but the same general purposes for *all* children, the objectives may vary but the *sequence* is the same for all. This makes planning a less complicated process than it would seem, once the teacher relates the program to the children's directions of growth: (1) eyes steering *all* movement, (2) upper, then lower, (3) midline, then "out there," (3) vertical, then horizontal, (4) large movements, then refined special movements (shoulder-whole arm, arm-hand, hand-finger). While not complete, this program of general movements does review the sequence of activities most often missed or inadequately performed in the early development of the retarded.

Most of the traditional seat-work activities of the curriculum for the retarded as well as many of the self-help skills call for *special movements*—combination movements of eyes and hands which permit manipulation of objects. Many authors and researchers have stressed the importance of the hands as tools of learning. Recent provocative research on training retarded children to enhance a functioning grasp skill by Friedlander states:

A child's hands are the most important tools he can ever possess in learning to adapt successfully to the tasks and opportunities for psychological growth that surround him in his daily life. Of course, his hands are effective devices for grasping and holding useful objects, but their importance for mental development goes far beyond these simple utilitarian functions. For an active child, his hands are the principal agents of his eyes and brain. He uses them constantly in the exploratory and creative activities of play and work by which he discovers the nature of physical reality. It is primarily with his hands that he gains competence at making and doing the countless number of things that give a child the experience of success as a participant in the life of his family, his friends, and his school. With his hands as well as his eyes he learns the rules of balance, gravity, size, weight, and texture that are the logical basis of thought. In this sense, development of intellectual abilities and the development of hand and finger dexterity often stimulate or delay each other's pace in the early years of growth. [Friedlander, 1966]

Gesell (1940) reminds us that "the infant takes hold of the world with his eyes long before he takes hold with his hands," but as Getman (1962) concludes, full performance and comprehension of "the world" cannot come until the eyes and hands are used in unified combination to probe, explore, and manipulate "the world." In providing practice in special movement activities, it is important to remember that the eye-hand movements are elaborations and refinements of the more total movements—that shoulder, arm, and hand movements directly affect finger movements. The developmental purposes of eye-hand activities are to facilitate manipulation and dexterity and enhance the sighting and steering skills in grasping, handling, inspecting, and moving objects in purposeful ways. Early experiences in reaching for and manipulating objects are apt to be sweeping arm movements with rather unsure, uncontrolled hand grasps. The reach is often short of or beyond the object in early trial efforts to capture, hold, and inspect (by eyes, tongue, or fingers) the objects of the young child's curiosity. But as general movements become more skilled, control of body parts more refined, and visual steering more effective in guiding general movements through space, there begins to be a more precise reach and a more controlled grasp of the objects of the world. Reaching in infancy is a two-handed activity. Over time and with cumulative experience, it becomes an alternating push-pull activity and finally a preferred hand activity. It is important to stress here that most eye-hand tasks are bilateral activities even when the major part of the task seems to be carried out by one hand. The activity of the opposite side (shoulder, arm, hand) in supporting the movement of the leading hand is as important to the task as the guidance offered by the two eyes "teamed" on the object. Catching a large ball with two hands should be practiced successfully before expecting that a child be able to catch a small ball with one hand. Here again, the one-handed act arises from the basic movement pattern learned in the two-handed catch. For retardates, large, heavy beach balls should precede standard playground balls in teaching children to catch. As they learn to estimate time and distance and are successful in controlling the reach and grasp of catching, a smaller ball can be substituted. When there is successful experience in the two-hand catch, the one-hand catch can be initiated.

Pegboard activities can combine both size and form sequences in developmental fashion beginning with large commercial pegboard (cut twenty inches or more square) and using wooden or plastic golf tees to reproduce the geometric forms in sequence. The standard preprimary pegboard with large pegs would be the next work board. When the sequence of forms can be successfully reproduced with large pegs, the task can then be performed on the standard eight-inch primary pegboard with small pegs. Success should be insured at each step before the next task of higher order complexity is expected. In this example, general movement patterns at increasing levels of complexity (creeping through, walking through, one-foot hopping) tracing the sequence of geometric forms on marked areas of floor or playground space, followed by general arm movement (both hands tracing a large blackboard form, then alternately tracing with one hand, then the other) would hopefully have built a concrete awareness, visual memory, and recognition of the forms to be reproduced with pegs. In like manner, the task demand in manipulating and placing small pegs to reproduce the forms would have been built through successively refined finger-dexterity skills growing out of general movement patterns. Tracing around large, then smaller stencils with chalk (at the blackboard), on large paper, then smaller paper is a related and effective way to build a motoric readiness for reading and writing. Such activity provides the nonpreferred hand a support role (in holding the form to be traced) while allowing freedom of direction and mobility of preferred hand and eyes in following visually and manually the arcs, angles, and lines constituting the geometric forms which are components of our language symbols.

Tactual recognition of familiar objects in the absence of "seeing" is dependent on former experience in looking at the object and tactually inspecting and manipulating it. Such "blind identification" activities demonstrate that one can "see" or visualize with fingertips general and special movement experiences which have originally been steered by eyes. Such activities are very useful in building visual memory of texture, size, and form, as well as helpful in developing vocabulary.

Attention to the selection of appropriate educational toys, devices, and equipment is inherent in teaching responsibilities. More often than not, the educational toys which fail to attract and hold the interest of retardates are those associated with "babyish" expectancies. Often the same principles of movement or dexterity required by a toy are incorporated in the real, life-size article which the toy duplicates. The wooden shoe toy designed for teaching lacing and tying of shoestrings is, in fact, less functional than a discarded large-size man's shoe, into which the child can place his own foot and thread the laces. The same holds true for nesting sets of cylinders or blocks. The older retardate who is learning size relationships and discriminations may consider the commercially available colored plastic sets of nesting forms as "baby stuff" and reject the activity on this basis. A home-made set of nesting cans or boxes of graduated sizes can offer a useful and less demanding method of achieving the same objectives. Further, size discriminations made with same-color cans or boxes are not as likely to be falsely "cued" by color sequence or order as are the multicolored plastic forms. In short, the selection of educational toys, materials of instruction, manipulative devices, etc., should be based on the purposes to be achieved by the activity and the potential of the materials to be appropriately and successfully employed in meeting these purposes. To make wise decisions in selecting and using toys, games, and devices, teachers must be able to analyze what the child can do (but should learn to do better), and how the toy or device can facilitate the child's performance (by providing developmentally appropriate experience). Task analysis, as a complement to child-behavior observations, will help teachers know *why* a particular activity is appropriate, *how* it can be implemented and with *what* materials, and *when* to use the "things" of learning. The what, why, when, and how are all predicated on the developmental status of the child and teacher sensitivity to his needs, interests, and strengths. In the absence of complete information on the child's readiness for a particular learning task or uncertainty about the functional merits of particular devices or materials, it is easy to misjudge the values of such educational equipment or to present materials too advanced for current skill levels.

In general, *construction-type toys* should be selected in terms of their durability and versatility. Wooden blocks (different geometric shapes) of graduated sizes are standard items of equipment. Many commercially available plastic interlocking units are useful and economical for classroom use, though it is well to purchase single-color sets to insure that the child sees (discriminates and associates) *shape* before color. The pull-apart or assembly-type devices are likewise easily available and economical as well as functional for eye-hand skill-building. Puzzles (three-piece to multiple-parts) in series of increasing complexity regarding parts, forms, and relationships provide opportunities for making form, size, and color discriminations, learning directional orientation, and making perceptual "match" between related parts. Lacing forms, sewing cards, and weaving looms have value in eye-hand coordination training in providing visual search and in manual reach opportunities.

Other activities providing eye-hand experiences in shape, size, texture, direction, and finger dexterity would include sorting and classifying (buttons, for example), bead stringing, paper folding and cutting, and tracing (around forms, within stencils, or on tissue over simple, one-line drawings). These activities will serve to supplement those eye-hand skills which are involved in the self-help program and the everyday transactions in the school and play environment—as, for example, in unlatching, locking, fastening doors, drawers, and lunch boxes. Stress on mastery of the manipulations required in the daily environment is important and constitutes a valid program priority. Teachers are reminded, however, that building on developmental readiness will insure more effective learning and carry over to related dexterity skills.

## Ocular Motility Training

Several pilot studies have demonstrated the value of ocular motility training. Simpson (1960) demonstrated a gain of nine to thirteen academic months with daily ocular pursuit training. A few activities are described here, but the reader is encouraged to refer to the writing of Getman (1962), Kephart (1960), Barsch (1965), and Simpson (1960) for other detailed examples of classroom activities in ocular motility patterns.

A styrofoam or plastic "wiffle" ball is suspended from the ceiling on a pulley (so that it can be lowered or elevated). With the ball suspended about sixteen inches from the child's eyes, set the ball in slow motion, keeping the arc within two feet. Move the ball first in the vertical direction, then horizontally, then on the diagonal. Encourage the child to keep his head still as he focuses eyes on the moving ball. (This routine may be varied by the posture of the child —prone, seated, or standing—or by having the child tap the ball lightly when it swings in full arc with a cardboard tube held with both hands.)

Holding his hands twelve to fourteen inches apart and about twelve inches in front of his eyes, have child hold up his thumbs. Signal him to look quickly from the right thumb to the left thumb, increasing the tempo of the pursuit to achieve rhythm and speed.

These activities help to improve the speed and efficiency of visual focusing and the ability to shift eyes quickly from one point in space to another.

Perhaps there is no more important learning space in the classroom than chalkboard space. Too often it is thought of as "training" space. Because the chalkboard lends itself so effectively to the freedom and direction of whole-arm, wrist-and-finger movements, chalk-form sequences provide general and special movements which are useful preparation for later writing. The sequence is patterned after the sequences of development of movement control beginning with the use of both hands in unison. To achieve proper posture for the chalkboard drills, the child should rest his elbow at his waist and extend his hand straight out in front of him to the chalkboard.

Direct the child, with chalk in each of his hands, to make large sweeping circles with both hands simultaneously through the developmental directions:

1. Right hand clockwise; left hand counterclockwise (ten circles)
2. Left hand clockwise; right hand counterclockwise (ten circles)
3. Both moving clockwise (ten circles)
4. Both moving counterclockwise (ten circles)

The form sequence (from circle, to square, to triangle) can then be traced after mastery of bimanual circles and lines described next. Prepare a large circle with dots at "hour" placement. In the straight-line sequence, the child draws horizontal lines from finger-tips to center of chalkboard with both hands moving at the same time. At the center with both chalks, both hands retrace the same line from center to periphery. Repeat the periphery-to-center then center-to-periphery movements with chalk for the "two o'clock"—right, "eight o'clock"—left, positions. Repeat for all possible horizontal, vertical, and diagonal positions with both hands at the same time.

Bimanual chalkboard drills are appropriate for retardates of all ages. For the younger child, such activities create the bilateral coordinations which assure more skilled manipulative movements. For the older child, they provide opportunity for relearning and refining the more discrete movements which may be deficient. The bimanual chalkboard sequence can be followed by large clear plastic template tracing at chalkboard and then translated to smaller stencil or template tracings on paper at the desk. Perceptual skills kits or programs which include follow-the-dot routines to build form perception through visualization of direction are appropriate and productive. Such follow-the-dot exercises should follow the developmental form sequence before other forms (like letters or digits) are introduced.

The activities which have been described are included because of their basic and important role in the development of other, higher level perceptual and cognitive skills. It cannot be overstressed that supervised periods of practice each day in the *basic* patterns of general, special, and ocular movements as they have been described here in some detail constitute a very major part of a developmentally sequenced curriculum.

While the subject of language is dealt with in chapters by Blanchard and Kluppel, it is important to note here the interdependent relationship of vision and audition in speech and language development. Audition is more than hearing, just as vision is more than sight. Audition and vision account for about 80 percent of the information received from the world and both are learned skills. Forms, similarities and differences, etc., exist in sounds that are heard (and interpreted) as forms that can be seen (and recognized). Lack of skill in auditory discrimination may lead to faulty interpretation and recall of words. Children who are not skilled in audition will confuse words that sound alike, "forget" directions, and often require repeated instructions. Some activities that come out of seeing and listening can extend skills in communication and are part of the language of the child's own action patterns. The naming of the objects he has moved toward, reached, grasped, and inspected with eyes, tongue and hands—the "label" language—comes first in developmental acquisition of speech. Naming and touching simultaneously combines vision and language. Doing and saying—moving and talking about the movement; seeing and naming; listening and repeating; inspecting and describing; visualizing and describing—all combine components of seeing and hearing, vision and audition, in the language sequence. It is very helpful, then, in carrying out any and all of the basic, special, and ocular movement routines to talk about the movements, directions, forms, positions, objects, relationships, etc., and to encourage the child to use words appropriately *with the action.* Such "listening-speaking-moving" experiences will build associations between audition and visualization, articulation and vocabulary, in language acquisition. Such associations have particular relevance in body parts references and in spatial terms, for example, upper-lower, left-right, large-small, here-there, near-far, etc. Slow and fast enunciation and articulation practices prepare retardates for blending sounds and aid in flexibility and control of speech movements. Many of the record and book series, or filmstrip and audio tape stories match actions and sounds, giving children visual impressions of what they hear. Getman (1962), Kephart (1960), and Barsch (1965) describe in detail many other activities which facilitate the perceptual match between audition and vision in language development. Specific sequences and techniques described by Blanchard utilize similar developmental principles in more structured language activities and provide the framework for the more informal language support for the perceptual-motor training periods.

The final stage in the perceptual-motor sequence is in the development of visualization patterns to substitute for action, speech, and time. Through the visual interpretation of symbols, the child recalls, relates, or restructures actual experiences he has had, as he brings these understandings to the printed material and gets meaning from the visual material itself. Visualization, as defined here, requires the ability to make visual comparisons, to store these in memory, and to project the visual image in the absence of sight (making a picture of remembered experience in the mind's eye). Moderately retarded children can and do learn to manage themselves, to observe routines, to learn by rote, and to do simple problem solving. Given more adequate opportunity for developmentally sequenced perceptual-motor training, they can, and hopefully will, learn to manage themselves more efficiently and effectively, to make more productive and satisfying use of their full (often unrealized) potential. The needs and characteristics of the mentally retarded make a developmentally sequenced program of perceptual-motor training the logical base for curricular activities.

Four contemporary trends give substantial support to the wisdom of the perceptual-motor focus of curricular effort for the moderately retarded.

1. Increasing attention to the cumulative research evidence on the role of early perceptual experience in the learning process. (Piaget and Inhelder's [1958] contribution, the revival of interest in Montessori [*The Montessori Method*, 1913], and the research of Bruner, Goodnow, and Austin [1956], Hebb [1949], and Mosston [1966] are notable examples.)

2. The application of research technology and automated teach-

ing devices in perceptual-motor training of the retarded. Friedlander's (1966) project demonstrated significant improvement in manipulative activities of forty-four moderately and severely retarded children from three and a half to twelve years of age after automated habilitation procedures.

3. The current curriculum organization and content reforms in special education, including grouping practices and implementation of the diagnostic teaching concept. Bateman (1964), Connor and Talbot (1966), and Quay Models (Werry and Quay, 1969) are examples of the trend.

4. The rapid expansion and availability of programs of care, service, and education for the preschool handicapped. (Legislative provisions, federal and state stimulation grants, etc., document both the unmet needs and the growth in programs.) Interest in the research on the effects of early sensory stimulation on mentally deficient or "high risk" infants is increasing here and in other parts of the world. Lorenzo (1967) reports a longitudinal study which utilized a home and clinic program of multisensory stimulation techniques carried out by a multidisciplinary team of professionals. Much of the perceptual-motor protocol is carried out by educators who work with mothers and babies.

These trends, the studies cited, and researchers quoted all serve to remind teachers that good pedagogy, like good research, must be systematically scientific. There is abundant scientific information about the growth and development of the child which education has neglected to apply in spite of lip service to the principles of human growth and development and the dignity and the worth of the child. Teachers working with retarded youth have unparalled opportunity to observe and analyze how children grow and learn by watching their pupils "live out" that predictable, sequential pattern in slow-motion fashion, like a film at low speed. If teachers observe closely enough they will learn from the retardates them-

selves how to guide their development—slow step by slow step—
but securely, confidently, and successfully to their own self-realiza-
tion.

### Suggested Films

*Lost in Space*—25 minutes, color, sound.
   Shows perceptual-motor techniques employed by multidisciplinary team
working with brain-injured children in residential camp-school project at
Stevens Point, Wisconsin, in 1960. Project was sponsored by Milwaukee
Society for Brain Injured Children and was co-directed by G. N. Getman
and Ray Barsch. Project was modeled after a similar program held in 1958
(Glen Haven Achievement Camp) co-directed by G. N. Getman and N.
C. Kephart. Available for rental from Society for Brain Injured Children,
Inc., 1601 West Greenfield Avenue, Milwaukee, Wisconsin 53294.

*A Movigenic Curriculum*—45 minutes, black and white, sound.
   Shows activities described by Ray Barsch in Bulletin Number 25, State
Department of Public Instruction, Madison, Wisconsin, 1965. Available on
loan from Bureau of Audio-visual Instruction, University of Wisconsin,
1312 West Johnson Street, Madison, Wisconsin. Address inquiries to Dr.
Maurice T. Iverson, BAVI.

*Why Billy Couldn't Learn*—40 minutes, color, sound.
   Illustrates classroom techniques of diagnosis and educational interventions used with "educationally handicapped" children. Dramatically demonstrates (in slow motion) perceptual and motor handicaps. Available for
purchase or loan from CANHC, P. O. Box 604, Main Post Office, Los
Angeles, California.

*Visual Perception and Failure to Learn*—20 minutes, black and white,
sound.
   Film uses Frostig Test of Visual Perception to demonstrate relationship
between disabilities in visual perception and various difficulties in learning
and behavior. Available through Churchill Films, 662 North Robinson
Boulevard, Los Angeles, California 90069.

Testing and Training Kits and Package Programs

Frostig, Marianne, and Horn, David, *The Frostig Program* for the Development of Visual Perception. Chicago: Follett Publishing Co., 1964.

Getman, Kane, Hallgren, and Mckee, *Developing Learning Readiness*. New York: McGraw-Hill, 1969. Manual and instructional materials —filmstrips, tapes, etc. for class of thirty children. Gives specific instructions and directions for perceptual-motor skills sequence in the five modes described by Getman and discussed in this chapter. While not specifically designed for retarded children, instructional techniques and devices can be appropriately adapted in curriculum for retarded.

Getman, G. N., School skills tracing board and form sequence cards with teaching manual. Designed for tracing in developmental sequence all form components and configurations required in writing (cursive or manuscript) and in reading. Board is designed for optimum freedom of arm-hand movement and stress-free vision of the eye-hand task. Available from: P.A.S.S., Inc., Box 1004, Minneapolis, Minnesota.

Getman, G. N. (Tape-recorded Lecture Series)
1. *The Four L's of Learning,* Part I, Part II (1966)
2. *Physiological Foundations for Academic Readiness* (1966)
3. *An Introduction to Visual Perceptual Skills* (1967)
4. *Visual Dysfunctions and their Relationships to the Basic Visual Perceptual Task* (1967)
Available from: Media, P.O. Box 2005, Van Nuys, Calif.

Helson, E.L.
1. *A First Course in Phonic Reading* (1965)
2. *A Second Course in Phonic Reading,* Books I and II (1965)
Available from: Educators Publishing Service, 301 Vassar Street, Cambridge, Mass.

Roach, Eugene, and Kephart, N.C., *Purdue Perceptual-Motor Survey.* Columbus, Ohio: Chas. Merrill, 1966. Text and survey forms.

Slingerland, Beth, *Screening Tests for Identifying Children with Specific Language Disability* (1964). Available from Educators Publishing Service, 301 Vassar Street, Cambridge, Mass.

Sutphin, Florence D.
1. *Perceptual Testing and Training Manual*
2. *Perceptual Testing and Training Handbook for First Grade Teachers*
Available from: The Winter Haven Lions Club Research Foundation, Winter Haven, Fla.
Valett, R. E.
1. Valett *Developmental Survey of Basic Learning Abilities.* Available: Scoring Manual, Scoring Booklet, Workbook, Demonstration Cards.
2. *Valett Psycho-Educational Profile of Basic Learning Abilities.* Available: Scoring Manual and Profile Forms.
Consulting Psychologists Press, 577 College Avenue, Palo Alto, Calif.

# References

Ayres, A. J. "The Role of Gross Motor Activities in the Training of Children with Visual-Motor Retardation." *Journal of the American Optometric Association* 33 (September, 1961): 121-125.

Barsch, R. *A Movigenic Curriculum* (Bulletin 25). Madison, Wis.: State Department of Public Instruction, 1965.

Bateman, B. "Learning Disabilities—Yesterday, Today, and Tomorrow." *Exceptional Children* 31 (1964): 157-176.

Bruner, J. S.; Goodnow, J. J.; and Austin, G. *A Study of Thinking.* New York: Wiley & Sons, 1956.

Connor, Frances, and Talbot, M.E. *An Experimental Curriculum for Young Mentally Retarded Children.* New York: Teachers College Press, 1966.

Frankel, M. G.; Happ, F. W.; and Smith, M. D. *Functional Teaching of the Retarded.* Springfield, Ill.: Thomas, 1966.

Friedlander, B. Z. "Three Manipulanda for the Study of Human Infant Operant Play." *Journal of the Experimental Analysis of Behavior* 9 (1966): 47-49.

Gesell, A. *The First Five Years of Life.* New York: Harper and Bros., 1940.

Getman, G. N. *How to Develop Your Child's Intelligence.* 7th ed. Luverne, Minn.: Research Press, 1962.

Getman, G. N. "The Visuo-Motor Complex in the Acquisition of Learning Skills." Edited by J. Hellmuth. *Learning Disorders.* Vol. 1. Seattle, Wash.: Special Child Publications, 1965.

Getman, G. N. *The Four L's of Learning* (Tape Recording). Van Nuys, Calif.: Media, 1966.

Hayden, F. *Physical Fitness for the Mentally Retarded.* Ontario, Canada: F. Hayden, 1964.

Hebb, D. O. *The Organization of Behavior.* New York: Wiley & Sons, 1949.

Kephart, N. C. *The Slow Learner in the Classroom.* Columbus, Ohio: Merrill, 1960.

Lorenzo, E. G. E. "Multi-Sensory Stimulation of 'High Risk' Infants." Paper presented at Charter Congress of the International Association for the Scientific Study on Mental Deficiency, September 1967, Montpellier, France.

Montessori, M. *The Montessori Method.* Baltimore, Md.: W. E. Richardson, 1913.

Mosston, M. *Developmental Movement.* Columbus, Ohio: Merrill, 1966.

Piaget, J., and Inhelder, B. *The Growth of Logical Thinking from Childhood to Adolescence.* New York: Basic Books, 1958.

Simpson, D. "Perceptual Readiness and Beginning Reading." Ph.D. dissertation, Purdue University, 1960.

Tannhauser, M. T., and Petersen, W. "A Diagnostic Test to be Administered by Teachers to Discover Potential Learning Disabilities." In *The Special Child in Century 21,* edited by J. Hellmuth. Seattle, Wash.: Special Child Publications, 1964.

Werry, J. S., and Quay, H. C. "Observing the Classroom Behavior of Elementary School Children." *Journal of Exceptional Children* 35 (1969): 461-469.

# 7

## ESTABLISHMENT OF SPEECH PATTERNS
## Irene Blanchard

The teacher of trainable mentally retarded (TMR) children is less concerned with speech therapy than with speech development. If, in the ongoing path of his development of verbal communication, the TMR child has stumbled and has not been able to take the next step, it may be necessary for him to start over again and trace the steps from infant vocalizing to the point in the developmental scale where he is stalled. With each step firmly fixed, he may proceed as far as his intellectual limitations will permit. Generally, TMR children first stumble at the articulation level of the development of verbal communication and have increasing difficulty at the higher cognitive levels required of language, seldom achieving the perfection of word and sentence formation that most children in the public schools are able to achieve.

When we concern ourselves with the verbal communication of trainable retarded children, we must be aware that their verbal speech patterns frequently are unlike those of normally developing children. Both patterns use sound symbols in English words, but the normal child uses twenty-three consonants and thirteen or more vowels, while a trainable retardate may use only three or four consonants and only one or two vowels to make up his whole vocabulary.

Development of the ability to combine consonants with vowels to form words follows a predictable pattern. The consonants that initiate the sequence are those whose production relates closely to the vegetative behavior of common structures. Following this there is gradual progression to *intentional* adaptation of the structures for infant activities other than merely vegetative ones, for example, to make words that are the symbols of meaning. This latter requires intelligent *forethought*, which, unfortunately, trainable children simply may not have in sufficient degree to manage the adaptation. Let us be realistic, then, in our planning for their speech training.

The social development of an infant leads him through experiences in the pleasurable expulsion of breath as he blows and vocalizes, bubbles and gurgles. These happenings are labeled classically as cooing and babbling. It cannot be said that his early pleasurable vowel-like cooing and syllabic babbling is communication, however important it is for readiness to communicate. More likely, it is reflex exercise of maturing structures, and becomes intentional only for kinesthetic-oral, and sensory-aural pleasure, and/or when it produces rewarding reaction in parent or sibling. The discovery of sounds one can make is accidental. Repetition reinforces the vegetative exercise as well as the aural pleasure. When the exercise becomes *intentional repetition of his own sound*, the result is labeled "lalling." Thus lalling and echoing usually are next in the sequence. One activity leads to another, and finally the sound symbols of spoken language are produced.

This lalling is not "slurred and defective" articulation (Van Riper and Irwin, 1958), or the substitution of *l* for *r* (Taber, 1956), or distortion of tongue-tip sounds (Van Riper, 1963), or a disorder of articulation (Van Riper, 1963). It is the phenomenon described by Berry and Eisenson (1956) as "the repetition of self-made sounds." It is heard often as perseveration of exercise of the tongue-tip that results in *l-l-l-l* or something that is perceived auditorially by adults who hear it as *l-l-l-l*. In this sense, lalling is an appropriate label.

This, too, is oral and aural fun. Children do it from infancy through childhood. It is considered normal behavior at these ages. Totally deaf children coo and babble, sometimes repeating the same movements over and over, not perceiving sound but enjoying the muscular exercise.

Echoing is probably the first *intentional* communicative vocalization. It is the term used to describe a child's imitation and repetition of sounds that he has heard uttered by other persons.

A fairly well-defined timetable for onset of these activities is outlined in Fokes' chapter on language development. A healthy, alert infant of six months should respond vocally to repeated syllables, spoken or sung. He will watch the speaker's or singer's face intently and will appear to imitate mouth movements. Soon, he should "talk back" when stimulated in face-to-face conversation. He will repeat in his lalling and echoing any sound in his native language and some sounds that he will never hear spoken. He invents complicated syllables and repeats them from one day to another, gurgling and spitting and laughing to himself. His only meanings are muscular accomplishment and aural delight and sheer somatic pleasure. The infant of nine months is eager to respond to sounds. He coos to music, sometimes changing his own melody to match changes in pitch. Occasionally he may harmonize with a prolonged tone. He vocalizes pleasure and displeasure, expectancy and disappointment. His syllabic utterance, repeated as babbling when he lies quietly in his crib, picks up speed and intensity at the approach of a familiar person. It stops abruptly when his attention is disturbed by a strange movement or sound.

All this time, he has been building up a fund of information about what he hears and sees, how it feels to do interesting things with his mouth, and the appreciative reactions to his experiments.

He has also built up a reserve of physical energy. His lips and tongue and all the other parts of him that he will need to use for speaking have been made strong and supple with sucking and eating and mouth play. His chest and lungs are exercised vigorously and his voice box can make sound. He is structurally capable of any movement needed to make his communication verbal.

Until the period of cooing and babbling blends via the process of lalling into intentional repetition of his own sounds, deaf, retarded, and normal children behave in much the same way. From this point on, verbalization requires a high degree of intelligence. The retarded child is somewhat slower to begin and stays longer at each step. It is the *intent* in intention that limits the retardate's learning. The lower the potential to *intend to change* habitual vegetative behavior (sucking) to conscious behavior (speaking), the slower and more abnormal the pattern of communication. Echoing, if perseverated beyond the emergence of meaningful words, becomes a pathologic sign of aborted development, usually signifying limitation of intention and intellectual stability.

By the time a trainable child comes to a special classroom, his senses, if his sensory equipment is working, have been stimulated for over five years. At least he has seen, heard, touched, and tasted, and it is likely that he has developed preferences of things he wants to see, hear, feel, and taste. His experience with a variety of stimuli has been defined by the conditions of his retardation, by limitations of nurturance, limitations within his culture and family economy. If he has felt hunger and thirst, pain and visceral discomfort, and has not known what he felt, he will be a problem not only to his teacher but to himself. If he is toilet-trained, he is surely able to recognize the sensations of fullness and pressure. Consider that the untrained youngster may not be able to recognize these sensations.

All development occurs in sequence. Due to the nature of child development, one uses as the basis for initiating training the child's native provision, his capacity for taking in information, and the equipment with which he organizes meaning and expresses them.

The child who will learn to talk needs *four* basic foundations: intelligence, hearing, social interaction, and organized structures.

(See the TMR Pyramid of Communication, Figure 1.) Upon these foundation blocks, he organizes meanings and then expresses them initially with his whole body, breath, and voice, then later with articulate syllables in words, and finally in language.

## Intelligence

The children discussed are handicapped, by the very condition that places them in the TMR classroom, by the human characteristic labeled intelligence. The human animal is the only one who possesses this characteristic. The human is the only animal who can speak. With his intelligence, he is able to translate thought into word symbols and to direct his hand to write these symbols, his lips and tongue to say them. With his intelligence, he is able to translate symbols he sees or hears into meaning. Intact intelligence is one of the first and foremost ingredients for articulate speech.

## Hearing

Of equal importance for developing speech is the TMR child's capacity to hear. An ear must receive sound before it can be transmitted. The avenue for conducting physical sound waves must be clear from the vast exterior to the tiny and precise inner ear, where the first step in translation begins. Accumulation of wax in the external ear canal, for example, can block the sound before it has a chance to be heard. Residue from upper respiratory infections can interfere with the articulation of the three tiny bones in the middle ear that transmit and refine the physical sound waves on their way to neural connections. The sound wave must pass through two membranes (the eardrum and the oval window) to the inner ear, then it must displace fluid jelly as it climbs up a spiral stairway and down again to reach the tiny nerve ending that is waiting to react

# The TMR Pyramid of Communication

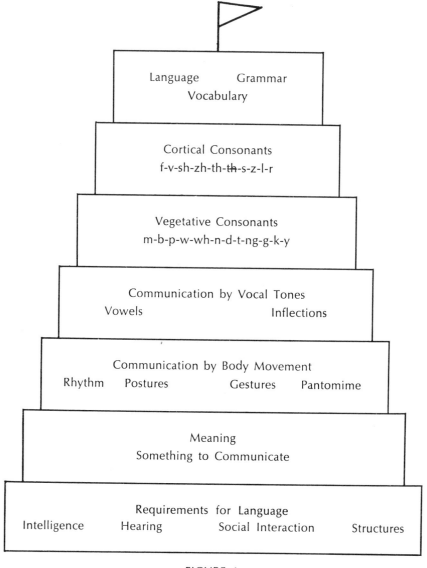

Language     Grammar
Vocabulary

Cortical Consonants
f-v-sh-zh-th-th-s-z-l-r

Vegetative Consonants
m-b-p-w-wh-n-d-t-ng-g-k-y

Communication by Vocal Tones
Vowels          Inflections

Communication by Body Movement
Rhythm    Postures     Gestures    Pantomime

Meaning
Something to Communicate

Requirements for Language
Intelligence    Hearing     Social Interaction    Structures

FIGURE 1

to precisely this wavelength. Then the sensation of sound is born, but it still has a long way to travel. It travels a minuscule nerve fiber, out of the bony labyrinth, and through a hazardous course of nerve and bone and blood vessels to the "seat" of auditory intelligence deep within the brain.

Much can happen along the way. Perhaps the most common damage to the neural part of hearing occurs when a neonate does not breathe vigorously at birth. In a matter of seconds, his brain tissue is deprived of nutrition and parts simply die of starvation. This infant may be deaf to only a few sounds that are part of the language he will learn to speak. Usually only the high-pitched sounds are affected, such as the hissing and whistling consonants *s, sh, th, f.* Since he cannot hear these sounds that are spoken in his presence, he establishes his speech pattern without them. He will call his sister *iter* or *titter,* and his shoe *oo* or *too.* He may answer to his name, to his mother's voice when she calls, to the teacher's instructions and to children's demands, but he hears only parts of their words, and he learns to speak them as he hears them. His teacher will do well to observe the kinds of sound such a child responds to and report her observations to the speech and hearing therapist. The therapist will verify the teacher's suspicion and teach the child how to put high-pitched sounds into words he uses. The longer he practices his incomplete speech pattern, the more fixed it will become and therefore more difficult to alter. If the infant does not respond to *any* sound, he should be sent to a teacher of the deaf as quickly as his disability is discovered.

## Social Interaction

The child who is stimulated by voice and words from his very first day is more likely to find pleasurable rewards in talking early than is the child who is seldom cooed and imitated. A generously equipped nursery in a far wing of a home is isolated from human sounds, the very sounds that will be invaluable in a baby's learning. Lucky is the baby who is held to be fed, who is joggled on his daddy's knee to rhythms of voice and jingle, who may be awakened by the laughter and play of his siblings, whose grandparents have joy in singing to him as they rock to the rhythm of a song. Not only is this lucky child hearing the sounds and rhythms of his native language, he is appreciating them and is perceiving the rewards, the joy, the usableness of spoken language. He will imitate the sounds and be further rewarded by smiles, hugs, and cuddling. His first words and sentences will be recorded and exhibited with pride.

## Organized Structures

The exercise that comes with a neonate's first intake of food is the very beginning of speech. He has been given only one set of structures to eat with and to talk with. Their first job is to suck nourishment into his tiny and totally dependent body. The most fortunate baby is breast fed. Not only is he feeling the security of his mother's body and the familiar throb of her heart, he is putting his mouth to purposeful activity. The structures he sucks with must work vigorously. This strong sucking organizes, at the *unintentional* (reflex) level of neural controls, the oral structures that he will manipulate at the *intentional* (cortical) level of controls to formulate meaningful sound symbols. His earliest words will be combinations of sounds that happen as he sucks. *Mama, baby, daddy, go, up, no*, are made by the same meeting of the structures over his outgoing breath that he has practiced since his first meal and repeated over and over in his babble.

When a spoon is offered to an infant, he sucks the food off as he will do for the rest of his life, closing his lips over the solid food, keeping them closed as spoon or fork is withdrawn. Both chewing and swallowing are instigated by this meeting of the lips. A speech-less child in a classroom, mouth agape and drooling, will need prompt reorganization of his sucking mechanisms before his limited intelligence can exercise controls over them to reshape them inten-tionally to produce a phoneme of his language. To achieve this reorganization, lips must meet from corner to corner, tongue well inside, as a healthy suck begins. Since sucking is a life-sustaining activity, the equipment for reorganization must surely be available for use. Meeting of the lips is the proper stimulator for reorganiza-tion. Even if they must be closed manually at first, their inborn nature takes over quickly. Bites of crackers and cookies are closed within the mouth, lips lightly meeting. Milk and juices are sucked from glass or cup. A child may have to learn to use a straw, but straws give lips and tongue fine, precise exercise at any age.

## Developing Meaning

The period of readiness for learning to talk passes very quickly in the infant's first year of life. If he should not show interest in communicating by his first birthday, it is likely that he has little meaning to communicate.

With all the foundation blocks sturdily in place, the climb to the peak of the pyramid (Figure 1) begins with a wide step: perception and sorting of meaning. Trainable children, at best, have but three solid foundation blocks and the one that's imperfect (intelligence) is the one most needed to perceive and sort meanings. A trainable mentally retarded child may have few meanings of his own, so we help him to find some.

The most obvious place to begin is with himself, with his own body and what it can do. If you ask him how he walks, he may say "with my feet." If his legs and hips are held so that they cannot move, he will be forced to learn that his legs and hips also help him to walk. When asked how he throws a stick, he will answer "with my hand." He must be shown that fingers, wrist, elbows, arms, and shoulders help, too. If he throws it far, his back and legs twist and push as well. When he pushes on tables with his hands, his feet push into the floor. When he pulls with arms, his heels dig into his shoes. Some parts of his body move, some do not. Some parts turn, some bend, some twist, some stay stiff, some can go limp.

## Suggestions for Perceiving Body Behavior

Meaning is first assigned to parts of himself and to objects in the immediate environment, but interaction between the child and the environment is necessary if portions of the body and if objects in his immediate surroundings are to be identified and correctly labeled. Some possible exercises are:

From the middle of a room, the teacher instructs and demonstrates and the children move their bodies to:

Push against the ceiling,
Push against the floor,
Push against the window,
Push against the door.

Where do you *feel* the push? Point to the parts of you that help you to push.

Lift a paper towel,
Lift a paper book,
A sweater from the table,
A coat from a hook.

Where do you lift? (the child replies) Where do you feel it? (reply) Some things are heavy, some are not, How can you tell? (reply)

The concepts of *I, mine, you,* and *yours* can be developed along with the discovery of what the body can do. For example, the teacher demonstrates:

I have a hand. You have a hand.
This is my hand. That is your hand.
You put your hand up, 'way up over your head.
This is my other hand. That is your other hand.
I can put both of my hands together. You put your hands together.
I can wave my hands, put them behind me, in front of me, etc.

Whatever is to be learned, whatever meaning is to be developed, must be presented to TMR children in its simplest form and as concretely as the teacher can manage, with much preliminary demonstration and follow-up repetition. Strong rhythmic activity used to introduce a concept organizes TMR children's physical selves and helps them toward relaxation and receptiveness (Hatcher and Mullin, 1967). A good start is with body bending, stooping, and squatting, to strong rhythmic direction. Example of such activities is found in the following:

Bend your body down, down.
You can tap the floor.
Head is heavy. Down it goes.
Bend and bend some more.

The instructions should be accompanied by *strong* rhythm, whether the lines rhyme or not. Even stronger rhythm, as required in the next example, is desirable:

That's the way. Heel to toe.
Walk. Walk. That's the way.
Heel to toe. Walk. Walk.

(Underscored words are emphasized.) It should be understood that in any activity in which TMR children are involved, the teacher should endeavor to establish some concept of things that are mentioned (*e.g., heel* and *toe* above).

Such activities must be repeated and repeated and repeated in precisely the same way each time. Every repetition reinforces the TMR child's response and deepens the pathways of learning so that he may retain in his neural memory both movement and meaning. With enough repetition, it is to be hoped that he will recall both at the appropriate stimulus.

## Bodily Action and Visual Cues

Firm recognition of what his body can do for him leads a speech-less TMR child to the expression of meaning by way of his body's movement. He has turned his head away from that which is dis-tasteful to him, telling clearly "I don't like that." He has shrugged his shoulders to say "I don't know" or "I don't care." He has tapped and tugged and pulled and clutched a hand to ask for attention. "See what I have," he tells without a word; or "Look what's hap-pening outside," or "I want you to know what I can do."

When body movement is stable, the child can proceed to the level of imitation; he can use his body to pantomime a meaning, to pretend that he is somebody else or feels like somebody else. Pre-tending is a form of symbolizing, and it is not easy for a TMR child. The child, however, thinks in terms of concrete objects and actions. He responds to stimuli that he can see and hear and feel. He can't see or hear or feel "pretending." The moderately retarded may even lack the concept of patterns that can be imitated, such as a person with a toothache, one with a sore foot, a hurt hand. He will know *tooth* and *foot* and *hand*, will identify them, exhibit his arm, and maybe call them by name if only by the vowels $\bar{oo}$, oo, and $\breve{a}$.

These children must be taught to observe the action of others and then to imitate it, but even imitation must be analyzed and presented in component parts. For example, attention may be directed to what Tommy does when his hand hurts. When Tommy's hand hurts, he holds it carefully, close to his body, to protect it from further hurt. He will likely reach out with his other hand to ward off a running playmate. How does Tommy look? Does this differ from the way he looks as he swings both hands and arms as he walks to school? If his hand hurts very much, he will tell it in his face. How does a face show hurt? How does Tommy look when he laughs? When he cries? How does he show he hurts? When the teacher demonstrates these "looks" she reinforces the children's memory of the "look" of somebody they have seen in pain.

Pretending happens when children imitate not only their teacher but an injured person that they remember seeing. They pretend they have hurt hands and protect them. They pretend they have sore feet and limp along, stepping and standing for a long time on the foot that is not sore. Each will note that his whole body leans toward the foot that is not sore. By pretending, each makes his body say "my foot is sore." Each will discover that his face looks sore.

If Betsy really has a toothache, she holds her hand to her face. Her head drops toward the cheek that hurts, her shoulders hunch and her body slumps. She *walks* slowly because her tooth aches. If Betsy pretends she has a toothache when she does not have one, she must command her body to do something very special so that it looks the way she felt when she did have a toothache. This is a great accomplishment. It is developed through imitation and practiced in play. At another time Pat may strut with chest thrown forward, feet and legs wide apart, thumbs hooked in his belt. "Who am I?" Batman, of course. Raymond clomps along, body bent at the waist, arms swinging together in front of him. He's an elephant.

Scott reaches, as though clinging to a branch, squats as though sitting on one, and scratches his tummy and under his arm as he has seen the monkey do at the zoo. Other children also have been to the zoo, and they call "Monkey"; some respond with a one-syllable vowel, some with two syllables, some with the whole word. This is the signal to repeat verbally whatever the child indicates by his motions. Let him know that there are words that say the same thing and let him know that some words are short, like *no* and *me* and *you*, while some have two parts, like *Bat-man* and *mon-key*.

It is possible that some TMR children cannot progress to acceptable verbal language. Their potential for expressing meaning may be limited to gross body postures and one or two vowels. For these children, stimulation must not cease. Encouragement to try the vowel sounds of name words and action words must be constant, each vocal response repeated and reinforced and rewarded. Even though these persons may not comprehend all that is going on they must surely take active part in big-body activity, circle games, dancing to music, clapping and drumming to rhythms. While their voices may not stay on pitch, they must be allowed to vocalize while other children sing simple melodies. These children could sit or stand next to the teacher, who could direct her own voice in the direction of their ears.

## Vocal Cues—Vowels

In the speech development of the TMR communication by vocal tones generally follows communication by body movement (Figure 1). For instance, Bobby may pull on your arm and hold out a pebble. You say, "You have a pebble. Bobby found a pretty pebble. You want to show me the pretty pebble. It is a very pretty pebble, a pebble." With a number of repetitions, Bobby should be expected to try the vowel *eh* in *pebble* and repeat it ad infinitum. It would be a good idea to find more pebbles. Each should be identified by the word *pebble* and Bobby should be encouraged to name each pebble with the *eh* vowel, until *pebble* means *eh* and *eh* means *pebble*. His vowel vocabulary enlarges on the occasion that he brings in a stone, much too large to be called a pebble. The vowel *ō* in stone is identified with the concept stone, and the two vowels appropriate to pebble size and stone size are differentiated. When a rock is discovered, the vowel in rock is identified with rock size.

Susie claps when she is delighted with the antics of a kitten. Her clapping says clearly "I am delighted." Her teacher remarks, "Susie likes the kitten, the pretty kitten, the kitten. The kitten makes Susie laugh. She laughs at the kitten, kitten, kitten." Susie may respond with the *i* vowel only, associating it with *kitten* and clapping in delight while watching the kitten at play.

At another time emphasis may be on the various ways in which you can say the single syllable *no* to carry different meanings. With only this one syllable, you can imply "I don't," "I can't," "I won't," "Don't do that!," "Is that so?," "You don't mean it!," etc. It is the melody of your voice that changes the meaning along with the force of utterance.

Additional consideration may be addressed to the various things a child's mother may mean when she calls his name. How does he know when his mother calls his name whether she means "I just want to know where you are." or "Are you into the cookies again?" or "Come here this minute!" or "Where does it hurt?"

Pretending to be hurt gives an excuse for remembering how one sounds when he is really hurt as Betsy pretends to have a toothache and Tommy pretends to have a sore foot. They probably utter a sound like *ow* in *ouch*, using only the *ow* vowel (actually two vowels *ah* and *ōō*). Hurt may be voiced in various ways. You do it by changing the pitch and loudness and melody of your voice. A short, sudden high-pitched *ow* happens when a short, sudden hurt happens, as when the doctor gives you a shot. A longer, louder *ow* happens when you get your finger caught in the door. When you fall on the gravel walk, and the hurt doesn't go away, your *ow* is low and soft and long and often. These changes in melody that change meaning are called *inflection*. Much of verbal communication is expressed by vocal inflections as well as by words. TMR children who are retarded because of Down's syndrome (mongolism) speak in a monotone, usually low in pitch. They lack variety of vocal inflection, and they seldom can carry a tune.

An effective way to introduce changes in melody is to speak contrasting melodies, up, up, up (with increasingly high pitch) and down, down, down (with increasingly low pitch) in rhythm, and accompanied by up and down body movements.

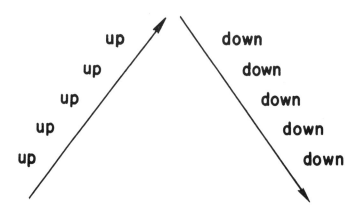

## Breathing

Prior to production of vegetative consonants (Figure 1) there must be control of emitted air. In order to establish this control of the breath, which makes speech sound possible, a trainable child learns that he has breath and that he can do something with it. Perhaps he needs some active pushing where his breath starts. His teacher can put one hand on his back, the other on his chest and give a sudden squeeze. A spurting voice will come. Repeated, the child can learn to make this same little grunt on his own *when he wants to make it.* He can learn to grunt without making a noise. This is gross control of the sort that is needed to begin articulate speaking.

His teacher will have a variety of things for him to blow. (These are rewards given to encourage him not to drool.) An easy way for the child to see the result of his breath is to let him blow into plain water through a tube. (A simple straw will do. Save blowing bubbles that float through the air *for a real reward.*) He can make the water barely move if he doesn't blow hard, whereas it becomes a veritable fountain if puffs are forceful.

Horns and whistles, especially the paper ones that unroll as you blow, are good practice and can be used in the rhythm band. To encourage finer controls, the cardboard core of paper towel rolls are excellent instruments for air-propelled races. Games that involve blowing crumpled tissues, Ping-Pong balls, round crayons, feathers, etc., can be invented. A simple chalk line to cross with a breath-propelled vehicle, several lines to stay between, a crayoned goal to reach, a taped line to follow on floor or table, a painted road to travel without crossing the edges are fun and require considerable skill in directing and controlling breath.

## Articulate Speech—Vegetative Consonants

Now, with success in the use of body breath and voice in order to express meanings, we climb the steps that lead to verbal language. Articulate speech sounds that compose words are made with *intention.* Combining them to make word symbols requires even more specific *intent.* In the sequence of learning to talk expect progress to be a hard one for the TMR. Taking it in sequence, as the unimpaired infant does it, the TMR six-year-old *with firm foundations and a meaning to express* may be expected to achieve *some* successful speech.

Speech sounds are made by stopping or shaping the breath, as it leaves the body. When we breathe, the air usually goes out through the nostrils. When we speak, most of it passes out through the mouth. There it is stopped or shaped by the same tongue and lips that have been exercised with eating. While there are some limitations to the shapes one tongue and two lips can make against otherwise nonmotile jaws and teeth and palate, an American child learns a hundred ways to do it. One tongue and two lips, with some help from soft palate, jaw, cheeks, and throat, contrive to shape and stop the breath to make twenty-three consonants and fifteen vowels and myriad combinations of consonants (blends), of vowels (diphthongs), and of both (syllables). From these speech musculators words are formed that are symbols of meanings.

Vowels are simplest to shape. With comparatively little up and down action of the tongue (with the jaw as in sucking) and familiar pursing and stretching of the lips, a variety of vowels (*ah, ōō, ee,* and twelve others) results. The infant coos with these "open" vowels. Then he manipulates tongue and lips to close off the open vowel sound to make babbling syllables. In the same sequence, the TMR child uses vowels in communication before he produces syllables and words. Repeating a statement made earlier, he may never proceed beyond the vowel stage of communication. It is imperative that he perceives appropriate vowels in "words" he uses.

As in all development, consonants are used in words in a fairly predictable sequence (Poole, 1934). The infant, as we have learned, makes all sorts of consonants in his babble and he may be able to repeat in his echoing almost any consonant alone and in combinations. But *until these consonants have become firmly established in word symbols that are meaningfully uttered,* they are not developed in language.

The sequence of consonant development, classically outlined by

Poole (1934) and essentially confirmed by Templin (1957), proceeds from a series of consonants whose primary production is practiced in the meeting and approximation of structures while sucking. Proof of this is very simple if you pretend that you are sucking and give attention to the tightening and relaxing of your lips. If you hum, you produce the consonant *m;* with only a small vocal sound before a quick opening (as in sucking) you produce *b;* with no voice, the same opening makes *p.* Add to these the consonant *h,* which is pure unshaped breath, and *w* and *wh,* which are almost closed by the lips (as in sucking), and we have the list of the earliest consonants to become established in English, French, German, Polish, Swedish, Dutch, Yugoslav, and, very likely, any human language (Poole, 1934).

If you continue pretending to suck, give attention to what is happening at the tip of your tongue. It is alternately pressing against the roof of your mouth and relaxing. With lips slightly apart, now as you hum, you make *n,* and with just a bit of voice before suddenly relaxing you make *d,* and with no voice at all, *t.*

Now consider what is happening at the back of your tongue during the same tightening and relaxing that occurs as you suck and swallow. With lips slightly apart, you hum and make *ng;* precede the opening with voice and you make *g,* and with no voice at all, *k.*

Because these twelve consonants approximate the meeting of structures for vegetative functions (sucking and swallowing) they may be called vegetative consonants. This is in contrast to other consonants whose production by the same vegetative structures is *different from the vegetative function.* Other consonants, which have to be produced intentionally, are termed cortical consonants (Figure 1). They are products of intelligent control of the structures. The vegetative consonant sounds are *h, m, b, p, w, wh, n, d, t, ng, g, k,* and *y.* All others are cortical consonants: *f, v, th, sh, zh, l, r, s, z.*

Since production of vegetative consonants is comparatively simple, it is small wonder that *mama, baby, papa, daddy,* and *bye-bye* are first words, or that so many of the most useful English words (even the "four-letter words") are predominantly vegetative: *good, and, no, one, pat-a-cake, toy, too, talk, go, come, home, man, woman, can, water, take, cat, dog, cup, eat, dinner, do, water, cake, cookie, bread, butter,* etc. Indeed, anthropologists Rzesnitzek (1899) and Keane (1920) report that the total verbal production of primitive people is made up of these consonants, a few vowels, and some vegetative "clicks."

In this respect, retarded children follow the patterns of primitive people. Two thirds of 150 children enrolled at one time in a residential school never progressed beyond the vegetative level of consonant production (Blanchard, 1964). Only one in ten achieved acceptable adult speech patterns (Figure 2). According to the Poole sequence, included in Fokes' outline of speech development, the establishment of vegetative consonants in words, for every normally developing child, should be complete by age four and one half. Many children, of course, accomplish this much earlier. Perhaps we should set the ultimate goals for speech development for TMR at this level of the normal (four and one half years old).

We can help TMR children who fail to achieve the four-and-one-half-year-old level to use *vegetative* consonants where they belong. They can make themselves understood *if* they speak simple words understandably. We would not expect them to repeat *Simon says* or *toothbrush* or *little* or *rattle.*

The teacher of trainables chooses things to do and things to repeat whose verbal symbols are combinations of *vegetative* consonants and vowels, and she would expect these names to be spoken whenever appropriate. Instead of "Simon says," she can play the game of "Hide a Button" or "Put a Cookie." Concepts of place and direction can be introduced as Bobby hides a button, while the teacher encourages him to say aloud: *in* a pocket, *behind* him, *on*

# Level of Language Development Achieved by Trainables
## (in percentages)

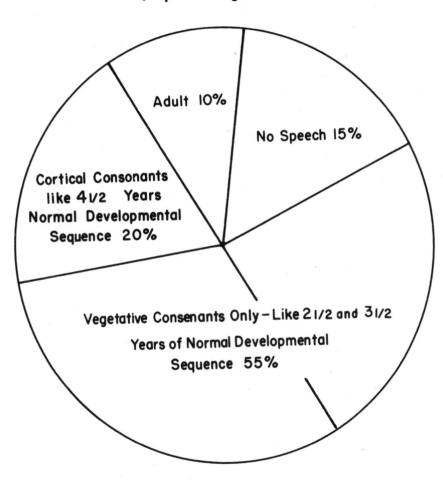

FIGURE 2

your head, *under* a book, *on top of* a paper, *behind* Tommy, *between* Betty and me, etc.

When counting, the TMR should be expected to say *one, two, eight, nine, ten, eighteen, nineteen, twenty,* etc., but not *three, four, five, six, seven,* until he has mastered all of the vegetative consonants in his speech and is ready to learn to make *th, f, v,* and *s.*

He can learn *one, two,* and *many,* and this much may be all he needs for his practical use. Whatever is to be counted should be real, visible, and touchable: *one penny, two,* and *many; one dime, two,* and *many; one domino* and *many.* The concepts three, four, five, six, seven may be introduced with dominoes, the children feeling the depressions that are the spots, seeing a line of spots from one to many, but *saying* only: *one, two, eight, nine.* The teacher can count aloud from three to seven, speaking clearly and in counting sequence. It is better that a TMR child should know that there are words he can't say, and is not expected to say, than to let him establish a pattern that is not understandable.

## Cortical Consonants

When the cortical consonants at the top of the Pyramid of Communication are approached we must take a long look at the TMR children in our classrooms. The potentials of each child must be assessed carefully before we expect him to take this difficult step. We must be realistic in our expectations. It is likely that limitations of intelligence will prevent more than half of the children in a TMR classroom (Figure 2) from making the essential intentional controls of their vegetative structures that produce the cortical consonants. Even normally developing children pause for a time at this level. (Note that in the Poole items, included in the Fokes schedule, only one consonant, *f,* becomes established in one year of development.)

To achieve these late-developing consonants, the smooth flow of

breath and voice must be disrupted in ways the vegetative structures have not practiced. Lips and tongue work together to occlude
the passage through the mouth, to narrow it or to block it almost
completely. These occlusions of the structures in new relationships
are intentional. They require intelligent, willful controls over the
structures. Intelligent, intentional, willful control is not an attribute
of TMR behavior.

We are committed to help the one trainable child in ten (Figure
2) who may reach adult standards of verbal communication. David,
who can use vegetative consonants regularly in words he knows,
now must add to his pattern of articulation the consonants that
require him to disrupt intentionally the orderly vegetative behavior
of his lips and tongue. Here David's intellectual limitations are
advertised. If David has the requirements to become the one in ten
who can put late-developing consonants in words, he needs much
help, help that is persistent, constant, consistent, and early. After
he has learned the essential disruption of structures to produce a
new consonant sound, he must be shown where the sound belongs
in words he wants to use.

The speech therapist can show David how to bite his lower lip
lightly and blow over it to make *f* and *v,* but she cannot follow him
through his daily activities to point out that the sound *f* belongs in
*fat* and *funny* every time he says *fat* and *funny;* in *four, five,
fourteen,* and *fifteen;* in *telephone* and *laugh;* in *if* and *afraid* and
*face* and *finger.* Nonetheless, the emphasis should be always on a
newly established consonant sound until it is firmly fixed in David's
pattern of speaking. One by one, David can add other cortical
consonants and learn where to put them in words.

The one-in-ten Davids, however, should proceed to the step of
cortical consonants. For subsequent disruptions of his vegetative
pattern, it is essential that David's teeth are in place. He will need
a blockage of teeth behind his lips against which to direct his breath
to make the sibilant sounds of *s, z, sh, zh.* It is virtually impossible

to produce these hissing sounds without teeth. Teeth help to narrow the breath passage for *th* and ~~th~~. Five-year-olds lisp when they lose temporary dentition. They try to fill the spaces where teeth used to be with their tongues, and instead of *s*, *th* happens; instead of *z*, ~~th~~ happens. This kind of lisp, which is not a speech defect in a five-year-old, is simply a substitution of *th* and ~~th~~ for *s* and *z*. It is the usual accompaniment to the loss of baby teeth.

It is likely that David and his classmates may be able to produce *th* and ~~th~~ more easily than the sibilant hissing sounds. These two consonants are useful to English speakers in ~~th~~at, ~~th~~an, ~~th~~e, ~~th~~ese, mo~~th~~er, in *th*umb and *th*irsty, in too*th* and no*th*ing. If David has learned to suck and to blow *at will* (this is *intentional* behavior, cortical rather than vegetative), he should have little trouble with making the sounds of *th* and ~~th~~. He almost, but not quite, bites his tongue and then blows over it.

As with all consonants in verbalization, the difficulty for David is not in being able to produce them in isolation, as the speech therapist teaches him to do, but in knowing where to put the sounds in words. Janie, who can read, will spot *th* and ~~th~~ easily because the two sounds are always spelled the same way. (Notice how many times this spelling appears on this page.) David cannot read. He has spoken imperfectly such words as ~~th~~is, ~~th~~at, mou*th*, o~~th~~er, *th*ings, and he will need constant reminding that he now knows the right way to say these words. Simply repeating a misarticulated word is reminder enough for Janie in the regular first-grade classroom, but David needs continual reminders. He needs repetition and review and reward and more repetition by every device a teacher can contrive: pictures and flash cards and drill and games and repetition.

This repetition and the understanding that patterns already set must be upset and other patterns established gives the teacher, and the parents, as well, something tangible to do. The speech therapist knows the tricks which will help David and Susie and Jimmy to place tongues and lips to produce the cortical consonants they can't make. This is her job but she sees each child a short time each day or each week. It is the people who are with these children when they are not with the speech therapist who help them to change their habitual patterns of articulation.

What of the nine out of ten trainable children who fail to make the difficult transition from vegetative to cortical control of their lips and tongues even to produce *f* and *v?* We must certainly stress the correct production of the vegetative, early-developing consonants in words they use often so that their jargon is at least partially understandable. Would it not be sensible to help these children to use baby talk (which is composed of early-developing consonants with vowels) as clearly as possible? Most of these children would say *hun* and *hat* and *hor* for *fun* and *fat* and *for*, and nobody understands them. The baby talker would say *pun* and *pat* and *por.* The substitution of *p* for *f* is a common baby-talk substitution. The three-year-old says *punny* for *funny* and *yap* for *laugh*, and *te-phone* for *telephone* and is understood. True, our TMR children are not three-year-olds, and the decision to be made is whether or not to let them talk in imperfect ten-year-old patterns, when they are unable to achieve perfect patterns, or to encourage them to speak well at the baby-talk level, the level at which they can perform and be understood. For those who lean to the latter horn of the dilemma, here is a list of the most common baby-talk substitutions:

*b* and *p* for *v* and *f,* as *bery* for *very, cop* for *cough,*
*d* and *t* for ~~th~~ and *th*, as *dis* for *this, tum* for *thumb,*
*d* and *t* for *zh* and *sh*, as *meadure* for *measure* and *too* for *shoe,*
*w* for *l* and *r*, as *witteh wabbit* for *little rabbit.*
s and z are usually omitted, as *ēe* for *see*, and *i* for *is.*

# Language

A detailed discussion of development of language appears elsewhere in this volume. The orderly arrangement of word symbols in English must be *learned*. All along the climb toward the peak of the pyramid, concepts of the names of things and of action words have become established, along with a few qualifying terms such as big and little, good and bad, pretty, warm and cold. The TMR child doesn't know a noun from a verb, a subject from a predicate, a clause from a sentence. He may, indeed, use the objective for the subjective in "Me want it." Repeated example, strong and clear and often, bombarding his ears with "I want it," may be the only way he will learn to say "I want it." Such an approach is practical, and the teacher can find or invent repetitive activities, always in rhythm, to help her children learn the difference.

Even if some TMR children can never reach the flagpole at the peak of the pyramid, there are stopping places along the way where they can perform comfortably. They can be good communicators with vegetative syllables or with vowels, or with pantomime. Even though the foundations may be incomplete, there is surely some meaning to be developed and some way to express it. TMR children can be helped to climb as far as they are able to go and should not be pushed farther.

# References

Berry, M., and Eisenson, J. *Speech Disorders.* New York: Appleton-Century-Crofts, 1956.

Blanchard, I. "Speech Pattern and Etiology in Mental Retardation." *American Journal of Mental Deficiency* 68 (1964): 612-617.

Hatcher, C., and Mullin, H. *More Than Words: Movement Activities for Children.* Pasadena, Calif.: Parents-for-Movement Publication, 1967.

Keane, A. H. *Man, Past and Present.* Cambridge, Mass.: University Press, 1920.

Poole, I. *The Genetic Development of the Articulation of Consonant Sounds.* La Verne, Calif.: Preston Printing, 1966.

Poole, I. "Genetic Development of Articulation of Consonant Sounds in Speech." *Elementary English Review* 2 (1934): 159-161.

Rzesnitzek, E. *Zur Frage der Psychischen Entwickelung eines Kindes.* Breslav: 1899.

Taber, C. W. *Taber's Cyclopedic Medical Dictionary.* 7th ed. Philadelphia: F. A. Davis, 1956.

Templin, M. *Certain Language Skills in Children.* Minneapolis, Minn.: University of Minnesota Press, 1957.

Van Riper, C. *Speech Correction: Principles and Practice.* Englewood Cliffs, N.J.: Prentice-Hall, 1963.

Van Riper, C., and Irwin, J. V. *Voice and Articulation.* Englewood Cliffs, N.J.: Prentice-Hall, 1958.

# 8

## LANGUAGE TRAINING

## D. D. Kluppel

For many years, most of the concern about the communication skills of the mental retardate was in the area of articulation. Heber (1962) categorizes speech skills under the general rubric of sensory-motor skills and then proceeds to define them as they relate to a lisp, to stuttering, or to stammering. Clearly, language ability or disability as opposed to speech ability of the retarded children is not specified. Even when discussing the importance of interpersonal relations and the impairment which the retardate suffers, Heber does not acknowledge the role of language as an essential in inter-personal behavior. As Schiefelbusch (1965) points out, Heber's statement is an extremely "restricted concept of speech disability."

The articulation of speech sounds is one of the overt manifesta-tions of language. Vocalization, in and of itself, may or may not have the underlying meaning and structure which is associated to sound sequences and which is the actual "language." The symbolic processes associated with oral communication involve the encod-ing, decoding, and integration of symbols by which an individual gives or receives information. In contrast with this is speech pro-duction, which is only one means of expressing language. Equally relevant and meaningful are other representations of language, written and gestural. The aspects of particular importance are the structure and the meaning, regardless of the mode of communication. These are elements that must be taught before it can be said that a person uses language.

The deficiency in symbolic processing in the mentally retarded, without specifically referring to language, has been reported so often as to become obvious. However, the view that the language disability is simply one more symptom of the overall condition has not been well explored. It is this aspect that will be stressed here.

For the mentally retarded child the focus must be on training those aspects of language which will be most easily learned and most useful. They should be the most easily learned, at least initially, so that the child is not frustrated in his attempts to acquire language, and therefore has a healthy attitude toward it. They should also be the most useful because the attempt must be focused to provide the child with a code which, when used, results in a reduction in the amount of effort or ambiguity. The child can then experience the greatest control over his environment and he will be using the system efficiently. The end product is a retarded child who performs not only as a function of his initial potential but also as a result of the training, of the educational techniques used with him.

One of the most crucial variables entering into the language training of retarded children is the assessment of the child's level of performance, which can be done by Fokes' Developmental Scale of Language Acquisition or Mecham's Oral-Aural Language Schedule (1963). After determining this, it is then possible to devise a program that will provide the appropriate model and level for the individual child. Assessment should be made of phonology, morphology, and syntax, as well as vocabulary. This assessment can be made through observations of the child.

In determining the child's phonological proficiency it is important to note what sounds he can make, which ones are left out, and whether or not he substitutes one sound for another. To try and teach him a word when he cannot make the sounds is frustrating for both the child and the teacher.

If the retarded child is making sounds into words, then the teacher must check to see if the child uses the plural, the possessive, verb tenses, and so on. Is the order of words the child utters in agreement with the adult's language? If it is not, where does the order break down? Can the child respond to the questions of "what," "where," "when," and "why"? Does the child have concepts such as time, space, and plurality? All of this should enter into the final assessment of the level at which the child is functioning. The necessity of determining each child's level and working from there cannot be overemphasized. It is possible, however, to have some group activities for vocabulary building or for working on concepts.

Reassessment from time to time is also a requisite, since rate of change will be individually determined by such factors as basic potential and motivation.

There are at least two conditions which must be met in order to have the most satisfactory situation for verbal communication to take place. First, there should be something to say, and second, there should be someone to say it to. Although these conditions are obvious, frequently they are overlooked.

One of the first requisites for oral language to occur is verbal stimulation. The child, normal or retarded, needs to hear language spoken. The model for oral language, therefore, needs to be at a level the child can understand and perhaps imitate. At the outset, sentences should be short and simple. Directions or instructions should be easy to follow. The teacher should accompany her dialogue with appropriate gestures and examples. Every possible sensory modality should be used to help the child experience his environment. Initially it is only through his direct experience that the child will learn about his environment. Gradually he can learn to attach the appropriate oral label to stimuli he experiences and eventually learn the meaning of words. In choosing those things to stimulate communication, *e.g.*, the things to talk about, care should be taken to make sure the objects, people, or events are at a level that the child can understand.

Providing the child with ongoing descriptions of what he is doing and what is happening in the classroom or what the teacher is doing is another technique for stimulation and for providing the child with new words. By example and association he can learn the meaning and the usage of words describing the ongoing activity.

If the language disability is viewed as a symptom, as one kind of behavior the child produces, then the teacher is free to treat the symptom. That is, she can deal with the language behavior without undue concern about *why* the behavior is like it is. For many educators, then, this approach provides a freedom to modify the behavior, that is, the phonetic and structural components of the child's language.

The freedom to modify the language behavior as a symptom may be compared, analogously, to behavior therapy—the modification of undesirable behavior into something more acceptable. This approach, then, also comes in for criticisms similar to those made of behavior therapy. Mainly, when you modify the language behavior, that is all you are doing; you are *not* correcting the cause of the behavior. At this time, this criticism should not be of concern. With the ambiguity of the research in the area of etiology and with the lack of knowledge concerning what is really going on when symbolic processing occurs, one should be content to modify the external overt behavior.

What are the conditions under which modifications of language behavior need to occur? For efficiency's sake, the technique should bring about maximum possible change in a maximum number of children. Therefore this program should be composed of children who can cope adequately for short periods in a group situation as well as individually. Specific IQ boundaries are not necessarily stated, since it has been demonstrated that children who test low on IQ tests may frequently demonstrate adequate social behavior, *i. e.*, "adaptive behavior." This approach is different, although theoretically similar, to the *two-person interactional therapy* approach suggested by Schiefelbusch (1965). It would be quite possible, indeed desirable, for these two programs to coexist.

What empirical evidence is there that behavior modification can be used with groups? Birnbrauer, Bijou, Wolf, and Kidder (1965) have demonstrated that specially trained teachers can use operant techniques, techniques that reinforce or reward a correct or desired response, in the control and modification of classroom behavior of retarded children. Hewett (1968) is currently directing a successful program using operant techniques in a classroom of children with special training disabilities. Some time ago, Ayllon and Michael (1959) demonstrated that operant techniques could be used by nurses to modify ward behavior of psychotic patients.

The rationale for the orientation of behavior modification has been given many times, notably by Ullman and Krasner (1965) and Bijou and Baer (1961), and further discussion is afforded in the chapter by Girardeau. The specification of why this orientation may provide gains, specifically in the area of language, is based upon the roles of reinforcement, both as an attitude modifier and as a feedback mechanism. It is also dependent upon generalization and discrimination, these latter two concepts at the semantic, syntactic, and conceptual levels.

The role of reinforcement as an attitude modifier should probably come first with most children. They have to learn that oral communication is a "good thing," that pleasant consequences result when they use oral language. The kinds of reinforcing consequences will obviously have to be geared to the individual group or child. Older children may work well for tokens, while younger ones may need more tangible rewards. Ultimately it would be desirable for the child to work for social reinforcers. It must be remembered that many of these children will have been extinguished or perhaps punished for their earlier attempts at oral communication. This is why reinforcement at this point must be seen in the role of attitude modifier. Later reinforcement can provide the useful information concerning the correctness of a verbal response. It serves then as a feedback mechanism; it gives knowledge of results. When generalization and/or discrimination is required, the presence or absence of reinforcement provides the information to the child, and he can modify his verbal behavior accordingly. These processes of generalization and discrimination will take place both simultaneously and successively when the child starts to formulate an utterance occurring on the phonetic or syntactic level. The resultant reinforcement or lack of it again operates to provide information to him.

Perhaps by now these points are obvious. Some teachers of the retarded may already operate this way. However it is necessary to insure that all teachers learn these skills. In contrast with the training given to a teacher of the deaf, and the approach so frequently used, the special teacher of retardates does not receive an educational orientation that places stress on oral communication. One knows he is working with a retarded child and perhaps expects communication difficulties. In a classroom for children with a hearing loss, every activity is planned so that the optimal usefulness of oral communication is there, whether it be in reading, games, or arithmetic. Not only is oral communication the appropriate response in most situations, but it eventually becomes the required response. Because of the group situation, the children are able to recognize that they are not unique in their communication difficulties and thus unnecessary anxiety is reduced. This focusing orientation on language skills has been demonstrated successfully with hearing-impaired children who have language disabilities. Therefore a similar orientation seems appropriate and useful for other children with language problems.

Previously it was stated that with the retarded child it is essential to teach those aspects of language that would be the easiest to learn and the most useful to the child. Perhaps a discussion of what kinds of concepts should be taught and more particularly how to apply the technique to the materials should be presented.

Exploring the notion of teaching the easiest things first, the child should be taught the names of things that he experiences in his environment. Initially these are those that he experiences as strong perceptual stimuli. The naming activity does several things: (1) it teaches the child a basic vocabulary; (2) it starts the child thinking in terms of "meaning"; and (3) it provides some of those units which ultimately will be put together to form discourse.

To start the child in the "naming" process, it is necessary, initially, to reinforce any attempt the child makes at vocalizing. Then reinforce him for vocalizing in association with the object. That is, reward him for producing any vocalization in the presence of the object to be named. After a vocalization is produced consistently as the object is presented, the teacher can selectively reinforce only those sounds that are appropriate to the object. For example, a *ball* may be called *ah* at first, and later the *b* sound should be reinforced —*bah;* still later the final *l* could be expected.

The wise teacher will choose the initial objects to be named after observing her children. The teacher should be aware of the developmental acquisition of sounds (phonemes) by normal children and of where the children are in the sequence (see Chapter 7 by Blanchard). The vowel in the example above is one of the earliest sounds that a child learns; the *b* is also an early consonant; but the final *l* is acquired much later in the sequence by normal children. As a result of this information, the teacher would expect *bah* to be produced much earlier than the complete *ball,* and she would accept the incomplete *bah* if she had observed that her retarded child could not produce the final *l.* Initially the emphasis is on accepting any sound the child makes and then shaping the sound gradually toward the particular sound or sound sequence that is appropriate to the stimulus.

When the child is at the stage of one-word utterances, it may make a statement or ask a question through the use of the single word. He does this by the inflection of his voice: *Ball* meaning *There is the ball.* Or *Ball?* meaning *Where is the ball?* How much more effective he would be if he could produce either of the two complete utterances! The teacher and his parents would not have to guess about which of these statements he is making.

The natural progression in language training is the combination of words learned. This can be taught in much the same way as the naming process. However, the teacher now should be dealing with the building up of the underlying structure (grammar) of the language. Random combination of phonemes or words does not constitute language. Rather it is the organization and structure of the phonemes or words that form language. After teaching the units, one demonstrates that the appropriate combination of words will form meaningful utterances. The major purpose of teaching the retarded child language skills is to provide him with the facility to communicate his needs and ideas to others. Language, therefore, is a means of manipulating his environment. In order for him to communicate effectively he must begin to sequence his utterances appropriately. It is necessary, however, for the teacher of retarded children to have a realistic view of what they will be capable of doing. Generally, the combination of words will be short and perhaps "telegraphic." Because the naming process will be taught and because of their obvious relevance, content words will make up much of the retarded child's vocabulary. Other words denoting action and relationships will be less apparent. These words will be learned and put into combinations more easily if they are made meaningful to the child. Demonstrate the action or relationship to the children and have them imitate it before and during the production of the words.

In general, before the sequencing of phrases or sentences takes place, there are some concepts the child should learn. These concepts make the acquisition of order and meaning much easier. For example, if the child knows the concept of time, it will be much easier to teach him verb tenses, since they are dependent upon chronology. If he knows the concept of spatial relationships, it will be easier to teach him certain relational prepositions. These concepts can be developed in the child while also working on naming objects. The use of a calendar of activities or the relevant physical location of known objects would be appropriate to this teaching. Other important concepts are size and shape. Knowledge of these concepts will help the child learn descriptive adjectives. Still another concept, which is perhaps basic to most of the others, is "same-different." Various kinds of games lend themselves to the teaching of this concept. Its relevance comes from such practical applications as dressing, for example, choosing socks of the same color; or eating—choosing a fork or spoon to pick up the food. More esoteric uses result in the ability to read and spell. The discrimination of these visual or auditory stimuli underlies the basic material included in the educational process for the retarded child. Of course, the need for reinforcement for success in using these concepts is obvious.

When these various concepts are acquired, the application of them to language should take place. The teacher can provide the model for simple phrases or sentences using various content words and relational or descriptive words—for example, "big dog"; "John runs." The child can either imitate or, when possible, construct phrases or sentences using his new concepts. Reinforcement or reward for correctly producing an utterance should immediately follow. The child needs the information about his verbal behavior.

In summary, it has been suggested that a training program be organized to provide verbal stimulation for retarded children. The teacher is to be a model for producing short and simple phrases and sentences used as directions and instructions. She also is the model for the imitation and learning of the names of things, for concepts such as time, relations, size, and shape, and for the learning of the underlying structure (grammar) of language. Reinforcement, or reward for desired response, is seen as a vital consequence of the verbal behavior of the child. Its use is as an attitude modifier as well as a source of feedback. Initially it follows any attempts at vocalization and subsequently occurs after phonemes, words, and combinations of words in correct grammatical order. The training program is developed after careful assessment of the level of performance of each child in the group. The central focus of the program revolves around all activities being seen as situations in which oral language is the appropriate response.

# References

Ayllon, T., and Michael, J. "The Psychiatric Nurse as a Behavioral Engineer." *Journal of Experimental Analysis of Behavior* 2 (1959): 323-334.

Bijou, S. W., and Baer, D. M. *Child Development: A Systematic and Empirical Theory.* Vol. 1. New York: Appleton-Century-Crofts, 1961.

Birnbrauer, J. S.; Bijou, S. W.; Wolf, M. M.; and Kidder, J. D. "Programed Instruction in the Classroom." In *Case Studies in Behavior Modification,* edited by L. P. Ullman and L. Krasner. New York: Holt, Rinehart, and Winston, 1965.

Heber, R. "Mental Retardation: Concept and Classification." In *The Exceptional Child,* edited by E. P. Trapp and P. Humelstein. New York: Appleton-Century-Crofts, 1962.

Hewett, F. "Resource Room Provisions for Exceptional Children." (Personal communication, 1968).

Mecham, M. J. "Developmental Schedules of Oral-Aural Language as an Aid to the Teacher of the Mentally Retarded." *Mental Retardation* 1 (1963): 359-369.

Schiefelbusch, R. L. "A Discussion of Language Treatment Methods for Mentally Retarded Children. *Mental Retardation*, 1965, pp. 4-7.

Ullman, L. P., and Krasner, L., eds. *Case Studies in Behavior Modification.* New York: Holt, Rinehart, and Winston, 1965.

# 9

## GOALS FOR SELF-HELP AND INDEPENDENCE

### Bernice B. Baumgartner

The objectives of self-help and independence for the trainable mentally retarded (TMR) may appear impossible to the uninformed, yet they are attainable by the child, teenager, or adult whose teacher or parent expects achievement and paves the way for success. The uninformed view self-help and independence as inconceivable because of the overwhelming negative implications of outmoded theories and the application of stopgap programs with limited expectations. Because of the misuse of intelligence quotients and mental ages, many boys and girls are labeled as retardates. Within the context of outmoded theories people use outworn practices as stopgaps. Unprepared teachers have been employed in mushrooming classes as a result of legislation and pressure, since there was no built-in readiness for such programs among educators.

## Outmoded Psychological Concepts

Hunt identifies six outmoded beliefs in psychological theories for disadvantaged children: (1) fixed intelligence, (2) predetermined development, (3) fixed and static brain function, (4) negation of experiences during the early years, (5) educational reactions based on instinctual needs, and (6) motivation of learning by homeostatic needs, painful stimulation, or acquired drives based on these needs. Such outmoded theories continue to be used with the TMR. In many institutions personnel either try to "get the child ready for education" or tend to wait until he has a mental age of three or a chronological age of eight (to meet requirements in public school classes). In many cases the most precious learning periods in the lives of these children are being wasted. Well-prepared professionals should be working with the child from the earliest time, for the child is ready for learning and education at birth (p. 258).

Every moderately retarded child *can* help himself and many *can* reach higher mental ages at earlier chronological ages *if* adequate experiences are provided. Compensatory education is indicated for the culturally deprived child because of his low socioeconomic environment. Compensatory education also is indicated for the child in the higher socioeconomic environments who is experientially deprived because of misconceptions.

## Stopgap Programs

A high percentage of TMR children are not profiting from their schooling. In addition to inadequate programs that are based on outmoded concepts such as those mentioned above, there are the inadequate practices resulting from the limiting aspects of the so-called objectives of self-care, social adjustment, and economic usefulness. By hiding behind the word *training* instead of seeking to provide real education and learning, many strange acts take place in TMR classes. Emphasis may be placed on social adjustment or the superficial "social graces" to the extent that these individuals become mimicking puppets, producing all the right words and actions at the right times in the most overprotected situations.

One illustration of this approach is the special "musical" in which the teacher said and sang the words behind a screen while the TMRs and even the EMRs pantomimed actions and words instead of learning to use the words they needed. However, when compensatory education was provided these persons' unused language abilities were called into being. With simple compensatory experiences, the mimicking young adults quickly learned to express themselves and presented hour-long programs that were unforeseen in the earlier artificial settings, where teachers were doing for these people what they could have done for themselves. After being expected to talk and sing, these young adults gained confidence. The independence of thinking and acting was reflected in everything they did—in learning to care for themselves as they were "allowed" to go out into the community on their own. The achievement of independence is also exemplified by teenagers in the Occupational Training Centers of New York City; they learn to ride the subways by themselves, to change from one subway to another, to become messengers for different firms. These people become different individuals; no longer are they overprotected puppetlike persons with a veneer of artificial social graces.

Many teachers also have used the "resting" activity out of context (Baumgartner, 1955). For instance, "resting" appeared to be the major activity in many classes. Periods of rest were observed to extend from one to two hours for socially and physically mature teenagers of sixteen and seventeen, whose learnings consisted of bringing in the cots and mattresses for an afternoon of sleeping.

The teaching of repetitive road signs (often quite different from those these children will ever see) and learning colors are other favorite but useless drill routines. Also, these individuals are found weaving mats by the hundreds, responding with infantlike and outmoded earlier behaviors because the adults responsible for programming expect no more. But, as we know, the IQ need not be considered a fixed entity—unless the school freezes it by not providing appropriate environmental experiences.

## Base for Self-Help and Independence

A broad base from which attainable objectives in self-help and independence can be nurtured should be established in an adequate physical and emotional climate and should include the following elements:

1. An open-ended philosophy which furnishes constructive guidelines in understanding the need, the development, and the interests of the individual.
2. The relating of goals to the basic philosophy in a manner that provides for the building of systematic procedures rather than fragmentation of effort.
3. The framework for bringing a systematic day-to-day approach into focus.

### An Open-Ended Philosophy

Basic to our expectations is "the conviction that many who are retarded in mental development have a potential, the limits of which are still unknown but highly dependent upon the ability of the training supervisor . . . to anticipate difficulties [and then] to analyze, and to teach those skills needed to overcome difficulties" (Baumgartner and Lynch, 1966). In such a context each person working with retarded individuals has "hope" for each child, teenager, and adult and has a commitment to expect unforeseen results —results that could not possibly be predicted in initial evaluations.

Expectations for those with whom we are working must be open-ended. They must include the realization that every child, teenager, and adult *is* capable of learning at every age from birth to death. Each person who is retarded in mental development or who is multiply handicapped should be evaluated as a total individual. The desire is to bring these persons to their highest levels of functioning in order that all may lead constructive lives, that remunerative work, self-help, and independence can become realities. Learning begins in infancy. But too often we are not ready to teach. We insist that a youngster fail and then spend years trying to rehabilitate him.

## Goals as They Relate to Basic Philosophy

The goals of self-help and independence need to be defined in terms of:

1. The abilities of the staff.
2. The ever-changing environment and the experiences needed in that environment to promote transition to the next higher step in social, physical, mental, and emotional development.
3. The emotional climate of the school with its expectations, acceptances, and attitudes (Baumgartner, 1965).
4. The current interests of each pupil as well as the experiences needed for more adequate achievement.
5. The experiential level of each pupil, his social level, and his physical level—not bringing other levels down to the level at which he is functioning mentally.
6. The underlying competencies which may eventually relate to the ability to succeed.
7. The understanding of the emotional impact of poverty, of inacceptance of the child in a home of high standards.
8. The pupil as an individual in his own right.
9. A plan which embodies short-term objectives for the child, his parents, and the teacher.
10. Involvement of everyone concerned with this individual as important "teachers," including the parent, from whom a great deal can be learned.
11. A group-gestalt approach to meet the child's emerging needs and abilities as all members of the training team synchronize their expanding expectations.

To the extent that all concerned can observe the strengths and limitations—and transmute the understanding of those observations into positive experiences in an expanding program—to that extent is it possible for the individual to find himself and his place in the environment where he can live [Baumgartner 1965].

## A Systematic Approach

A systematic approach comes into focus by building a framework that is based on sound knowledge of growth and development that advances each individual to his fullest potential at each stage of his existence. The program most realistic: the needs of each person are considered as teachers learn to build a bridge by (1) *studying the child*—observing the child's level of development and his growth patterns and (2) *matching*—finding the proper methods, people, and experiences to help this individual advance toward the next step in his growth and development.

The teacher learns to study the child, teenager, and adult by seeing, listening, and continuing to observe the reactions of the individual as he moves, utters sounds, uses his body, in the time he needs to move from one activity to another, in his reactions at different times of the day, in the way he responds to his peers, and in the things that make him a personality in his own right. The teacher needs to identify the level of present behaviors and to pinpoint the next step of functioning for this person.

By means of systematic study and programming the teacher learns to obtain information sufficiently detailed to discern:

*How* the child grasps what has been presented.
*Where* he has success.
*When* he reaches his frustration level and when he is ready to learn to take frustration.

*How* his strengths are expanded and his weaknesses (errors)
are minimized or overcome.

Areas in which to view pertinent growth patterns through which
each child can be guided include:
1. *Concept of Self.* There should be a systematic evaluation of
the mental health of each person (at each age). There is also a need
for each to develop trust and autonomy and to find people with
whom to identify. There is a need for the teacher to know when the
child reaches his frustration level, how he views life *now,* how he
handles life situations during strategic crises, and how he relates to
adults, to peers, to a group. There is need for the teacher to know
how to change himself in order to adjust to the child. There is need
to eliminate unfounded fears in the child, and in the parent, and to
eliminate stigma and "disability labels."
2. *Physical Movement Patterns.* Children should be encouraged
not only to move but to learn to move effectively. The muscles of
the body respond to sensory perceptions or to the lack of them.
Various movements help make bones, muscles, and joints stronger.
Individual programs are planned toward the development of agility,
balance, flexibility, and strength. Motor development is part of all
areas of activity—play, rhythms, swimming, dancing, music, art,
language arts, and school-work study.
3. *Sensory-Motor Perception.* Ongoing comprehensive evaluation of skills and changes in the child leads toward special planning
to meet needs for sensory perception including skills in auditory-
motor, visual-motor, and tactile perception, as well as kinesthetic
perception, olfactory perception, and gustatory perception.
4. *Cognitive Appraisal and Language Development.* This includes communication, both nonverbal and verbal, as it is discussed in
the chapters on cognitive and language development, and all academic subjects in which one learns to observe, listen, imitate, verbal-
ize, converse, read, write, compute, be creative, and be oneself.

5. *Environmental Manipulation.* Careful scrutiny of culture, socioeconomic factors, parents' attitude toward child, acceptance of the community, foster home placement, court action, residential placement, parent involvement—conferences, reporting to and from teachers, home visits, consistent interaction between home and school—all contribute to this area of top priority.

6. *Social Interaction.* Social communication cuts across all matrixes as the individual is assisted in learning to get along with others, to take directions, to develop good work habits, to participate in group activities with his peers, to communicate and interact with adults, to care for self, to cope with change, to assume responsibilities, to evaluate self, to participate in recreation and other community activities, to use public transportation, and to become a useful citizen.

# Building a Dynamic Open-Ended Curriculum

The experiential curriculum, which encourages the development of self-help and independence, emerges through people, as well as from and through events, values, and needs. With goals clearly in mind, lessons emerge in which patterns of development point the way toward growth in needed skills. The following format can be used for lesson plans to provide adequate experiences:

## Lesson Plan

1. *Class:* Nursery School, Elementary School, Secondary (Circle one)
2. *Objectives* (Circle those that apply)
Self Concept                    Physical Movement Patterns

Sensory-Motor Perception        Cognitive Development
Environmental Manipulation      Social Interaction
How are you guiding such growth?    _____

3. *Motivation* and *attention:*    _____
_____
_____

4. *Materials:*    _____
_____
_____

5. *Procedures:*    _____
_____
_____

6. *Evaluation* (after the lesson): _____
_____
_____

7. *Related Activities, Follow-up:* _____
_____
_____

8. *Recording Observations*

   Daily observations are desirable; at the least, weekly observations of children should be recorded. _____
_____
_____
_____

## Summary

Outmoded concepts and stopgap programs must be eliminated if the person rather than the TMR label is to survive.

The ingredients of an educational program are similar in nature for any child, teenager, or adult who, due to specific limitations, must have a unique prescriptive plan designed to meet his particular needs. No one should be excluded from such an educational approach. We are far beyond the simple objectives of self-care. We know that expecting only limited self-care activities destroys and retards the progress of the person who needs special techniques to help him grow. Second-rate programs are acceptable no longer.

There is the need now to take time to analyze what is happening. Each individual needs opportunities to find circumstances to match his own particular interests and stages of development. The teacher needs to determine whether prescriptions for teaching match what the child has in storage, to classify and clarify the range of activities, to provide a framework for finding out what is worth doing, to eliminate the deficits in present efforts, and to reconceptualize and replan what needs to be done.

Mere words defining the approach to the transition of experiences from one level to the next are not enough. But with actual demonstrations with children and with carefully planned and executed practice teaching that is geared toward compensatory and developmental experiences at every age, there can be progress.

How well students learn self-help and independence depends in a large part on the expectations of teachers and parents. These expectations count more than the materials used in teaching.

## References

Baumgartner, B. B. *A Curriculum Guide for Teachers of Trainable Mentally Handicapped Children.* Springfield, Ill.: Department of Public Instruction, 1955.

Baumgartner, B. B., and Lynch, K. D. *Administering Classes for the Mentally Retarded: What Kinds of Principals and Supervisors Are Needed?* New York: John Day Co., 1966.

Baumgartner, B. B. *Guiding the Retarded Child.* New York: John Day Co., 1965.

Hunt, J. McV. "The Psychological Basis for Using Preschool Enrichment as an Antidote for Cultural Deprivation." *Disadvantaged Child,* Jerome Hellmuth, ed. Seattle, Wash.: Special Child Publications of the Seattle Sequin School, Vol. 1, pp. 222–260.

# 10

## TRAINING FOR SELF-HELP AND INDEPENDENCE
## Beth Stephens

The ultimate aim of training programs for the moderately retarded is to assist these persons in the attainment of the highest
level of independence for which they are capable, but basic to this
aim is the realization that the skills that promote such independence are highly interrelated. Self-help skills are acquired as the
person develops motorically and perceptually. Social skills are acquired as the person interacts with others, first through facial expressions, gestures, and intonations, and later through language.
While cognitive development is necessary in the acquisition of
academic and vocational skills, it also is a necessary prerequisite for
social skills and language. This chapter considers self-help, social,
and academic skills and the methods that have proven successful
in establishing these abilities in persons who are moderately retarded.

## Self-Help Skills

The primary learning tasks of early childhood are self-help skills.
These are the skills that must be learned if a person is to cope

successfully with daily occurring personal needs. Although not explicitly identified under this heading, a large portion of activities included in the Montessori program, discussed by Banta in Chapter 14, are either self-help skills or activities basic to their acquisition. Procedures for instilling these abilities are presented by Rosenzweig and Long (1960). The areas included in their listing are:

1. *Feeding* is initiated with the ability to eat solid foods with a spoon and proceeds to the ability to eat and drink various foods and liquids appropriately without spilling or soiling.

2. *Dressing* starts with pulling on garments and continues until there is ability to dress oneself unaided, including buttoning and tying.

3. *Toileting* initiates with recognition of need to go to the toilet and is complete when the individual is self-sufficient, can wait until the appropriate time, and observes privacy.

4. *Washing and grooming* progresses from attempts to wash and dry face and hands to bathing without assistance and to caring for hair and nails.

5. *Brushing teeth* starts with rather superfluous brushing of front teeth and is considered a skill when teeth are brushed correctly and regularly.

6. *Using handkerchief* commences with trial attempts, usually when reminded, and is considered established when handkerchief or tissue is self-initiated and successfully used at appropriate times.

7. *Controlling self* initially is concerned with obvious dangers in the daily environment; later there is ability to work or play without supervision for extended periods and ability to avoid common dangers.

8. *Following instructions* is first noted in response to simple commands and develops into the ability to execute a sequence of

instructions over a period of time that may extend over days, weeks, or even months.

9. *Completing tasks* at its inception is the ability to finish the chore at hand; at a higher level there is self-sufficiency in the initiation, performance, completion, and appraisal of new as well as familiar tasks.

10. *Employing self* is first noted in short-term activities and proceeds to skillful planning and execution of projects.

11. *Holding temper* is considered to initiate in acceptable expression of anger and proceeds to the ability to express displeasure through language rather than physical acts.

Prior to embarking upon a program to instill self-help skills there is need to determine the precise nature of each task (*i.e.*, does the activity involve gross motor functioning, eye-hand coordination, finger dexterity, etc.?) and to determine the child's level of attainment in these areas. Ideally the task should be sufficiently in advance of the present level of functioning to be challenging or motivating, but not so much in advance that it will prove frustrating. When Connor and Talbot (1966) sought to develop a curriculum for the preschool retardate they presented a group of young retardates with a task specific to the area in which development was desired, *e.g.*, self-help skills, and then analyzed the gradation of behaviors observed when each child's performance was compared with that of others. From these observations five-point descriptive scales were devised for each task; thus, rather than according a pass-fail score, each child's level of performance was noted. For example, the five levels for the curriculum item "Hand Washing" (Connor and Talbot, 1966, p. 171) are listed in Table 1.

## Table 1
### THE FIVE LEVELS OF THE CURRICULUM ITEM—HAND WASHING

| 1. exploration | 2. use of soap | 3. washing palms | 4. washing whole hand | 5. consideration of clothing |
|---|---|---|---|---|
| **DESCRIPTION OF BEHAVIOR OBSERVED AT EACH LEVEL** | | | | |
| 1. Child explored and manipulated washroom equipment: water, soap dispenser, towel dispenser, waste can; dabbled fingers in water; spilled, splashed, rubbed wet fingers together. | 2. Child used liquid or bar soap to produce suds. | 3. Child rubbed palms together, inspected palms (resoaped sometimes), rubbed palms together with towel held between them to wipe. | 4. Child used soap on whole hand, inspected results. He might still wipe just palms. | 5. Child turned up or pushed up sleeves, was careful about splashing. |

### PROGRAMMING
### TEACHING PROCEDURES TO ESTABLISH READINESS FOR NEXT LEVEL

Teachers gave help with sleeves and cuffs before and after washing, until child assumed responsibility; also checked to be sure that backs of hands were dry.

| 1. exploration | 2. use of soap | 3. washing palms | 4. washing whole hand | 5. consideration of clothing |
|---|---|---|---|---|
| 1. Help with proper use of faucets, soap dispenser, towel dispenser, and waste can. Teacher participation or help to child, to show use of soap. Verbal help during washing process. Verbal attention to appearance of palms. | 2. Verbal attention to suds, child's washing movement. Inspection of palms of hands. Suggestion for washing again; suggestions for rinsing. | 3. Verbal attention to palms, fingers, backs of hands. Suggestions for washing part of hand missed; suggestions for wiping hands. Attention to water dripped on floor. Gradual withdrawal of supervision. | 4. Class discussion. Noticing hands, after child's return to classroom (smelling soap, noting dampness, cleanness). Noticing clothing; reminders about cuffs, sleeves, dress front. | 5. Class discussion. When to wash hands: (after using toilet, after use of clay, paint; before eating and cooking, or handling items apt to get dirty). Discussion of reasons (appearance, hygiene). |

The self-help items selected by Connor and Talbot (1966) to use in the training of preschool retardates included:

*Dressing*
Buttoning, unbuttoning, snaps, zipper, tying and untying knots, tying and untying bows, hats on and off, boots on and off, shoes on and off, mittens on and off, gloves on and off, open-front garments on and off, dress on and off, slipover garments on and off, snow pants on and off, scarf on and off.
*Hand Washing*
*Toilet Education*
*Juice Time*
Setting table, pouring juice, passing crackers, helping self to more food, clearing table, washing table, washing and wiping dishes, putting dishes away.
*Feeding Skills*
Using spoon, fork, knife, and drinking.
*Appearance*
Combing hair, brushing teeth, wiping nose.
*Care of Clothing*
Hanging clothes, placing overshoes.
*Housekeeping Activities*
Putting toys away, opening and shutting doors, cleanup after activity.
*Safety in Classroom*
Caution with sharp instruments, safety with hot water, safety on stairs, holding on to banister, protection of head from bumps.
*Safety on Playground*
Avoid accident with slides, swings, see-saw, steps, sandbox, and wheel toys.
*Independent Travel*
In building.

Each of the above activities is analyzed by the method set forth in the above description of the hand washing task. Behavior is described at each level, and teaching procedures are listed which serve to establish readiness for the next level. The emphasis given

the Connor and Talbot approach in the present writing is not a
suggestion that it be followed slavishly, but rather that the techniques used for analysis of task performance and of task development are appropriate regardless of curriculum area or age of
students. Moreover they are particularly pertinent for the moderately retarded children who proceed to task mastery not by global
accomplishment, but by a frequently halting progression through
minute steps of achievement.

## Social Skills

Because it is reasonable to give intensive training in those skills
that matter most in adult life (Gunzburg, 1958), social skills are
emphasized in a curriculum for the moderately retarded. Indeed,
social incompetence serves as one of the major criteria for mental
deficiency (Rosenzweig and Long, 1960). Early realization of the
importance of development in this area is reflected in Doll's (1953)
provision of the Vineland Scale of Social Maturity, which sets forth
a sequential ordering of social skills needed for a person to conform
to patterns of social living present in our American culture. Basic
to the acquisition of social skills is the ability to reason in social
situations and to let this reasoning govern action. Since reasoning
is a cognitive function, retardates would be expected to experience
difficulty in this area. Nonetheless, acceptable social performance
can be achieved by the moderately retarded, but the goals will be
directed more profitably toward conformity than toward originality
or resourcefulness. Although conformity in normals frequently is
regarded as passive or unimaginative behavior, in retardates it frequently represents concentrated effort to conform to social mores
set by and for normals (Stephens and Peck, 1968). Equipped with
the needed powers of reasoning the gifted person may exhibit social
sensitivity and use his creative ability to perform brilliantly in social

situations. The retarded, who also may have the urge to perform creatively but who lacks the reasoning power to exercise social selectivity, may produce social responses which are regarded by others as bizarre behavior. The goal is not merely to teach the retardate stock phrases and mechanical behavior; however, goals must be realistic; there must be a realization that the social finesse of a diplomat is not possible for someone performing at a five-year level.

The social skills included by Rosenzweig and Long (1960) in their goals for the dependent retarded child include:

1. *Considering others* originally consists of regard for others only as this relates to personal needs but develops into recognition that others have rights and feelings as well as responsibilities and into expectation of reciprocal action from persons encountered in daily living.

2. *Receiving help* emanates from recognition of one's own inability and from requests for help; later these requests are selectively bestowed and gratitude is expressed to the respondent.

3. *Imitating others* initially requires attending to the action of others; after this the observed behavior is imitated; still later imitation may be evoked by verbal description or direction.

4. *Playing and working with others* is evidenced at its onset in selected activities which call for group play, later in cooperative teamwork and play which may or may not have competition as a motivator.

5. *Helping others* is noted in appropriate responses to a request for help; at a more advanced level there is recognition of another's need for help and satisfaction in the provision of assistance.

6. *Comparing with others* initially is noted in competition which is prompted by desire for status or prestige and later includes group as well as individual competition.

7. *Being courteous to others* begins with simple verbal courtesies and proceeds to appropriate observance of established courtesies.

8. *Obeying rules* proceeds from initial conformity to rules in which the necessity for obedience is understood to the acceptance of rules as behavioral guideposts which may be modified.

9. *Kindness to animals* is originally displayed as the child identifies or empathizes with them; later interest prompts care and protection of pets.

Items to promote social development selected by Connor and Talbot (1966) were:

Relatedness to children and adults
Sharing
Consideration of others
Receiving help
Respecting property rights
Expressions: please, thank you, you are welcome, apology, greeting, offering
Attitude toward and participation in juice time
Food preparation
Group games
Trips: planning, participation, and traffic safety

As in self-help skills, five levels of the curriculum item were given. Those under Respecting Property Rights (Connor and Talbot, 1966, p. 89) are listed in Table 2.

Preparation of the moderately retarded for adult living implies functioning in an adult world. If these persons are to be accorded the opportunity to participate in such activities they must be equipped with the social acumen that makes such participation both possible and ongoing. To this end social training proceeds.

## Academic Skills

The relationship between cognitive development and academic skills long has been established. Yet, academic programs for the

## Table 2
### THE FIVE LEVELS OF THE CURRICULUM ITEM—RESPECTING PROPERTY RIGHTS

| 1. claiming ownership | 2. identification of own possessions | 3. recognition of others' possession | 4. respects others' property with reminders | 5. respects own and others' property |
|---|---|---|---|---|
| **DESCRIPTION OF BEHAVIOR OBSERVED AT EACH LEVEL** | | | | |
| 1. Child claimed toys he liked and wanted, toys similar to some he had at home. Sometimes child wanted to take (or took) school toys home. | 2. Child recognized objects he had brought to school or wraps worn to school. | 3. Child named owner of object he had or wanted, but did not necessarily return it to owner. | 4. Child accepted teacher's reminder to return property to owners and to put away school toys. | 5. Child identified own and others' property. Gathered up own belongings to take home, returned other objects to owners or stored school things in cupboards. |
| **TEACHING PROCEDURES TO ESTABLISH READINESS FOR NEXT LEVEL** | | | | |
| 1. Verbal attention to toys chosen. Conversation about personal toys at home. Discussion of school toys. Planning for use in school: putting away at end of activity or at end of session. | 2. Verbal attention to child's possessions. Designating shelf for safe storage. Focus on toys brought to school, providing for ownership by various children. Providing opportunity for child to permit others to inspect and return personal items. Playing games at close of school: "Whose coat is this?" "Who brought this to school?" | 3. Continued provision of opportunities for inspecting personal toys, returning toys to owners, storing toys on "checking" shelf. Continued assembling of possessions at end of each session, returning to owners. | 4. Provision for inspecting, borrowing, returning, putting away things belonging to various individuals. Teacher "loans" of various items. Teacher gifts of various items. | 5. Activities looking toward citizenship. Circulating library activities. Joint projects (e.g., bringing materials for grocery store; cooking activities). Caring for, cleaning and repairing materials for group use. |

moderately retarded frequently presuppose skills that are not present in persons functioning at the preoperational level of reasoning. It is not by chance that academic skills which require concrete reasoning generally are acquired by normals who are beyond the age of six. Their acquisition occurs after a period of rapid perceptual development and after the flexibility of the operational process required in grouping and categorization, as well as the reversibility required for arithmetical subtraction, are achieved. Realistic academic aims for the moderately retarded have as their goals the acquisition of those skills usually realized by persons who function at the preoperational level. These include reading readiness or beginning reading, number concepts which involve twenty, ten, or fewer objects, and functional writing which includes the pupil's name and address. Basic to each of these is language development; therefore, training efforts should include improvement of underlying language difficulties. Because suggestions for speech and language training are presented in chapters by Blanchard and by Kluppel, present consideration is addressed to the development of reading, handwriting, and arithmetic skills.

## 1. Reading

During the sensory-motor stage, which generally occurs in normals prior to their second year and in the moderately retarded prior to their sixth year, the child should have achieved the visual-motor (see-do) and visual auditory (see-hear) coordination which serves as a basis for later perceptual development. According to Piaget (Flavell, 1963), perception develops not alone but as a subsystem within the larger structure of sensory-motor intelligence; perceptions are assigned meaning as the objects one observes (stimuli) are differentiated. Differentiation is brought about through their assimilation by the mental structures of the sensory-motor stage. Even in simple stimulus situations a subject may not learn at all if he does not possess the mental structures necessary for assimilating the input. Thus viewed, it is sensory-motor intelligence, not perception, that provides the initial framework for later intellectual development. As objects are perceived and manipulated by the child in his daily environment they acquire meaning—a sock becomes something to wear and a ball something to throw. During the sensory-motor stage the child should make the initial transition from concrete objects, socks and balls, to symbolic representations (photographs or pictures) of socks and balls; that is, the meaning or recognition assigned to the familiar concrete object also should be assigned to its pictorial representation. However, if there has been cognitive difficulty in assigning meaning to the concrete object or in associating the concrete object with a picture of the object, the transition to meaningful symbolic representation will not be realized. Consequently, even at the sensory-motor stage a child may be falling behind schedule in the sequence of abilities related to reading readiness. Because the development of reading derives from more basic cognitive abilities it follows an ongoing, evolutionary process. Ability to make the transition from the concrete object to its pictorial representation is not an end in itself but merely serves as a starting point for the transition from pictorial representation to a higher form of symbolic representation, word recognition (Stephens, 1967).

During the stage when transition is made from reading readiness to beginning reading, new words are associated not only with pictures, but also with a sequence of symbols (letters). Likenesses and differences are detected in these symbols as they become clues to auditory and visual recognition and memory (Ingram, 1960).

Differentiation of written characters from one another is accomplished prior to decoding—that is, if a letter is to be interpreted correctly it must be perceived as being different from other letters, and these differentiating features must remain invariant regardless of such factors as change in type, size, and brightness. Selectivity is required, but retardates frequently are unable to direct attention to the significant aspects of visual and auditory stimuli or to exclude less relevant stimuli (Stephens, 1967). Therefore, training in discrimination is an appropriate reading-readiness task.

Perhaps the difficulty encountered when effort is made to teach the moderately retarded to read is best understood when one remembers that generally the optimum development for these persons does not go beyond a reading-readiness level, and in instances where reading skill is acquired it usually involves the recognition and recall of single short words or short sentences. This does not mean that some of these persons will not advance further in reading skills, but in general single-word recognition is a realistic goal.

At a readiness stage the child should be able to recognize pictures of common objects. Then, after training in recognition of pictures of *chair, car, table,* etc., a card with a picture of *car* is presented. This is followed by a card which bears the word car. The child should respond *car* to the picture card and later to the word card which immediately succeeds the picture card. Simultaneous presentation of the picture card and the word card is not recommended; when this occurs the child tends to attend to the picture rather than the word. Words appropriate for young trainables to read include "car, boy, hat, play, ball, see, toys, coat, run, dog, candy, book, hands, face, party, milk, cake, doll, girl, mother, daddy, the, water, and my" (Kolburne, 1965, p. 100).

As learning proceeds, charts which contain two or more words replace the single-word flash cards. However, prepositions and pronouns usually are best introduced with flash cards. As these cards are used to introduce a functional reading vocabulary, cards containing letters of the alphabet may be interspersed with word cards. A flash card bearing *a* may precede one bearing *dog* and the child's attention called to his reading of the phrase *a dog.* However, the question "What is this *letter?*" should be the question that accompanies the flash card containing a letter if the child is to distinguish between letters and words. After letter concept is established simple spelling can be attempted. When a basic reading vocabulary is acquired the child may use standard preprimers and primers, but to avoid frustration new words should continue to be introduced by the method described above (Kolburne, 1965).

Because a phonetic approach to reading involves logical multiplication it is not appropriate for moderately retarded persons who perform at the preconceptual level. It is not realistic to expect these persons to understand that one letter can stand for more than one sound, for example, *a*te and *a*rm, or to understand that in see*s* the *z* sound, but not the *z* letter is present.

## 2. Writing

To attempt to teach moderately retarded persons to write before they have acquired the concept of letters as symbols brings to mind the story of the man who was asked if he could read and write. His reply was, "Can't read, but can write." When requested "to write something" he filled the page with unintelligible scribbles. The onlooker asked, "What have you written?" the man replied, "Don't know. I told you I couldn't read."

Basic to writing skill is motor development at a sufficiently advanced level to assure eye-hand coordination and finger dexterity. By thirty months the average child generally holds a pencil by thumb-finger apposition rather than in the fist; for the moderately retarded who may be advancing at one third the normal tempo, approximately ninety months or seven and one half years would be the expected age. During initial training efforts Bruner's (1966) enactive level (*i.e.*, guiding the learner through the motions) of instruction is appropriate.

In a concise presentation of an approach to teaching handwriting to the moderately retarded, Kolburne (1965) notes that the first step after proper grasping of the pencil is pencil control. As the beginning exercise Kolburne suggests that the child be required to place his pencil on a fairly large dot. Here again, physical guidance of the child's hand by the teacher may be necessary. After the dot is touched the child is requested to remove the pencil from the paper (in order to prevent aimless scribbling). The procedure is repeated at different sittings until the task can be performed on dots of diminishing sizes without guidance. Following this the child is requested to draw a vertical line in order to join two dots. Guidance may be provided to assure that marking stops when the second dot is reached. As skill develops, the space between the dots is increased and the direction of the drawing varied from bottom to top, then top to bottom (see Figure 1). Later dots are spaced so that either slanted or horizontal lines must be drawn. Still later, arcs which result in circular lines are used to join dots (Figure 2). Emphasis all the while is directed to stopping *on* the dot rather than going beyond. Guidance by the teacher may furnish directional help. Later, stencils may be used to structure the response (Kolburne, 1965).

After formation of lines and arcs positioned at various angles is achieved, letters of the alphabet are made by joining dots, starting with letters made from combinations of straight lines; later straight and slanted lines are involved, and then there is progression to letters formed by curved lines; and last to letters written by a combination of curves or curved and straight lines (Figure 3) (Kolburne, 1965).

Initially the teacher starts the stroke in the right direction; later the child may trace letters independently. As skill is acquired the use of dots is phased out. When skill in the formation of letters via this method is established the next step is to *copy* short words, but these should always be words the child can read to prevent a "can-write-but-can't read" situation. Work should be checked for spacing and accuracy, and aimless scribbling should be discouraged. The next step after the copying and reading of single

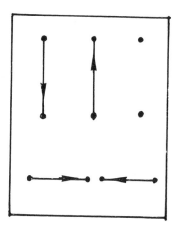

Figure 1
(adapted from Kolburne,
1965, p.109)

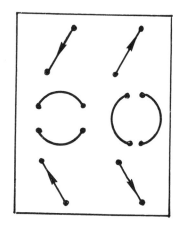

Figure 2
(adapted from Kolburne,
1965, p.109)

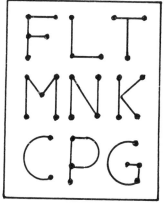

Figure 3
(adapted from Kolburne,
1965, p.109)

words is the copying and reading of short sentences. Work by Kolburne (1965) found that after a two-year training period a person whose IQ was 27 learned to write without dots, and that some children between IQs of 35 and 50 went one step further and were able to make the transition to manuscript writing after progression through the series of steps outlined above. A realistic goal is for the moderately retarded to exhibit reasonable speed and accuracy while copying short paragraphs, later while being dictated short sentences, and still later while expressing their own thoughts in words and short sentences (Kolburne, 1965).

## 3. Spelling

If independent self-expression is to be achieved, the next step after learning to read and write a word is to learn to spell it. The approach suggested by Kolburne (1965) is a continuance of the method used to establish reading skill. In teaching spelling a flash card which contains the word is presented briefly; after its removal the pupil attempts to spell it. If he is unsuccessful the flash card is shown again and another spelling attempt is made. The procedure continues until it is possible to spell the word without the aid of the card.

Another variation on the above technique which was found by Kolburne (1965) to be effective is to write a word, *e.g.*, *dog*, while the student observes. Then the teacher observes while the pupil copies the word immediately below the model. Social or tangible reward is given if the child copies correctly; if he copies incorrectly he is assisted to assure correct reproduction. When the word has been correctly formed two times in succession attempt is made to write the word without looking at the model. When this is achieved a previously learned word is dictated and then is followed by dictation of the newly learned word. The procedure is repeated several times during that lesson and during lessons on succeeding days.

Introduction of additional words should utilize the same technique and the same sequence of learning—first reading, and then writing and spelling.

## 4. Arithmetic

A teacher of the moderately retarded should seek to understand and diagnose the development of number-relevant capabilities, capabilities more subtle and basic than those involved in the elementary operations of counting, rote addition, and subtraction. The skills with which to be concerned are those that have to do with the fundamental properties of numbers. Because of the early age at which they are acquired these properties seem almost innate to most adults.

In the beginning of quantification "one" object becomes distinct from the group "more than one." Later one-to-one correspondence is initiated; a napkin is placed beside a cup, another napkin is placed beside the next cup, and still another beside the next until a one-to-one correspondence exists between two rows of elements. One-to-one correspondence has been fundamental in the construction of the integer. Counting on the fingers and the exchange of one object for another both demonstrate the part played by correspondence in the origin of number.

When Freidus (1966) analyzed the development of mathematical concepts attention to the following sequence was listed:

1. *Sets and Matching*—Objects need to be grouped into sets so that they can be arranged or counted. "The same" may deal with size, color, or form. The amount of experience required for task mastery will vary from child to child. Certain ones may need repeated experiences in sorting red beads from blue ones, blocks from balls, and pictures of dogs from pictures of cats.

2. *Relationship Concepts*—Matching and sorting prepared the way for comparing and relating. Prior to age five, a child usually has

learned to understand the terms bigger-smaller, nearer-farther, and heavier-lighter, but the moderately retarded child probably will not have done so. Grasp of the relationship concepts is basic to understanding number concepts.

3. *Measuring and Pairing*—After assimilating what is necessary for grouping objects into sets and learning to compare individual objects the child begins to compare sets. Will the water in this container fill that one? Does this shoe go with that one? Is there enough candy for each one to have a piece?

4. *Counting*—The repeating of numerals in proper sequence helps a child to match an object to its number symbol. However, work should be closely supervised to avoid pointing to the same object as the "one, two, three" is verbalized. Ideally he should pick up an object and move it to emphasize that each object is a unit.

5. *Sequential Values*—Awareness should develop of how each numeral derives its value (*i.e.*, two comes next after one and means that there are now two objects rather than just one). The child should work with sets containing the same number of elements (two feet, two shoes); later he should move to threeness and fourness.

6. *Relationship of Parts to Whole, Parts to Each Other*—Let the child discover that when two given quantities are combined they always equal the same larger quantity. In Montessori schools work with water serves to establish part-whole understanding.

7. *Operations*—As the numerical ordering of objects up to ten is mastered, fluency is gained in expressing and manipulating them symbolically.

Effort by Rasmussen (1964) to apply theory to method resulted in the acquisition of a mathematics laboratory equipped with such devices as rods, blocks, measuring devices, and objects for counting. Teaching was not merely a verbal dialogue, but was composed of doing, of discovering situations. In other instances a schoolroom store afforded excellent opportunity for grouping and matching merchandise as it was placed on shelves. Articles would be counted as they were purchased; the sale involved the exchange of money. The minimum arithmetic goals for the moderately retarded as outlined by Kolburne (1965) are:

1. Understanding of numbers through five as they are associated with concrete objects; after the concept of oneness, twoness, etc., is established effort centers on reading and writing these numbers. Number sentences are made by writing "one and one make two" in arithmetical terms, "1 + 1 = 2."

2. After mastery of the first five digits the task is increased to include five through ten. Again the child works with concrete objects as he composes number sentences to describe what is being accomplished: "2 (blocks) + 2 (blocks) = 4 (blocks)." Thus the addition facts through ten are learned. After this accomplishment individual worksheets, tailored to each child's knowledge and needs, are prepared which give exercise in calculating sums up to ten.

3. If the child can perform most addition facts up to ten but has difficulty with one sum, say 7 + 3, Kolburne suggests that a paper be prepared containing 7 + 3, which is presented to the child, and that he be assisted in obtaining the correct answer. Immediately following this the problem should appear on the sheet several times with the answer omitted. The child may refer to the previous problem for the answer. Efforts should result in such tangible rewards as gold stars, or by writing the grade in colors, as well as by praise.

4. After mastery of addition facts through ten the task may be increased to include addition facts through twenty. Flash cards may be used after the concept has been established through experience with concrete objects. Initially the side of the card without the answer is presented, then the side containing the answer is revealed; then the card is returned to the original position as the child again gives the answer. Only one or two new facts should be introduced at any one time, and drill on previously learned sums should continue.

5. With mastery of addition facts through twenty the child is ready for single-column addition. When the moderately retarded child is given the problem "$9 + 2 + 4 = \_\_$" he will have difficulty in mentally retaining the sum of $9 + 2$ (or 11) while he adds 4 to it. For this reason it is well to permit him to write the 11 and then proceed to add 4 to 11. When skill is acquired in work with three addends the task is increased to include four or five. An abacus or other concrete device should be used to establish the concept symbolized by the sum. After mastery of single-column addition, two-column addition *with no carrying* is introduced. Along with these exercises effort continues to establish meaning to numbers between twenty and fifty, and then later between fifty and one hundred.

6. When skill is gained in the above processes double-column addition may be introduced. There is acknowledgment that many of the moderately retarded will not achieve this level.

7. Because subtraction requires reversibility of the thought processes (example $7 + 3 = 10$; therefore $10 - 3 = 7$), a mental process that generally is not achieved until the stage of concrete operations, the moderately retarded probably will have difficulty with the concept. Again, initial attempts should involve grouping and withdrawing objects as the activity is recorded as an arithmetic sentence, "$10 - 3 = 7$." If the child can achieve reversibility of thought processes he proceeds to worksheets and the other sequential steps outlined for work in subtraction. Detailed discussion of techniques to use in establishing subtraction skill is available in Kolburne's work (1965).

8. Because even limited independence involves the handling of money the moderately retarded should recognize the various coins and smaller bills. Discrimination learning techniques can be used to advantage in this task, but the value concepts that account for the differences in coins and bills is more difficult to achieve. The counting of five and then ten pennies proceeds in the same way as the counting of other objects. When this is accomplished children

are taught that five cents are equal to a nickel. Then they are shown that the nickel can take the place of the first of five pennies in a row, and that the penny that is in line immediately after the nickel remains the sixth cent. Later counting includes a nickel and two pennies (seven cents), a nickel and three pennies (eight cents), etc., until the tenth cent is reached. Following this the fact that a dime equals ten pennies is introduced; only after understanding of this concept is assured is the fact that a dime equals two nickels presented or that a dime can also equal a nickel and five pennies. Next the child learns to count a dime and a penny, two pennies, three, four, and five, or a dime and a nickel. Thus he proceeds by sequential steps until he realizes the various coins that can combine to make twenty cents and then twenty-five cents. To count change which involves amounts in excess of twenty-five cents is difficult for these persons; for those who can proceed the approach is the same as that used for smaller coins and sums.

Practical utilization of change-making skills can begin with store-type situations in the classroom which provide purchasing experience. Later there should be provision for supervised shopping experience in stores. Still later the person may *make* small purchases independently.

## Summary

When an effort is made to establish skills which lead to self-help and independence in the moderately retarded, the training must start at the level at which the individual is then performing, but ultimate habilitation goals are also considered. For a young normal child who learns to read first one word and then many more, the usefulness of the first read words is not of prime concern. In the moderately retarded, where acquisition is more limited, usefulness of the knowledge is of prime concern. Self-help, social, and academic skills are taught which are absolutely basic requirements for everyday functioning. After these are achieved the acquisition of less critical skills should be considered.

# References

Bruner, J. S. *Toward a Theory of Instruction.* Cambridge, Mass.: Harvard University Press, 1966.

Connor, F. P., and Talbot, M. E. *An Experimental Curriculum for Young Mentally Retarded Children.* New York: Teachers College Press, Columbia University, 1966.

Doll, E. A. *The Measurement of Social Competence (A Manual for The Vineland Social Maturity Scale).* Washington D.C.: Educational Testing Bureau, 1953.

Flavell, J. H. *The Developmental Psychology of Jean Piaget.* Princeton, N.J.: D. Van Nostrand Co., 1963.

Freidus, E. S. "The Needs of Teachers for Specialized Information on Number Concepts." In *The Teacher of Brain-Injured Children,* edited by W. M. Cruickshank, pp. 111-125. Syracuse, N.Y.: Syracuse University Press, 1966.

Gunzburg, H. C. "Educational Problems in Mental Deficiency." In *Mental Deficiency,* edited by Ann M. Clarke and A. D. B. Clarke, pp. 328-354. New York: The Free Press, 1958.

Ingram, C. P. *Education of the Slow Learning Child.* New York: Ronald Press, 1960.

Kolburne, L. L. *Effective Education for the Mentally Retarded Child.* New York: Vantage Press, 1965.

Rasmussen, L. *Mathematics Laboratory Material* (Primary Edition). Chicago: Learning Materials, Encyclopaedia Britannica, 1964.

Rosenzweig, L. E., and Long, J. *Understanding and Teaching the Dependent Retarded Child.* Darien, Conn.: The Educational Publishing Corp., 1960.

Stephens, W. B. "The Influence of Deficient Cognitive Development on

Reading Skills." *Education and Training of the Mentally Retarded* 2 (1967): 113-120.

Stephens, W. B., and Peck, J. R. *Success of Young Adult Male Retardates* (Monograph). Washington D. C.: Council for Exceptional Children, 1968.

# 11

## HABILITATIVE RECREATION

## B. L. Freeman and C. Jean Mundy

During the past seventy-five years many changes have been experienced in the programming and care of the mentally retarded. In the beginning these individuals were the sole responsiblity of the family. However, as parents banded together and exerted greater influence, state and local governments began to accept more responsibility for the care of the mentally retarded. Establishment of special schools and institutions for the handicapped stand as evidence of these efforts. During the ensuing years, there has been a trend from large, centralized institutions to small, regional programs; as a result, today's emphasis is on such community-based programs as public school special education classes, sheltered workshops, and day care centers.

The changing setting for the care of these individuals has been accomplished by a decided change in the philosophy underlying most programs for the mentally retarded. Many of the early attempts at providing services were characterized by what might be called a "custodial" approach; the prime emphasis was on providing pleasant surroundings and keeping the child clean and healthy. The larger portion of any programming (if indeed there was any) was devoted to medical and paramedical activities such as physical and occupational therapy. Now, however, the custodial approach is gradually giving way to a philosophy that is training or habilitation oriented. One operating from this frame of reference is primarily interested in helping the retardate, no matter how limited he is, move up the ladder of skills. In other words, if the child is profoundly retarded and has been left in bed most of the time, he would be assessed in terms of motor development; then the initial step probably would be to involve him in activities that would strengthen his back and neck muscles and allow him to sit up. From there he might progress to a wheelchair, and effort would be made to involve him in an ambulation program. If the person functions at a higher ability level, efforts might be directed toward the development of self-care, social, or even academic skills.

As one would expect, when basic philosophies concerning mental retardation change, so do the roles played by those involved in the program. Where social workers were previously involved in gathering family histories and providing some supportive therapy, they now spend much of their time seeking adequate home placement for persons in vocational training. Social workers also expend a large portion of their efforts in casework with retardates who are disturbed by environmental problems. Psychologists are no longer viewed primarily as psychometrists but are being utilized more as program developers and program consultants.

What about the recreator? His role is also changing. The unfortunate thing is that, like many other professionals, the recreator is not always prepared and willing to accept his new responsibilities. This can be partly attributed to administrators' attitudes toward recreators and their expectations of a recreation program. At a recent meeting, administrators in the field of mental retardation were asked to justify the practice of having both a department of physical education and a department of recreation in the same table of organization. Their explanation was that this was necessary because physical education provided training for the children and recreation was "just for fun." With this attitude, it is not surprising that the recreators in our day care centers generally have very little training in their area of specialization and many times are high school and college students who work only on a part-time basis. Recreators must be willing to accept part of the responsibility for the layman's view of recreation for the handicapped. A recent questionnaire sent to recreators employed by institutions for the retarded in the southeastern region of the United States asked them to list justifications for their program. The three primary justifications which evolved are:

1. Recreation is fun and it gives the residents a break from the monotony of the day-to-day schedule.
2. Recreation gives the cottage personnel a daily break from the responsibility of caring for the residents.
3. When the resident is kept busy and given the opportunity to participate in varied activities, he presents fewer behavior problems.

It becomes evident that even many of the recreators in mental retardation view their services as something extra and not necessary to the training needs of the retardate. This does not have to be the case. With the new emphasis on skill development, the recreator can become an integral member of the training team. In order to do this, he must broaden his horizons and incorporate some new approaches with his traditional methods. Recreation is fun but it can also be a skill builder.

## The Purpose of Habilitative Recreation

The purpose of recreation for the retarded within the habilitation context has been expressed in varying terminology. *Recreation and Physical Activity for the Mentally Retarded* (American Association for Health, Physical Education and Recreation, 1966) states, "The basic aim of the overall program is to cultivate varied capacities so that the individual is always progressing toward greater degrees of social independence, physical well-being, emotional stability, and intellectual advancement." Avedon (1966) talks of "the plus factors in recreation which can be put to work to help prevent many types of physiological and psychological impairment in retarded children. These plus factors can also contribute to a successful economic and social adjustment." In essence, these two statements express the general opinion among professional recreators today who view the aim of recreation for the retarded to be the development of the individual, socially, emotionally, physically, and intellectually through the use of recreative experiences.

Data is presently being gathered which will substantiate the recreators' contribution in these areas. Oliver (1965, 1966a, b, c, 1967) and others have clearly shown that improvement in the areas of strength, skill ability, and physical achievement can be prompted through recreational activities. A program of activities for the trainable, which resulted in improved social behavior and intellectual skills, has been outlined by Bennett (1967). Improved motor abilities, as a result of a six-month program of recreation and physical education activities in a day care setting has been reported by Gross (1967). Evidence is accumulating which will support the recreator as a vital member of the training team.

## What Habilitative Recreation Includes

Ordinarily when one speaks of recreation, large group activities such as baseball, basketball, and swimming are envisioned and, if one has had association with an institution, bus rides, dances, movies, hot dog parties, and billiards will be included. The term recreation also will bring to mind leisure-time activities such as cards, dominoes, and checkers. Habilitative recreation, however, is much broader in scope. Arts and crafts, for instance, which has generally been considered the domain of the occupational therapist or the classroom teacher, is a fruitful area for the recreator. Weiner (1954) states, "The contribution of arts and crafts to the cognitive development of retarded children deserves primary emphasis. The mentally retarded child, like other children, learns of the world about him through direct contact with it. When such opportunity is provided and encouraged, he discovers the 'fact' of color, shape, size, texture, and spatial and structural organization, and he learns to note likenesses and differences, congruencies and incongruencies, consistencies and inconsistencies. Further understanding becomes possible when he is allowed to grasp, move, and alter the conditions of those things which come within his reach." It should also be noted that certain components of social behavior, such as enthusiasm for new activities, team participation, and sharing, are emphasized in an arts and crafts program.

Musical activities should also enjoy a place of importance in an habilitative program. Through such activities the retardate can develop improved auditory perception. Clapping, stamping, swaying, and marching to clearly defined rhythms helps the individual gain increased control and coordination of body movements. Dramatics can also be used to give meaning and focus to isolated parts of the total recreation program. For example, skills learned in arts and crafts can be utilized in the construction of simple costumes and stage sets. Simple dramatics should be incorporated into a program of musical activities, and through simple dramatics the retardate can learn the importance of group responsibility, sharing, and cooperation. From a psychological standpoint, the retardate can gain in self-confidence and feelings of self-worth as a result of having planned, produced, and successfully performed in a program for the rest of the student body.

Another group of activities that should be included in the total recreation program involves planned events such as summer camp-outs, field trips, parties, and simple snacks or treats. As in the case of dramatics, much of the benefit from these activities, other than just the fun, derives from the preparation. Camping activity brings the retardate face to face with the importance of good planning and workable rules for group living. His comfort is dependent not only on how well he carries out his job but also on how effectively others meet their responsibilities. The importance of sharing and good cooperation is emphasized.

# Is Habilitative Recreation Different?

Surely by now everyone is poised and ready for an emphatic *yes!* However, if the average layman or even the average recreator were to visit a day care center or an institution in which a habilitative approach to recreation was being utilized, he would notice very few differences. In fact, his comments after such a visit would probably follow this line: "I had heard a great deal about their recreation program so I decided to make a visit and see it in action. I was a little disappointed because they are really not doing anything different. Their students are involved in arts and crafts, music, swimming, field trips, and other group activities, just like the ones we use."

Such a reaction would probably be a fairly valid observation because the big difference is not in *what* is done, but in *why* and *how* it is done. There are differences in philosophy and selection, not only of students but also of activities. The three characteristics that distinguish habilitative recreation from other recreational programs are:

1. Habilitative recreation is goal oriented.
2. Habilitative recreation is based on evaluation.
3. Habilitative recreation is sequential in nature.

The remainder of this chapter is devoted to a detailed discussion of these three characteristics.

## Goal Orientation

What is meant by a goal-oriented recreational program? This term simply implies that each activity is chosen for a purpose. It would probably be less than correct to imply that the typical recreation program does not have a goal, but it is a general goal that is applied to the total program, and the intent is to provide the retardate with diverse activities which are enjoyable. A case in point is Considine's (1955) description of the "Detroit Plan," a plan that follows no critical or academic pattern. Actually, the Detroit Plan does nothing more than give the retarded child an opportunity to be happy, to feel that he belongs, to feel that his rights are the same rights as those of the normal youngster. No one would take issue with these general goals. However, in the case of habilitative recreation, goals are needed which are specific and are the basis upon which activities are chosen.

In many of today's receational programs for the retarded, activities are chosen somewhat haphazardly, the only criteria being that they be fun and involve most, if not all, of the students. In the case of habilitative recreation, an activity is included in the program only if it helps improve a particular skill in which a child is weak. A beanbag activity may be chosen which rewards the retardate for throwing the beanbag through certain shaped openings (squares) while he is bombarded verbally with the word *square*. Before he receives credit for satisfactory performance he might be required to tell the name of the particular shape. The activity would also be appropriate for a child who is experiencing difficulty in gross motor coordination; in this instance focus would be on the throwing motion. In keeping with the goal of improving form discrimination, the retardate may be involved in an arts and crafts activity in which he pastes colored pieces of string around different-shaped figures. The figures may then be filled with pebbles or dried corn.

One of the required skills of a habilitative recreator is capability in activity analysis, that is, the ability to break a recreational activity down into its component skills. If there is a guiding principle or philosophy, it is that all activities are made up of several skills and if a successful habilitative program is to be established the recreator must be cognizant of these subdivisions of a given activity. For example, if a retardate is to participate successfully in a game of volleyball, he must possess, among other things, adequate balance, good ocular movements, and acceptable eye-hand coordination. Moreover, these skills cannot exist in isolation; the individual must be able to integrate them into one response pattern. The complexity of any given task is suggested in Kephart's (1960) account of the skills required to complete the simple task of drawing a circle. It is the activity analysis which allows the recreator to select activities which will enable him to carry out the goals of his program.

## Evaluation

The second distinguishing characteristic of the habilitative approach to recreation is the fact that such a program is based on evaluation. Before an individual is placed in activities he undergoes a series of tests to determine his strengths and weaknesses. These are then closely analyzed and the student is placed in a recreational group based on his needs. Although the approach may appear to be simple on the surface, there are some inherent problems. For instance, what is an acceptable evaluation instrument? Although there are a number of instruments available which supply information in this area, most of these either exist as subdivisions of other scales or they are in the experimental stage and are not available in large numbers. Examples would be selected parts of the TMR scale, the Purdue Perceptual Survey, and the experimental Florida State University Recreational Inventory. Most recreators, however, have declined to use such scales, because when only a portion of a test is used the normative standardization data is not applicable. One also must remember that tests are much like theories in that they cannot be good or bad, only useful or not useful. If the recreator can forget his quest for a score and use these subscales as simple checklists of skills, he will be provided with much useful information concerning strengths and weaknesses of the retardate. Limited space does not allow one to take a combination of these subscales and show how they can be useful in planning a recreational program. In a habilitative recreation program the question is not whether you emphasize strengths or weaknesses; the answer is "both." Recreators would probably do well to take a page from the special educators' book and begin with activities that place emphasis on the individual's strengths and gradually progress to instructional activities that focus on weaknesses. During the final minutes of the recreational period the recreator should again revert to activities that the retardate can successfully perform, thus ending the period on a positive note. It is this evaluative process which allows us to select our groups, set our goals, and plan our programs.

## Sequential Development

One of the basic assumptions of the habilitative approach is that all activities are made up of a number of component skills and that the individual must possess each of these in order to complete the task satisfactorily. Here again, it is important that the recreator be able to perform an activity analysis, for it is this procedure which allows one to identify the weak link in the chain of skills which prevents the individual from carrying the task to completion. For example, through the evaluation procedure it becomes obvious that a child is unable to throw a ball with any degree of accuracy. His performance may be the result of difficulties in grasping the ball, bringing the arm back to the proper position, utilizing the forward throwing motion, release of grasp, or coordination of all of these procedures. The activity analysis enables the recreator to choose tasks which will afford practice in each of these skills in isolation and then in a coordinated effort.

Once the particular area of weakness has been identified the habilitative program should progress in a sequential manner. What does this mean? It implies that the skill-building program must be organized in a number of ordered steps and that each step must provide the basic skills or building blocks which are necessary for learning at the next level. The following example should clarify the concept of sequential development.

A certain group of young trainable retardates are known to be weak in the area of form concepts. The recreator who adheres to the habilitative approach decides to attack this problem through the use of recreational activities. As a result of his knowledge of child development, he knows that his program must begin at a very concrete level and gradually progress step by step to an abstract level. He also knows that to a very young child the concept of directionality has very little meaning except when related to one's own body. For instance, the concepts of *up, down, right,* and *left* have no meaning to the young child except when interpreted in terms of his physical body. Therefore the beginning activity should be concrete in nature and should attempt to teach form in terms of actions involving one's entire body. A game of Follow the Leader fulfills these requirements.

The children are asked to follow chalk lines or pieces of tape which have been placed on the floor in the form of various geometric shapes such as circles, squares, and triangles. This activity gives them kinesthetic, visual, and auditory cues concerning certain form concepts as well as relational ideas as they march *in, out,* and *around* the circles and squares. At the next step in the program the children would play games of tag, Drop the Handkerchief, etc., around or within groups of individuals who have joined hands to form certain geometric figures.

The next set of activities in a sequential development of form perception would remain at a concrete level but would restrict activity to parts of the body rather than to the body as a whole. Manipulation of puzzles and form boards involves hand movement and also is an excellent opportunity to involve the children in arts and crafts. Geometric figures can be traced with crayon and then either colored or filled with corn, beans, grout, rice, etc. One might also create modern art posters by cutting geometric figures from construction paper and pasting them on poster board.

If the task is drawing geometric figures, then emphasis should be placed on varying the activities along the concrete-abstract continuum. As indicated above, the initial step is to trace motorically, with both hands and feet, a continuous line which forms a specific geometric figure. In order to increase the degree of abstractness the child uses his hand to trace along a broken line and eventually he connects isolated points on the border of the figure. At this point in the program the retardate may be asked to copy a circle or square which is used as a model and eventually to reproduce such figures from memory. Much of the tracing activities can be incorporated into work with leather, copper, etc. The child has now progressed from the concrete to an abstract level and in doing so has accomplished developmentally sequenced tasks. The same type of programming can be utilized in developing skills involving colors, numbers, balance, and eye-hand coordination.

# Implementation of Habilitative Recreation Programs

The following is a step-by-step guide to the implementation of planned habilitative recreation programs for the child with retarded mental development.

**Step One:** Assessment or evaluation of the individual's abilities and performance to determine the appropriate recreation activities for his level of development.

It is possible to use informal observations of the individual's functioning in various activities as well as previously collected data from other professionals. However, since recreation is a distinct and unique discipline, this information should be used to supplement the data gleaned from formal testing that is specifically directed toward the assessment of the individual's recreative functioning. Some instruments that can be used in evaluating the recreative functioning of the mentally retarded are the Purdue Perceptual Motor Survey, Fokes Motor Development Scale, and The Mundy Recreation Inventory for the Trainable Mentally Retarded.

The Purdue Perceptual Motor Survey is an instrument of a global nature which assesses the perceptual-motor development of the individual. It deals with areas such as balance, body image, ocular control, and form perception. The Fokes Motor Development Scale is an assessment of motor development which starts at birth. The Mundy Recreation Inventory is geared toward assessing specific skills and concepts which are related to recreation activities. It includes areas such as action concepts, amount, position, place and space concepts, color concepts, rhythmic abilities, and various manipulative and motor skills. These three instruments, used along with other tests as a battery of assessments, complement each other and provide a well-rounded, wide range of information which can be utilized to determine the individual's strengths and weaknesses and, therefore, his recreative functioning.

**Step Two:** Individuals are grouped into homogeneous units based upon the evaluation of their strengths and weaknesses. In most institutional recreation programs grouping has been done on a cottage basis. While one cottage was at the swimming pool, another cottage would be at the playground. However, a fluid method of grouping is used in habilitative recreation programming. Each individual is placed in many different groups, each possibly with a varied group of participants, in order to be with other persons who are at his same level of functioning according to the components of the activity being undertaken. For example, one participant may be in a high-functioning group when the activity involves balance, throwing, or kicking, but in a medium-functioning group when ocular control, catching, or form perception skills are involved. Fluid grouping makes it possible to diminish ability ranges and to handle larger groups without sacrificing a developmentally oriented and sequential program.

**Step Three:** General goals and specific educational and behavioral objectives are stated for each individual or group of homogeneous participants.

Well-defined goals and objectives are among the most important ingredients in habilitative recreation programs. However, they are the elements which are most consistently overlooked in planning the program. Goals and objectives provide guidance and direction to the planned program and also serve as the basis for later program evaluation. In order to be effectively utilized in the program, the goals and objectives must be broken down into specific details and expressed in behavioral terms. For example, if one of the program goals is to develop and improve perceptual-motor functioning, the educational objectives are arrived at by determining *which* perceptual-motor skills are to be included and taught in the program. The educational objectives may include "to improve the participant's form perception," "to improve the participant's body image," "to improve the participant's balance," etc. In order to arrive at workable behavioral objectives, the next step is to state specifically what behavior the participant would exhibit if each educational objective were reached. With a goal of improving perceptual-motor development (educational objectives of improving form perception, body

image, and balance) behavioral objectives might include, "to reproduce a circle, triangle, and square accurately from drawn models," "to move over, under, around, and through equipment without
touching it," and "to be able to maintain balance while walking a
straight line on the floor."

**Step Four:** The component parts of recreational activities are
analyzed in order to select activities which will bring
about the attainment of the stated objectives.
Following through with the example mentioned above, if a
behavioral objective is "to move over, under, around, and through
equipment without touching it," the planner must then determine
which activities involve these body-image skills. The selected activities must then be arranged into a sequential program. Some of
the activities which would help meet this particular objective would
be work on playground equipment, relays involving over, under,
and through activities, Follow the Leader, Simon Says, and obsta-
cle-course work.

**Step Five:** Selecting methods of presenting the activities in the
recreation program.
After activities have been selected and sequentially ordered, it is
necessary to determine the most appropriate methods of presentation. Some of the elements to be considered are level of concrete-
ness, type and level of sensory input (such as kinesthetic, auditory,
visual input, etc.), group size, and length and frequency of the
participation periods.

**Step Six:** Periodic, systematic evaluation to assess the program
and individual growth.
Since social, emotional, physical, and intellectual goals and
behavioral objectives have been stated, it is possible to determine
the extent to which the objectives and, in turn, the goals have been
reached. Case studies, behavioral observations, staff conferences,
and test-retest results can be utilized for evaluative purposes. This

information is then utilized as a basis for making changes in either goals and objectives or in the program.

In summary, this article has been written in an attempt to acquaint the reader with the purpose of all recreation programs for the retarded: to provide the individual with opportunity to progress toward greater degrees of social independence, physical well-being, emotional stability, and intellectual advancement. There can be no second-class members of the training team. Each discipline must step forward and join hands with its sister professions in a cooperative effort to reach this common goal.

# References

American Association for Health, Physical Education, and Recreation. *Recreation and Physical Education for the Mentally Retarded.* Washington, D. C., 1966.

Avedon, E. M. *Recreation and Mental Retardation.* Arlington, Va.: U.S. Department of Health, Education, and Welfare. 1966.

Bennett, F. W. *Results of an Experimental Cottage Activity Program.* Paper presented to the American Association of Mental Deficiency, May 1967, Denver, Colo.

Considine, J. J. "Happiness Through Recreation." *Recreation* 48 (1955): pp. 230-231.

Gross, L. *The Development of a Physical Education Program for Trainable Mentally Retarded Children and Young Adults.* Progress report, Office of Education, U.S. Department of Health, Education, and Welfare (Project no. 6-8564, grant no. OEG2-7-068564-0272), 1967.

Kephart, N. C. *The Slow Learner in the Classroom.* Columbus, Ohio: Merrill, 1960.

Oliver, J. N., and Chesworth, A. "Subnormal Boys Are Helped by Logs." *Special Schools Journal,* 3 (1965): 20.

Oliver, J. N. *Sport and Recreation in the Education of the Mentally Handi-*

*capped.* Paper presented to Related Sciences Section, Conference on Sport in Education and Recreation, July 1966a, London.

Oliver, J. N. "Road Work with E. S. N. Boys." *Special Education* 55 (1966b): 25.

Oliver, J. N. "Pilot Investigation into the Effects of Circuit Training on Educationally Sub-Normal Boys." *Research in Physical Education* 1 (1966c): 11.

Oliver, J. N., and Keogh, J. F. "Helping the Physically Awkward." *Special Education* 56 (1967): 22-25.

Weiner, B. B. "A Report on the Final Academic Achievement of Thirty-Seven Mentally Handicapped Boys Who Had Enrolled in a Prolonged Pre-Academic Program." *American Journal of Mental Deficiency* 59 (1954): 200-219.

# 12

## VOCATIONAL TRAINING FOR
## THE MODERATELY RETARDED

### Keith E. Stearns

The successful attainment of the objectives of education for any individual is determined by his ability to function in whatever environment he finds himself (*i.e.*, to achieve in an educational program, to interact socially with others, and to participate in employment). Educational programs focus upon increasing the development of skills, knowledge, and attitudes necessary for individual and social competency. If individual and social competency is to be attained in our work-oriented society, the individual must be vocationally adequate. Broadly defined, vocational adequacy may be demonstrated in a variety or combination of situations. This could include functioning in the home, in the community, in competitive, noncompetitive, or sheltered employment, or by continuing an education in school or in an adult activity center. The global educational objectives have equal validity for retarded and nonretarded individuals. Implementation of global objectives at a behavioral or operational level and the degree to which objectives are obtained may vary, but the final test of the validity of objectives for retarded and nonretarded individuals depends upon the extent to which such objectives meet the needs, present or future, of the individual.

The preceding statement may cause one to assume that the writer is totally ignoring the objective limitations that accompany moderate intellectual subnormality as a disability condition. These limitations have been extensively documented in the literature of mental retardation in terms of language and conceptual development, physical-motor development, and specific social skills. For at least the last twenty years preservice teachers of the mentally retarded have been able to recite the litany of limitations of the trainable. In their preservice training teachers of the mentally retarded have been provided with information which indicates that:

Public schools can organize custodial classes within the public school system for the care, training, and supervision of the trainable mentally deficient [imbecile]. Such an organization would attempt to assist parents in caring for the child at home and would supervise the child for several hours during the day. . . . [Kirk and Johnson, 1951]

An issue of prime concern is where to meet the needs of the "trainable" mentally retarded child, who is capable of learning only to care for his personal needs. [Magary and Eichorn, 1960]

With the moderately retarded [Binet IQ, 36 to 51; adult MA, 6 years 1 month, to 8 years 5 months], self-care rather than independent employment becomes the focus of attention. [Robinson and Robinson, 1965]

It is hoped that the trainable will improve their mental, physical, and social behavior after training and will learn to protect themselves from common dangers. [Fitzgibbon, 1967]

Since it is expected that most of the trainable mentally retarded will be dependent or semidependent all their lives, the objectives of their school programs are limited. [Telford and Sawrey, 1967]

The cumulative effect of preservice training programs which emphasize the limitations of the moderately mentally retarded has produced a generation of teachers who frequently view their task as custodial rather than educational. Curriculum development for the moderately mentally retarded has become narrowly defined and limited to attempts to improve self-care skills and language deficiencies. Slight consideration has been given to what happens to the moderately mentally retarded individual when he reaches legal school-leaving age. The educational program largely has ignored helping the moderately mentally retarded develop specific skills and has ignored orienting him to the world of work.

At this time programs of vocational habilitation are severely limited by the negative orientation commonly held by special educators toward the abilities of the moderately mentally retarded. Such negative attitudes have been nurtured by preservice training programs which stress disabilities rather than abilities. The primary limitation of such programs derives from the negative attitudinal orientation of the special educator rather than the objective limitations which accompany moderate mental retardation.

## Vocational Accomplishments of the Moderately Retarded

Despite the negativism of the past concerning the potential vocational accomplishments of the moderately mentally retarded there does exist a body of literature which indicates that some of these individuals have obtained a degree of vocational adequacy. Further, the implication of this literature is that the degree of success in obtaining vocational adequacy (both in terms of the level of accomplishment and the number of individuals habilitated) could be increased through the development of improved programs of habilitation and training. Such evidence is generated largely from three sources: follow-up studies relevant to the community adjustment of moderately mentally retarded adults, reports of the achievements of the moderately mentally retarded in various sheltered work situations, including sheltered and activity workshops and residential facilities, and experimental studies which attempt to assess the effect of various working conditions on the productivity of the moderately mentally retarded. Space requirements demand some degree of selectivity. For more complete coverage one might refer to Wolfensberger (1967), Huddle (1966), Cohen (1966), Clarke and Clarke (1965), Cobb (1969), and Windle (1962).

One of the first clear indications that the moderately mentally retarded could develop some degree of vocational adequacy (*i.e.,* participate in gainful employment, perform worthwhile tasks around the home) was provided in a follow-up study of former Beta class students in St. Paul, Minnesota (Delp and Lorenz, 1953). In reviewing the current life status of this group, Delp and Lorenz found that forty-two of the eighty-four former students demonstrated some degree of vocational adequacy. Of the seventy-three living students at the time of the report sixteen (approximately 22 percent) were either currently employed or had been employed. Of this group two were on full-time jobs, three held regular part-time jobs, five were doing odd jobs, and six of the institutionalized were on an unspecified payroll basis for adequate performance of institutional jobs. The highest levels of vocational success were indicated by one individual with nine years' tenure as a hospital janitor at a salary of $145 per month and a second individual with four years' tenure in a department store commissary. Of the unemployed group, twenty-five individuals living at home and eleven individuals in institutions were able to complete useful tasks which went beyond mere development of self-care skills. Duties successfully completed by the unemployed group included washing dishes, general house cleaning, yard work, and assisting in the care of dependent individuals in the institution.

Further evidence that the moderately mentally retarded can live productive lives was provided by Saenger's (1957) study of former students enrolled in New York City classes for the trainable from

1929 to 1956. Saenger drew a stratified sample of 523 subjects from an available census of 1,725 subjects for his in-depth study. Of this sample 66 percent were living in the community, 26 percent in residential facilities, and 8 percent were deceased. Of those living in the community 27 percent (94) of the sample group were currently employed and 36 percent (127) were either currently working or had been employed since leaving the school program. Of the currently employed group 85 percent (79) worked in the community while 15 percent (14) worked in some type of sheltered environment.

While the relationship between amount of pay and type of work was not clear, it was evident that regular work paid better than part-time work. Of the working sample 45 percent were earning in excess of $20 per week, with half of this group earning in excess of $40 per week. The ninety-four moderately retarded young adults who were employed engaged in a variety of tasks ranging from custodial-domestic to light industrial work. The largest single employment category was messenger service and deliveries. This accounted for 36 percent (32) of the employed group. An additional 37 percent (33) were employed in such light industrial tasks as store work, assembly, and general unskilled labor.

The achievements of this group can probably best be illustrated by presenting edited versions of Saenger's (1957) indication of optimum levels of employment for the moderately mentally retarded.

F. was a presser of sweaters earning $40.00 per week. At age 32 [time of study] his Binet IQ was reported to be 42. He had no observable physical handicaps. F. has held his job for 13 years. He started as a winder for $8.00 per week. As the minimum wage increased his wage increased from 40 cents an hour to 75 cents and then to $1.00 per hour. His father obtained the job through friends.

Unidentified male has been employed as a maintenance worker for six or seven years. At the age of 28 [time of study] his Binet IQ was reported to be 44. He has unspecified visual and hearing defects. His maintenance work consists largely of odd jobs, repairing, painting and cleaning. Initially his earnings were $10 to $15 per week. He currently earns $40 to $50 per week. [pp. 128-129]

In addition to paid employment outside the home a significant number of the moderately mentally retarded in the Saenger sample assumed regular responsibility for a large variety of household tasks. Data on those occupied with household tasks indicated that 19 percent of the sample served in roles similar to those characteristic of live-in domestic help. Twenty-six percent of the remaining group provided regular assistance in the maintenance of a home. Even the majority of the remaining 50 to 60 percent, who were described as being of "minimal" assistance, did assist in household tasks in a manner which saved the parents time and effort.

Faced with the type of information generated by Delp and Lorenz and by Saenger some specialists in retardation may tend to deprecate the validity of the information. They may cite inadequacies of design, of sampling, and of the diagnosis of moderate retardation used by those conducting the studies (Blatt, 1966). However, one must attend to the consistency with which other researchers have reported similar results (Tizard and Grad, 1961; Kaplan, 1961).

Kaplan (1961), in reporting on the importance of the moderately mentally retarded to the work force of the mental retardation residential facility, found that nearly 58 percent were "employed" (without remuneration) as institutional aides. The weekly work schedule indicated that work hours for this group of aides ranged from three and one half to over eighty hours per week. Areas of work included patient care, household and food service, general building maintenance, and outside work involving farm and garden work. The quality of the patient's work was rated on a four-point scale (poor, fair, good, excellent) by supervising attendants.

In discussions on vocations for the mentally retarded, the unpaid work of the moderately mentally retarded in the residential facility is frequently ignored. Kaplan's data on the quality of the moderately retarded as institutional aides underscores the significance of this group to the economic well-being of the residential facility. Over 25,000 hours of aide work per week, which was rated fair or better, was produced by 663 moderately mentally retarded individuals (approximately 40 percent of the moderately retarded population of the institution). Moderately retarded aides who obtained performance ratings of "good" or "excellent" accounted for 11,500 hours of work per week. From a slightly different perspective and considering only moderately retarded aides with "good" or "excellent" performance rating, 258 moderately retarded aides (16 percent of the institution's moderately retarded population, 27 percent of the moderately retarded work force) working an average work week in excess of 44 hours provided a work force equivalent to 287 men working a standard 40-hour week.

In addition to the previously cited sources, other investigators (Cohen, 1962; Kagin, 1967) have discussed the feasibility of developing viable vocations for the moderately retarded in various domestic and personal-care type service occupations. While the demonstrated ability of the moderately mentally retarded to function adequately in service areas remains important, it is equally important not to overlook the ability of this group to succeed with light industrial work.

For the moderately retarded industrial work may offer certain advantages not found in domestic type service employment. Interaction with parts to be assembled, rather than with people, reduces the necessity for a high level of receptive-expressive language skills and interpersonal relationships. The repetitive nature of many industrial tasks makes them appropriate for highly detailed training programs which facilitate the learning of the individual who is retarded. Staff training and supervision are generally of higher quality in industrial concerns than in service-oriented organizations.

Studies which indicate that the moderately mentally retarded can be trained to complete industrial assembly tasks successfully have been reported by Loos and Tizard (1955), Clarke and Hermelin (1955), and Huddle (1966). Successful completion of light industrial work in sheltered workshops has been reported by Tobias and Gorelick (1963), Blue (1964), and Baroff and Tate (1966).

Loos and Tizard (1955) sought to determine if adolescent and young adults, moderately mentally retarded, could be taught to complete a simple industrial task. Using existing shop personnel and conditions, Loos and Tizard found that a group of six moderately retarded adults (mean IQ 32, mean CA 20) could be taught to complete satisfactorily a simple box-folding and gluing assembly task. The fact that the group had little previous work experience makes this report still more significant. Further, through manipulation of working conditions Loos and Tizard found that by organizing the moderately retarded workers into teams (where they worked as peers with mildly retarded workers) productivity was enhanced. In a follow-up study, reported as part of a series of studies by Clarke and Hermelin (1955), the six subjects had been employed as box folders for a two-and-one-half-year period. During this time the average weekly production was 30,000 to 40,000 boxes. The follow-up also indicated that the need for supervision was minimal and that, when necessary, the group could significantly increase the production rate.

The Clarke and Hermelin (1955) follow-up of the Loos and Tizard study was an attempt to determine the upper limits of industrial assembly trainability for the moderately mentally retarded. The first phase of the experiment required that the workers use a simple guillotine to cut insulated wires into ten-inch pieces. By the end of the second training period the moderately retarded workers were achieving substantially the same level of productivity as the mildly retarded workers who had had a long period of experience with the task. The second phase of the study required that the moderately retarded workers master a complex soldering task. This task required the workers to solder four different-colored wires to the correct terminals of an eight-pin television plug. Despite the fact that at least three of the six workers could not correctly name colors they mastered the task. Their final level of productivity (in terms of potential earning power) approached that of the simpler wire-cutting task. The final industrial assembly task required that the workers assemble a bicycle pump. This task required nine operations which had to be completed in the proper sequence. Initially the workers, with assistance, required from approximately four minutes to eleven minutes to assemble the pumps. By the thirtieth trial the moderately retarded workers, without assistance, required from approximately one minute to two minutes to assemble the pumps without error.

Further confirmation of the ability of moderately mentally retarded adults to complete sequential industrial assembly tasks effectively was reported by Huddle (1966). In order to evaluate the effects of competition, cooperation, and monetary reward, Huddle taught a group of institutionalized moderately retarded adults to assemble a television rectifier. Assembly of the rectifier required that the subjects complete a seventeen-step operation. The sequence involved placing five spacers, five corrugated aluminum washers, and five plates in a predetermined sequence upon a central fiber rod. Initially Huddle taught the task to 112 subjects who met his selection criteria (IQ range 30–60, CA range through 39, absence of severely limiting motor or behaviorial disabilities, four months' residence in the institution). Of this group Huddle found that only eleven of the 112 subjects failed to meet a criterion of at least nine complete assemblies of the rectifier in two of the ten training sessions. From this pool of subjects Huddle selected a final sample of forty-eight moderately mentally retarded adult males for his final study. Huddle's study does provide a limited opportunity to compare the assembly rates of moderately retarded adults who have not participated in competitive employment with the assembly rates of normal factory workers (limited in the sense that Huddle's subjects worked only forty-five minutes per day). During the experimental period the mentally retarded workers in the reward subgroups had mean production rates of 40.29 units while the production rate for the nonreward subgroups was 33.31 units. Normal factory workers for the same period had mean production rates of approximately 61 units. Of the forty-eight subjects in the study, seven averaged more than 40 units per period, eight averaged more than 50 units per period, and three averaged more than 60 units per period. The highest performance record was achieved by a subject in a nonreward subgroup who averaged more than 80 units per period.* Consistent with the reports of Loos and Tizard (1955) and Clarke and Hermelin (1955), Huddle (1966) found that the error rate was infinitesimal and that strict supervision of the moderately retarded workers was not required.

In addition to the data obtained from follow-up studies and experimental studies the vocational abilities of the moderately retarded are apparent in reports from various types of shelter service agencies such as sheltered workshops, adult activity centers, and occupational day centers. Admittedly much of this type of information is lost in the fugitive data of informal and embryonic workshops conducted by local associations for retarded children, specific projects conducted by special class teachers, and reports from workshops serving heterogeneous populations. Tobias and Gorelick (1963) investigated the feasibility of training a group of

---

*This study further underscores the feasibility of industrial assembly tasks as a workable vocational area for the moderately retarded. The author has observed young adults who are moderately retarded achieve levels of efficiency in the assembly of electrical switches which equal or exceed local factory production rates.

moderately retarded adults to complete a simple salvage task. Although the group consisted largely of adults who traditionally have been considered to be "unsuited for vocational activity" they found that the majority of the group was able to master the salvage task (removing a wing nut from a threaded bold and thus freeing a washer). Inspection of their report indicates that productivity was related to measured intelligence. Blue (1964), in describing a program designed to enhance transition of moderately retarded adolescents from the school program to the workshop's program, indicates that with proper preparation moderately retarded individuals are adequate workers in a production-centered workshop. Paralleling previously cited studies a sequential industrial assembly task was the major task completed by the workers.

The most complex industrial assembly task completed by moderately retarded workers is reported by Baroff and Tate (1966). Like many projects with the retarded, necessity (or opportunity) proved to be the mother of innovation. Baroff and Tate needed forty relay panels for research apparatus. Such panels may be purchased commercially at a cost of about $50 per relay, or they could be fabricated by a research assistant. Fabrication of the relay panels requires twenty different operations, including cutting plastic sheets, drilling holes, attaching fuse clips, relays, neon lights, and making and soldering sixty-two wire connections. As an alternative to purchase or graduate assistant fabrication of the panels Baroff and Tate decided to train residents of the Murdoch Center (a North Carolina institution for the retarded) to manufacture the relay panels. The current work force of twenty-six residents with a median IQ of 52 was described as an adult population with a history of institutionalization and little likelihood of community return. While Baroff and Tate fail to provide information about specific production performance the success of their project maybe noted by its growth. At the time of the report (nearly two years after the project began) the workshop had expanded to the point where it was necessary to hire a half-time supervisor, several projects had been added, and equipment was being purchased by psychologists located in thirty-five different institutions.

Planning programs of vocational education and habilitation of the moderately mentally retarded must be based on positive expectations rather than the negative expectations of the past. When one takes into account the demonstrated abilities of the moderately mentally retarded the following points would provide a reliable basis upon which to develop programs of vocational education and habilitation.

1. Our society is work oriented. Status is conferred upon those who produce. However, productive work is not an either-or proposition. Productive work is a continuum of activities ranging from those who produce products or services over a sustained period of gainful employment to those who are able to produce only part of the time but in so doing reduce the amount of time others need to use to care for them. The moderately mentally retarded may obtain various levels of adequacy within this continuum. The level obtained is as much a function of the opportunities and training offered them as it is a function of the abilities and disabilities they bring to the work situation.

2. Individuals who are moderately mentally retarded have demonstrated the ability to complete successfully the task demands over a sustained period of time on a wide variety of industrial jobs. While the limits of trainability of the moderately retarded have not been established, present evidence tends to indicate that repetitive assembly tasks may serve as an optimal employment opportunity.

Present evidence indicates that optimal vocational opportunities may exist in a variety of patient care and related activities in institutions and hospitals, domestic work, routine maintenance work, and various aspects of food service.

3. Continuous supervision of all aspects of a specific job is not a necessary condition for employment success of the moderately

mentally retarded. The degree of supervision required is a function of the work conditions, the nature of the task, and the level of the training of the individual, rather than any inherent quality which may be considered to be an attribute of mental retardation.

4. Some of the moderately mentally retarded, because of a lack of opportunity or the presence of other handicapping conditions, will not be able to participate in competitive or shelter employment or in work activity centers. Such individuals should find their work in the completion of regular household chores which go beyond mere self-care skills.

## The Curriculum and Vocational Training

In the introductory chapter to this book, Lance indicates that the development of curriculum is the foremost issue facing special educators responsible for programs for the moderately mentally retarded. As one reviews the curriculum examples that Lance cites, it becomes apparent that his comment is highly relevant to vocational habilitation as a part of the total curriculum for the moderately mentally retarded. All too frequently, curriculum plans for the moderately mentally retarded appear to be developed without serious consideration being given to the postschool placement of the learner. Those plans which give consideration to development of prevocational skills frequently assume that one must wait until the learner reaches some magic age (usually CA 14 to 16) before such skills are introduced.

Preparing the moderately mentally retarded for maximum vocational habilitation or independent living requires that all professionals, including special educators, recognize that this can be achieved only by developing a continuum of services. At the preschool level, developing behavioral readiness for group participation, direct teaching of self-help skills, and communication development all lay the basis for later prevocational training. During this entry point the teacher has the opportunity to develop a positive task orientation which includes extending time on task, task completion, and the ability to engage in parallel and group activities. Direct teaching of self-help skills at this level extends the degree to which the child has mastery over his environment, reduces his dependency on others, and aids the child in developing a more effective concept of self. During the school years the teacher should extend and refine the learner's task orientation. Significant stress should be placed on the completion of tasks requiring extended work periods and self-evaluation of quality. At this point the teacher should introduce and develop those academic skills which are the precursors of vocational training. For example, travel training (Cortazzo and Sansone, 1969), as a skill essential to competitive employment and participation in a variety of adult programs, presupposes knowledge of people, objects, protective vocabulary, numerals, and various signals. This should be a normal part of the school curriculum. Delivery of all elements of the curriculum should be based on a carefully structured contingency system which will not only strengthen personal and social habits but will also serve to reflect the contingencies of the real world.

It would be possible to extend the discussion of the relationship between the experiences which one provides for the child at age three, five, seven, nine, and so on, and the later vocational and social habilitation of the individual. All too frequently, the teacher of the public school class for the moderately mentally retarded works in splendid isolation, reinforced only by minute behavioral changes on the part of her learners and an occasional pat on the back for her demonstrated resources of patience and sympathy. Under such circumstances it is possible that even the most highly motivated teacher might fail to recognize that her efforts are part of a continuum of services. Indeed it is likely that in the course of her preservice preparation the concept of a continuum of services, if mentioned, was never fully described. Specifically, the point being stressed here is that the curriculum for the moderately mentally retarded is sequential in nature, leading to the development of skills that will assist the individual in gaining mastery over his environment.

To illustrate this point, Figure 1 is a representation of the continuum of services necessary to obtain maximum habilitation of the mentally retarded. Each part of the continuum has some relationship. For example, Education of the Public appears under the heading Prevention. However, if in a vocational sense you plan to develop programs which use community placements (Cohen, 1962; Kagin, 1967), it is as necessary to provide an educational program for the prospective employer as it is for the employee. As indicated in Figure 1, the first step toward providing services for the mentally retarded begins with identification because in a real sense education and training begin with this identification. Early in the diagnostic period the parents of retarded individuals must become actively involved in both long-term and short-term planning. However, as Galazan (1966) has indicated, a parental attitude of overprotection frequently is established during this period. Overprotection, according to Galazan, creates persistent barriers to the development of independence and as such has a negative effect on vocational habilitation. For illustrative purposes the services necessary for the habilitation of the mentally retarded have been presented under the headings Prevention, Identification, Treatment, and Rehabilitation. It should be clear, without drawing overlapping circles or double-headed arrows, that each service contributes and is interrelated to every other service in the attempt to achieve maximum habilitation of the mentally retarded.

At this point it is necessary to extend the concept of the continuum of services one additional step. Public school educators frequently deal in terms of programs for "school-age, school-eligible" children, and as a result tend to ignore the necessity of devel-

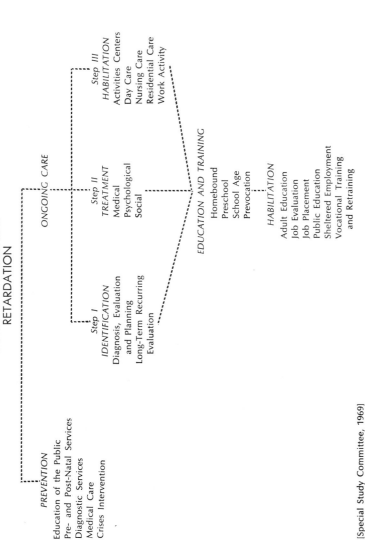

DIAGRAM OF SERVICES
RETARDATION

*PREVENTION*
Education of the Public
Pre- and Post-Natal Services
Diagnostic Services
Medical Care
Crises Intervention

*ONGOING CARE*

*Step I*
*IDENTIFICATION*
Diagnosis, Evaluation
and Planning
Long-Term Recurring
Evaluation

*Step II*
*TREATMENT*
Medical
Psychological
Social

*Step III*
*HABILITATION*
Activities Centers
Day Care
Nursing Care
Residential Care
Work Activity

*EDUCATION AND TRAINING*
Homebound
Preschool
School Age
Prevocation

*HABILITATION*
Adult Education
Job Evaluation
Job Placement
Public Education
Sheltered Employment
Vocational Training
and Retraining

[Special Study Committee, 1969]

oping a complete sequential educational package. Schematically, Figure 2 is a generalized representation of a sequential educational program for moderately and severely retarded individuals. It should be noted that each level assumes progression to another type of program. As with individuals who are of normal intelligence, program progression for the moderately mentally retarded is not a homogeneous occurrence. Experience, training, and opportunity as available in the community result in a variety of exit points from the school program.

The purpose of Figure 2 is to provide a generalized outline of the scope of sequential educational services for individuals who are moderately or severely retarded. However, the information provided is still too generalized. In order to develop more effective habilitation programs it is still necessary to specify components. For example, it is all well and good to say "tool subjects where applicable" or "prevocational education," but specifically what tool subjects and under what conditions? What is prevocational education? Following are illustrative examples of what could be included under such headings.

Kagin (1967) has described a program (The Mimosa C Project) that was developed to prepare moderately mentally retarded adolescent girls for discharge from Parsons State Hospital and Training Center in Parsons, Kansas. Twenty-seven girls ranging in CA from fifteen to twenty-one, measured intelligence from approximately IQ 22 to 55, were involved in the project. The major objective was to prepare this group of young adults to function effectively in community living and employment placements. While the Kagin report contains a readable discussion of the operant methodology employed, the curriculum outline is of special significance for this chapter. The rationale for including various elements in the skill curriculum is described by Kagin as:

## Figure 2
### Sequential Educational Programs: Pattern for Development of Services for the Moderately and Severely Mentally Retarded

| Referral From | To Program Level | General Objectives | Progression To |
|---|---|---|---|
| Diagnosis-Evaluation<br>Parent Education Programs<br>Head Start | Preschool | Behavioral readiness for group participation<br>Language and communication development<br>Direct teaching of self-help skills<br>Psycho-motor development<br>Differential diagnosis of special learning abilities and disabilities | Classes for the educable<br>Classes for the trainable<br>Other types of special classes<br>Regular classes<br>Day-care center<br>Residential care |
| Diagnosis-Evaluation<br>Preschool Program<br>Parent Education Programs<br>School Classes<br>Residential Care | School Age | Language and communication development<br>Self-help skills with emphasis on competence in home and community settings<br>Behavioral adjustment in home, community and school<br>Tool subjects where applicable<br>Prevocational skills<br>Continued differential diagnosis of special abilities and disabilities | Regular school classes<br>Special education classes<br>Day care<br>Activity centers<br>Sheltered workshops<br>Adult Education programs<br>Residential care<br>Combination programs<br>Vocational Rehabilitation<br>Training Programs and other types of post-school vocational education training programs |
| Diagnosis-Evaluation<br>School-Age Program<br>Community Referral<br>Community Agencies<br>Residential Care | Adult Education | Correlated educational activities as related to the needs of various adult programs (i.e., development of skills not previously developed that are most effectively programmed in an educational setting) | Re-referral to various programs, including:<br>Activity centers<br>Sheltered workshops<br>Community placement<br>Residential care<br>Vocational Rehabilitation and Training Programs<br>And other types of post-school vocational education training programs |

[Special Study Committee, 1969]

The demonstration project's major objective is to demonstrate and implement procedures for training the adolescent girls in personal, social, educational and occupational skills. These skills relate to adaptive behavior elements of independent functioning, individual responsibility, and civic and economic responsibility. As the girls are trained in the above skills, their adaptive behavior is likely to improve and they are less likely to appear retarded to other persons. As their retardation becomes less visible, their chances for leading more independent lives outside of the hospital increases. [Kagin, 1967, p. 6]

*Mimosa C Project Skill Areas*

A. Personal Skills
  1. Personal Hygiene
  2. Posture and Movement
  3. Grooming
    a. Selection and maintenance of wardrobe
    b. Hair care

B. Social Skills
  1. Formal Communication Skills (verbal behavior, both expressive and receptive)
  2. Social Interaction
  3. Heterosexual Interaction
  4. Desirable Attitudes (pleasing verbal behavior, facial expressions, "helpfulness," etc.)

*Comment*

Direct teaching of self-help skills is discussed in an earlier chapter. However, it should be noted that at this level part of the instruction should be directed to the use of community services, such as barber shops, beauty salons, and laundromats.

Inadequate social adjustments account for the largest number of vocational failures among the mentally retarded. While it is not possible to detail all factors, the educational program can increase approach tendencies toward communication activities. The overprotection of parents, schools, and institutional programs has frequently prevented the development of normal heterosexual interaction patterns. This must become a programmed part of the curriculum.

C. Educational Skills
1. Reading
2. Writing
3. Arithmetic
4. Time telling

The emphasis for these academic skills is on material related to recreational, occupational, and self-help activities in a community setting.

Functional mathematics skills, including telling time, use of the numeration system, use of the monetary system, and use of measurement, and functional reading skills lead to the development of independence. As Kagin (1967) and Baumgartner, in Chapter 9, suggest, such training must be based on the real-life situation and not be presented as a "classroom exercise."

D. Occupational Skills
1. Basic household skills (for use with family, in own home, or for utilization in a work placement)
2. Nonhousehold skills
   a. Training in caring for persons less able to care for themselves— *e.g.*, bedfast patients.
   b. Training in cooperative work habits—*e.g.*, for sheltered workshop work.
   c. Training in basic job skills—*e.g.*, time keeping

This listing is as valid for adolescent boys as it is for the girls of Mimosa C. At an early school age the teacher may begin to provide the instruction basic to these skills.
However, attainment of the implied objectives in a school setting will require close coordination with the home.

As indicated in the comment on educational skills, adequate implementation requires using the community beyond the school walls as the classroom.

Athough the Mimosa C Project curriculum was designed for a specific group of adolescent girls who were being prepared for termination from a residential facility for the mentally retarded, the subject area headings that appear under the four skill areas are appropriate for similar age groups of moderately retarded individuals in public school programs. Perhaps the most significant omission from the Mimosa C curriculum is the area of travel training as a skill. This criticism may be somewhat unfair, as travel training may not have been appropriate in their particular setting (or it may have been assumed as a component of one of the four skill areas).

While the Mimosa C curriculum is more specific than the global objectives outlined in Figure Two, it still requires that the teacher supply explicit curriculum components. Further development of the curriculum can be facilitated by reviewing the types of activities provided by activity training programs for moderately and severely retarded adults. Cortazzo (1968) has analyzed the types of activities provided by sixty-eight activity programs for mentally retarded adults. These programs were at the time of the report providing services for 1,154 retarded adults with a CA range of sixteen to sixty-two years and an IQ range of 12 to 60. The major global objectives of the centers were mental health, training in daily living areas other than work, parent relief, and the development of skills necessary for workshop placement.

The types of activities which the various programs report closely parallel typical school curriculum for the trainable mentally retarded. One can only speculate as to the manner in which the effectiveness of various training programs for adults who are retarded might be increased if school programs were accountable for obtaining the objectives. If one needs further guidance as to the content of the prevocational curriculum for the moderately mentally retarded the following abridgment of the activities reported by Cortazzo should be useful.

| Types of Training Activities Provided by Programs (quoted in condensed form from Cortazzo, 1968, p. 33) | Comment |
|---|---|
| Self-Care<br><br>   Grooming<br>   Dressing<br>   Personal hygiene<br>   Select clothes to wear<br>   Safety<br>   Care of clothes<br>   Shaving (males)<br>   Apply cosmetics | The activities listed here should be broken down into fairly explicit instructional packages. If the teacher is able to describe the activities in terms of behavior to be produced, then she is more likely to obtain her objectives.<br>This is not considered to be a complete listing. Local conditions, including the population to be served, will require local additions. |
| Useful Home Skills<br><br>   Washing dishes, etc.<br>   Use cleaning equipment<br>   Meal planning<br>   Clean and set tables<br>   Making beds<br>   Ironing<br>   Sewing | One might envision ideally designed classrooms for the moderately retarded which include all of the facilities to implement this part of the curriculum. However, if effective, such *skills* must be usable in the individual's home living environment. If necessary, the skill is introduced and taught at school. Eventually, transfer must be made to the home. This will require a higher level of parent-school interaction than currently exists in most programs for the retarded. |

Academics

Count objects
Identify coins
Make change
Identify numbers
Tell time
Write signatures
Identify functional words
Fill applications
Recognize signs
Recognize symbols—cooking
Use measurements

Huddle (1966) and Barrett, Relos, and Eisele (1965) have indicated the importance of knowledge of the value of money and the ability to recognize money as powerful adjuncts to vocational training. The importance of these skills in the development of independence has been discussed by Cortazzo and Sansone (1969). The stress must remain on the functional development of the skills in real-life situations. All too frequently the special class teacher thinks a skill has been learned only to find that the use of the learned skill is limited to the classroom.

Recreation

Dancing
Parties
Basketball
Swimming
Bowling
Excursions—trips
Spectator sports

To paraphrase a point which Kagin (1967) stresses, successful adjustment to the community may be contingent upon the mentally retarded individual's effectiveness in social situations during nonworking hours or during the hours spent away from the closely supervised environment of school or workshop. In the coming years those responsible for developing total habilitation programs for the retarded must place at least as much effort, time, money, and creativity into this area as we have devoted to other aspects of the curriculum.

Community Skills

Dining out
Shopping
Use of recreational
    facilities
Crossing streets
Asking directions
Community courtesies
Travel training

The above section is a rather traditional layman-like view of recreation. However, professional recreation is a powerful ally in obtaining curriculum objectives. Those in this section are particularly relevant to the field of recreation. The relationship between dining out, shopping, and travel training and the academic areas of the curriculum should be obvious.

Communication

Group discussion
Current events
Use of telephone
Language development

The area of communications is usually stressed in public school programs for the moderately mentally retarded. However, as in other areas, the teacher must be careful that the skill is developed in a manner that will be useful in environments other than the classroom.

Paid Work

Subcontract
Salable products
Service

Some authorities (Huddle, 1966) assert that paid work may not be possible in the school environment. However, this is largely a matter of unsnarling administrative red tape. Learning to work productively for pay is a significant pre-vocational skill and should be included in the school curriculum as a normal event.

Crafts

Paper craft
Woodworking

Craftwork with the retarded is frequently downgraded. As with other elements of the curriculum the element of purpose and relevancy should be the issue. The inherent motivational quality of some craft projects may serve to enhance fine motor development. The peer and at-home payoff of successfully completed projects may be used to assist the individual in the development of a more effective concept of self and of task orientation.

At this point, it would seem appropriate to provide an explicit, highly-developed curriculum and label it the "prevocational-vocational" curriculum for moderately retarded adolescents and adults. However, the current state of knowledge precludes such closure. As one reviews a variety of nonschool programs (Barklind, 1969; Bitter and O'Neil, 1967; Cortazzo, 1968; Cortazzo and Sansone, 1969; Kagin, 1967; Tobias and Cortazzo, 1963) that have been provided for adolescents and adults who are moderately mentally retarded, a partial picture of what should constitute the school prevocational-vocational curriculum begins to emerge.

With full knowledge that many will find the listing somewhat less than complete, the following areas are offered as a *minimum* school-based prevocational-vocational curriculum for the moderately mentally retarded:

1. The program should assist the individual in developing an adequate concept of self as an adult and a productive worker. Continued reference to adolescents and young adults who are retarded as "children" is reflective of an attitude that limits the development of independence. Development of a reward system by the teacher which uses "pleasing the teacher" or "not embarrassing" the teacher as the major contingency system tends to perpetuate or develop childlike relationships between the young adults who are retarded and other adult authority figures, such as job foremen and work supervisors. While this may be useful in the school setting, the long-term consequences may be damaging to the vocational competency of the retarded worker.

2. The program should provide the individual with direct travel training to enable him to get around the community alone for recreational, work, and training purposes. Behaviorally this is a much more specific objective than number one. However, it does involve some risk taking and requires weaning parents and teachers from their tendency to overprotect the retarded learner. Independent travel skills could be an important part of obtaining a more generalized objective such as that stated above. Cortazzo and Sansone (1969) have developed and reported a rather explicit set of procedures for travel training.

3. The program should develop specific functional academic skills which will be transferable to independent and semi-independent living and employment conditions. Such academic training should include, but not be limited to, the following:

a. The ability to read signs, names, labels, pictorial directions, numbers (including addresses, phone numbers, route numbers and public conveyance numbers, prices, etc.).

b. The ability to: use the number system, including counting objects; establish the relationship among objects counted; package items singly or in multiples; use simple measurement; and the ability to use the monetary system at least to the extent of using the coinage system and dollar bills.

    c. The ability to recognize, make discriminations, or groupings on the basis of color, size, shape, or multiple factors.

    4. The program should develop maximum communication effectiveness. Objective three is basically part of communication effectiveness. Specifically, direct attempts should be made to increase receptive and expressive oral language skills of the individual. Use of oral language as a recreational or socializing tool should not be overlooked.

    5. The program should develop maximum self-help, self-care skills for the individual. Skills revolving around dressing, eating, and personal hygiene are obvious and usual components of curriculum. Skills requiring preparation of one's own meals, care and maintenance of clothing, and selection of leisure-time activities are too frequently ignored and should be included as a curriculum component.

    6. The program should assist the individual in learning and observing the rule-oriented world of work. Lytle (1963) suggests that there are at least four areas of rule-observance environments. These areas include rules of conventional courtesy, honesty, and cleanliness; rules regarding time schedules; rules relevant to quantity and quality of work; and safety rules.

    7. The program should provide the individual with instruction and practice in using common tools, simple machinery, and household appliances. Developmental activities should be programmed into the curriculum. As skill levels increase, progression may be made to the production of salable skills or objects.

    8. The program should provide the individual with an introduction to the realities of the world of work. This could be accomplished by extending current work-study programs for the mildly retarded to include the moderately retarded. For those not ready

for this level of participation, classrooms for adolescents could be organized to simulate workshop or industrial situations.

9. The program should provide the individual with training and direct experience in using the recreational facilities of the community. This should include directed experiences in using public-for-profit resources such as movie theaters, bowling lanes, and restaurants as well as public facilities such as city parks and recreation departments, swimming pools, YMCA's or YWCA's, and churches.

## Specific Methodology Applicable to Vocational Training

One of the basic problems in designing instruction for the moderately mentally retarded is to break the task to be taught (the learnable task) into its simplest steps. The method used to accomplish this is usually some form of task analysis (Mager and Beach, 1967). As a method of instruction, task analysis is frequently used as a tool to teach workers (normal as well as retarded workers) to complete specific industrial tasks. Silvern (1963) describes the use of task analysis to train retarded workers as "object analysis and action synthesis." Gold (1968), in describing the development of preworkshop skills for the trainable, refers to the process as a sequential technique. Crosson (1969) uses what he refers to as a "taxonomy of sequential operants" to describe the use of task analysis for training severely retarded workers.

Without regard for what each author calls his particular form of task analysis, they all have common features. Each task analysis deals with a learnable task. By definition (Gole, 1970) a learnable task is a task which (1) has a definite starting point, (2) has a definite ending point, and (3) is performed because certain conditions exist. When the tasks analyzed are being performed in an operational context (Silvern, 1963; Gold, 1968, Crosson, 1969), direct observation is the most important data source for the analyst. Specifically, the analyst looks for cues which call for responses, objects to be used, manipulations to be made, and feedback to be used. The task description then specifies when the individual is to do something, what he is to do it with, what action he is to take, and what feedback exists to indicate that the behavior has been performed adequately. Thus one might view task analysis as a detailed description or ordering of the subtasks that are necessary to complete a learnable task. Implicit in the process is the assumption that learner failure is the fault of the training procedure rather than the fault of any inherent flaw in the learner.

## Predicting Vocational Success

It is standard operating procedure for vocational training programs to run prospective clients through batteries of tests prior to accepting them in the program. Such tests usually include individual psychological examinations and social and medical histories and may be expanded to obtain work samples over a several-week period. Though many of us would like to behave as if such examinations were useful in predicting vocational success, to date, no individual test or multiple-criterion battery can be demonstrated to be of sufficient practical use to justify the time and energy sacrificed to obtain the data. Patterson (1964), Wolfensberger (1967), and Cobb (1969) have reviewed the state of the art relevant to predicting vocational success for the mentally retarded. The Patterson review is primarily a descriptive (what and how to do it) review, while the Wolfensberger and Cobb reviews represent critical evaluations of the literature. Wolfensberger cites five major deficiencies in the literature relevant to job success prediction. Briefly, the major deficiencies are poor design and control, lack of cross-validation

(Wolfensberger was able to find only one study that was at least partially cross-validated), lack of confirmation across studies, emphasis on variables associated with the mentally retarded individual with little attention being paid to variables associated with training, placement, or the placement situation, and weakness of some of the predictors. Cobb (1969), in summarizing the predictive studies, indicates that:

> It should be noted that in the majority of the analytic studies, the point of application of criterion measures is within the training-assessment process and does not extend appreciably into subsequent post-training adult life. . . . Insofar as predictive validity over time is concerned, there is no study which establishes the validity of predictors from pre-training or training phases of development to the post-training adult phase. In some instances, validity has been established to criteria at the terminus of training, but not into subsequent placement. [Pp. 142–43]

Patterson, in concluding his 1964 review, indicates that the 1956 summary of the O'Connor and Tizard studies seems to be appropriate. The final sentence of the Patterson review is a quotation of the 1956 O'Connor and Tizard work: "Under these circumstances, it would be wise . . . to give all feeble-minded boys a trial at simple repetitive work rather than . . . to attempt some selection which at present must be based on unreliable tests and criteria . . . [p. 149]."

The reviews of Wolfensberger and Cobb suggest that the 1956 conclusions of O'Connor and Tizard remain as valid today as they were in 1956 and 1964. To view the problem in another way, Cobb's advice to the vocational counselor is that "the evidence suggests that it is more appropriate to make an assumption of positive adaptation to employability and social integration until negative evidence appears rather than assume a poor prognosis until positive evidence appears" (Cobb, 1969, p. 149).

At this point one might ask, "Where do we go from here?" Since the Wolfensberger and Cobb reviews, studies of other efforts have been reported by Bae (1968), Elkin (1967), and Sellin (1967). Bae's major conclusion, that greater consideration should be given to differential vocational efficiency rather than global measures of vocational efficiency, was based on the finding that retardates judged to be unfit for one particular program were considered to be highly suitable for other types of programs, even though the levels of abilities required by the programs were similar. As each of the 113 trainees in the Bae program was placed in at least four of the eight training programs, it would be interesting to determine if temporal order of placement was relevant to success.

In addition, Levine and Elzey (1966, 1968) have developed a thirty-item scale, The San Francisco Vocational Competency Scale (SFVCS), designed to yield a total vocational score. The purpose of the scale is to assess vocationally relevant sociopersonal, cognitive, and motor behaviors. This rather heterogeneous group of items includes expressive-receptive language items (*i.e.*, following verbal directions, explaining tasks), use of the symbol system (*i.e.*, reading ability, measuring), task orientation (*i.e.*, initiating task, correcting errors, and reaction to supervisor), and several specific skill type items. At this point, it is doubtful that the SFVCS would be a useful screening instrument to add to the ritual of preadmissions examination. However, the SFVCS is useful in terms of suggesting prevocational curriculum components and in terms of providing a tool to evaluate attainment of prevocational curriculum objectives.

Like the SFVCS, the TMR Performance Profile (DiNola, Kaminsky, and Sternfeld, 1963) may prove to have some usefulness in evaluating the vocational readiness of individuals. Discussion of this profile is found in Delp's chapter on social development. As a teacher-administered observational tool rather than a psychologist-administered tool, the TMR Performance Profile allows the teacher to make an ongoing evaluation of the pupil's progress in areas that are relevant to typical curriculum outlines for classes for moderately and severely retarded children.

In view of the fact that current methods of predicting vocational success have limited validity, and in view of the evidence generated by Clarke and Hermelin (1955) that the initial ability of retardates on industrial tasks is not a good predictor of final ability (thus casting doubt on work sample methods), alternate methods of selecting individuals who are moderately mentally retarded for vocational training and placement are needed. Therefore until methods with demonstrated validity are developed, it is suggested that those responsible for vocational training and placement employ what shall be called, for lack of a better title, "The Wolfensberger Rubrics" as the guiding principles in selecting retarded individuals. Briefly stated (paraphrased from Wolfensberger, 1967, p. 233) the Wolfensberger rubrics are:

1. The mentally retarded individual who is capable of basic self-care is almost certainly capable of at least sheltered work.

2. The mentally retarded individual who can profit from arts and crafts components of the curriculum or who is capable of purposeful play is likely to be capable of at least sheltered work.

3. Inability to walk, inability to use both hands or sit erect in a wheelchair, lack of speech or language, and even incontinence are not necessarily indicators that a retardate is incapable of sheltered work.

To these statements, two additional statements must be added:

4. The mentally retarded individual who is capable of assisting in providing care for dependent individuals or who is capable of independently completing household tasks is probably capable of competitive employment.

5. The mentally retarded individual who is capable of learning in a sheltered environment to complete simple or complex indus-

trial assembly tasks and who is capable of sustaining production is probably capable of competitive employment.

## Some Final Thoughts

The burden of this chapter has been to demonstrate that the individual who is moderately mentally retarded has vocational potential and can become a contributing member of society. From the author's prospective as a former teacher of children who were moderately and severely retarded, as a trainer of preservice teachers for the mentally retarded, and as a consultant to local associations for retarded children, the major difficulty in obtaining vocational adequacy for this group is the attitudinal orientation of those of us, professionals and parents, who have a deep commitment in our work with the retarded. It is necessary that we abandon the stereotypes of the past which have led to patterns of negativism and overprotection. It is necessary that we look to the problems of the future.

For the adult with work potential, Wolfensberger (1967, p. 232) has proposed the motto "a full day of work—happiness usually will follow." While this sounds good, it is not entirely true. One cannot review the literature relevant to the postschool adjustment of the trainable without being struck by the bareness of their social life. Away from the work situation, and this is particularly true if the work situation happens to be a sheltered workshop or a work activity center, they have few associates and seldom more than a single friend. The mentally retarded adult, who needs more assistance, probably has the least assistance of any member of our society in terms of providing for leisure-time activities. Even though we may in the future develop the most sophisticated vocational habilitation programs, which result in optimum training and vocational placement for the mentally retarded, these programs will be of no use if we do not also make significant advances in assisting the mentally retarded adult in the management of his nonworking time.

# References

Bae, Agnes Y. "Factors Influencing Vocational Efficiency of Institutional-ized Retardates in Different Training Programs. *American Journal of Mental Deficiency* 72 (1968): 871-874.

Barklind, Kenneth S. "Work Activity as a Context for Education and as a Legitimate Vocation for the Trainable Retarded Adult. *Education and Training of the Mentally Retarded* 4 (1969): 11-16.

Baroff, George S., and Tate, Bobby G. "A Demonstration Sheltered Work-shop in a State Institution for the Retarded." *Mental Retardation* 4 (1966): 30-34.

Barrett, Albert M.; Relos, Ruth; and Eisele, Jack. "Vocational Success and Attitudes of Mentally Retarded Toward Work and Money." *American Journal of Mental Deficiency* 70 (1965): 102-107.

Bitter, James A., and O'Neil, Lawrence F. *Habilitation of the Retarded.* Saint Louis, Mo.: Jewish Employment and Vocational Service, 1967, ED 015 608.

Blatt, Burton. *The Intellectually Disenfranchised.* Boston, Mass.: Division of Mental Hygiene, 1966.

Blue, C. M. "Trainable Mentally Retarded in Sheltered Workshops." *Mental Retardation* 2 (1964): 97-104.

Clarke, A. D. B., and Clarke, A. M. "The Abilities and Trainability of Imbeciles." In *Mental Deficiency,* edited by A. M. Clarke and A. D. B. Clarke, pp. 356-384. New York: The Free Press, 1965.

Clarke, A. D. B., and Hermelin, B. P. "Adult Imbeciles: Their Abilities and Trainability." *Lancet* 2 (1955): 337-339.

Cobb, Henry V. *The Predictive Assessment of the Adult Retarded for Social and Vocational Adjustment.* Vermillion, S. D.: The University of South Dakota, 1969.

Cohen, Julius S. "Community Day Work in a Vocational Training Program." *American Journal of Mental Deficiency* 66 (1962): 574-579.

Cohen, Julius S. "The Sheltered Workshop." *Mental Retardation Abstracts* 3 (1966): 163-169.

Cortazzo, Arnold D. "An Analysis of Activity Programs for Mentally Retarded Adults." *Mental Retardation* 6 (1968): 31-34.

Cortazzo, Arnold D., and Sansone, Robert. "Travel Training." *Teaching Exceptional Children* 1 (1969): 67-82.

Crosson, James E. "A Technique for Programming Sheltered Workshop Environments for Training Severely Retarded Workers." *American Journal of Mental Deficiency* 73 (1969): 814-818.

Delp, H. A., and Lorenz, M. "Follow-Up of 84 Public School Special Class Pupils with IQ's Below 50." *American Journal of Mental Deficiency* 58 (1953): 175-184.

DiNola, A. J.; Kaminsky, D. P.; and Sternfeld, A. E. *T.M.R. Performance Profile for the Severely and Moderately Retarded.* Ridgefield, N. J.: Reporting Service for Exceptional Children, 1963.

Elkin, Lorne. "Predicting Productivity of Trainable Retardates on Experimental Workshop Tasks." *American Journal of Mental Deficiency* 71 (1967): 576-580.

Fitzgibbon, Walter C. "Public School Programs for the Mentally Retarded." In *Mental Retardation,* edited by A. A. Baumeister, chapter 11. Chicago: Aldine Publishing Co., 1967.

Galazan, Michael M. "Vocational Rehabilitation." In *Prevention and Treatment of Mental Retardation,* edited by Irving Philips, pp. 294-307. New York: Basic Books, 1966.

Gold, Marc W. "Preworkshop Skills for the Trainable: A Sequential Technique." *Education and Training of the Mentally Retarded* 3 (1968): 31-37.

Gole, Barbara S. "A Simplified Form of Task Analysis for the Teacher of the Mentally Retarded." Mimeographed. Bloomington, Ind.: Center for Educational Research and Development in Mental Retardation, 1970.

Huddle, Donald D. "Work Performance of Trainable Adults as Influenced by Competition, Cooperation, and Monetary Reward." Ph.D. thesis, Indiana University, 1966.

Kagin, Patricia, E. "Experimental Discharge Planning for Trainable Adolescent Girls: Implications for Social Work." *Project News* (Parsons State Hospital and Training Center) 3 (1967): 1-12.

Kaplan, Sidney. "The Growing Importance of the Trainable in an Institutional Setting." *American Journal of Mental Deficiency* 66 (1961): 393-398.

Kirk, Samuel, and Johnson, G. Orville. *Educating the Retarded Child.* Boston, Mass.: Houghton Mifflin, 1951.

Levine, Samuel, and Elzey, F. F. *Personal-Social and Vocational Scale for the Mentally Retarded.* San Francisco: San Francisco State College, 1966, ED 010 594.

Levine, Samuel, and Elzey, F. F. "Factor Analysis of the San Francisco Vocational Competency Scale." *American Journal of Mental Deficiency* 73 (1968): 509-513.

Loos, F. M., and Tizard, J. "The Employment of Adult Imbeciles in a Hospital Workshop." *American Journal of Mental Deficiency* 59 (1955): 395-403.

Lytle, Howard G. "Pre-Shop Groundwork for Retarded." *Rehabilitation Record* 4 (1963): 28-29.

Magary, James F., and Eichorn, John R. *The Exceptional Child.* New York: Holt, Rinehart and Winston, 1960.

Mager, Robert F., and Beach, Kenneth M., Jr. *Developing Vocational Instruction.* Palo Alto, Calif.: Fearon Publishers, 1967.

Patterson, C. H. "Methods of Assessing the Vocational Adjustment Potential of the Mentally Handicapped." *Training School Bulletin* 61 (1964): 129-152.

Robinson, H. B., and Robinson, N. M. *The Mentally Retarded Child.* New York: McGraw-Hill, 1965.

Saenger, Gerhart. *The Adjustment of Severely Retarded Adults in the Community.* Albany, N. Y.: New York State Interdepartmental Health Resources Board, 1957.

Sellin, Donald F. "The Usefulness of the I.Q. in Predicting the Performance of Moderately Mentally Retarded Children." *American Journal of Mental Deficiency* 71 (1967): 561-562.

Silvern, Leonard C. "Object Analysis and Action Syntheses Methods in Developing a Program for the Assembly of a Television Antenna in a Sheltered Workshop." *Mental Retardation* 1 (1963): 140-147.

Special Study Committee. *The Ins and Outs of Planning for the Mentally Retarded.* Indianapolis, Ind.: Indiana Association for Retarded Children, 1969.

Telford, Charles W., and Sawrey, James M. *The Exceptional Individual.* Englewood Cliffs, N. J.: Prentice-Hall, 1967.

Tizard, J., and Grad, J. C. *The Mentally Handicapped and their Families: A Social Survey.* London: Oxford University Press, 1961.

Tobias, J., and Gorelick, J. "Work Characteristics of Retarded Adults at Trainable Levels." *Mental Retardation* 1 (1963): 338-344.

Tobias, J., and Cortazzo, A. D. "Training Severely Retarded Adults for Greater Independence in Community Living." *Training School Bulletin* 66 (1963): 23-37.

Windle, C.D. "Prognosis of Mental Subnormals." *Monograph Supplement, American Journal of Mental Deficiency,* 1962.

Wolfensberger, W. "Vocational Preparation and Occupation." In *Mental Retardation,* edited by Alfred A. Baumeister, pp. 232-273. Chicago: Aldine Publishing Co., 1967.

# 13

## RECREATION AND LEISURE TIME

## David W. Anderson and Beth Stephens

Statements of broad educational goals for the trainable mental retardate usually center around producing an adequately adjusted and socially acceptable person—acceptable in the home, school, and community (Molloy, 1963). Specific skills geared toward achieving these goals tend to be classed under the following categories: physical growth, emotional growth, social growth, and intellectual growth (Molloy, 1963; American Association for Health, Physical Education, and Recreation, 1966). As noted by Freeman in the chapter on habilitative recreation, physical education and recreation can help to increase the retardate's degree of socialization through stimulating growth in each of these areas.

Each individual must, of necessity, adapt to the norms of society, if he is to be accepted in the community. Each individual, however, is also subject to certain physiological and psychosocial needs with which he must cope. The process of socialization can thus be considered one of adaptation, in which the individual learns and accepts the basic values of the society in which he lives and finds means of satisfying his needs in ways that are acceptable to that society.

Present interest is centered on psychosocial needs, which can be subdivided into security needs and adequacy needs (Katz, 1968).

Security needs are those of companionship (affiliation), love (for self and for others), and acquisition (possessions). Adequacy needs include achievement (feelings of worth), prestige (status), and independence strivings. Katz holds that "failure to satisfy psychosocial needs is likely to lead to failure in community living [1968, p. 74]." This is certainly no less true for the retardate than for the child of normal intellectual functioning.

A general state of mental or emotional health is essential for the retardate's acceptance by society—as well as for his own acceptance of his role in society. He must have an adequate understanding of his capabilities and limitations, recognition of his own worth as an individual, respect for the rights of others, ability to function responsibly in group situations, and ability to make good use of his leisure time. Profitable use of his leisure time is of special importance when considering the adult retardate. In special education programs much emphasis has been placed on training the moderately retarded for competitive employment so that he can be partially self-supporting (though possibly in a sheltered environment). However, more concern must be placed on how the retardate functions after working hours. For the student of school age, the concern is for the *after* school hours, time which the child may be forced to spend at home because of lack of interest, lack of knowledge, or lack of community acceptance and provision.

Unless direction is provided, constructive use of free time by retardates is not common (AAHPER, 1966). Yet there is no reason to assume that the retarded individual has any less need to spend time in creative, healthful activities than the normal person. Active participation by the mentally retarded in community recreational activities will benefit not only the individual, but also his family and the community. If the retardate uses his leisure time to participate in scouting, YMCA, or other community organizations, or to engage in bowling, swimming, dancing, etc., it follows that he will become less self-conscious and more self-sustaining in his relationships with others; in turn this will lead to a more self-satisfying and worthwhile life. The fact that he is mentally retarded, while still a basic impairment, becomes less of a handicap.

The level of social functioning achieved by the retardate has been recognized as one of his most serious handicaps, but there seem to be few professional services available to enhance his social development or to meet his leisure-time needs (Schreiber, 1968). Not knowing how to make use of his free time, the retardate becomes an added burden to his family and community. The relationship between retardation and antisocial behavior has been studied by Dybwad (1964), who reported that inferior intelligence is often a factor in delinquent behavior. Lack of leisure activity not only hinders the emotional and social growth of the retardate, but it also has a deleterious effect upon sibling relationships, family economic conditions, and continued feelings of guilt or resentment on the part of the parents (Farber, 1968: Katz, 1968). With the presence of a severely retarded child, entire families tend to "disengage themselves from community relationships and to focus their attention on problems within the family" (Farber, 1968, p. 174).

Often the retardate is not able to participate in community recreational activities because he is not aware of their availability (if they are available), or because he has had no training in the various skills required. These factors are multiplied by his history of failure in competition, general slowness in learning (which makes him less able to understand the mechanics of the game or activity), poor communication skills, social and/or cultural deprivation, and poor motor coordination and physical strength. Play and recreational programs need to be included in the educational structure in order to provide the retarded with knowledge and skills for leisure-time use. At the same time, such training provides experiences which stimulate social maturation and aid the child in meeting psychosocial needs. In a discussion of planned leisure Ginglend (1968) states that these programs meet the psychological needs of the retarded by: helping him gain a sense of identification, broadening social skills as well as individual and group functioning ability, and fostering learning for growth at each stage of development. Highly important by-products of recreation are pleasure, success experiences, and self-assurance (Happ, 1967). Following five months of individualized physical fitness and recreation training with junior high school educable level retardates, Giles (1968) found positive effects included improved attitudes, self-image, level of confidence, and interpersonal relations. These reported changes were based on teachers' and parents' observations of the children's present behavior as compared with previous behavior characteristics.

Physical education and recreation training serve two important functions for the retarded: they enable the child to perform on a higher physical, mental, emotional, and social level, and thus to become more competetive in terms of employment, and they provide him with social, aesthetic, and personal satisfaction (Kelly, 1967). The value of such programs is summarized in this statement:

> Play and recreation are essential to the education, training, and therapy of the mentally retarded. Through active participation in these activities there are gains in physical well-being, redirection of drives, guidance in emotional development, reshaping of habit patterns, and establishment of socially acceptable attitudes. Along with these therapeutic values, the retardate attains greater feelings of personal satisfaction and reaches higher levels of social maturity. [AAH-PER, 1966, p. 23]

The two basic areas of learning suggested by Kelly (1967) in teaching recreational and leisure-time activities to retardates are basic vocabulary and meaning as related to the various games and activities which would probably be discussed in social situations ₅(baseball, football, etc.), and physical skills which help develop self-confidence and encourage the persons to be more at home with the learned vocabulary. Such coordination of verbal and physical skills helps the mentally retarded gain flexibility in social interaction and reduce a tendency toward stereotyped behavior.

In developing a program of recreation education geared toward carry-over into leisure-time activities for the retarded, it will be necessary to consider individual needs, interests, abilities, and limitations. Degree of retardation, physical fitness, present social adjustment, and past experiences will all influence the structure of the program. In terms of individual assessment, it will also be necessary for the teacher to observe the child's current level of play—individual play, parallel play (side by side with the same objects, yet independently), or group play where cooperative effort is made. In all areas, the desire is to determine the level at which the child is presently functioning and to plan the necessary steps to bring him to the next higher level of performance.

For older retarded children, recreational education can center on developing interest in hobbies or camping (Baer and Stanley, 1969), but for the younger child, play activities may be central. Research supports the thesis that retarded children just as normal ones experience growth and development through play activities which provide opportunities to be with others, to establish identity, to accept and contribute to group goals, to enhance eye-hand coordination, to learn precise body movements, and to refine sensory preceptions (Sessoms, 1965). Even in the nursery school, activities can be designed and selected which aid in the accomplishment of these goals.

> Play and recreation can be the stimuli, the synthesizing agents, and the common, binding thread where the individual uses meaningful, symbolic, and nonverbal activities to express himself and to learn. The individual participates in his own therapy; he is fully involved in it emotionally, socially, intellectually, and physically. [AAHPER, 1966, p. 19]

The concept of socio-recreative programming (Avedon and Arje, 1964) is built upon the use of recreation as a means for promoting the process of socialization. Such a program provides a continuum of structured experiences which gradually introduce the retardate to various levels of activity. This type of programming focuses upon showing the retardate, his family, and the community how recreation can be used as a means of promoting physical and mental health, enhancing the potential for continued mental and social development, and developing realistic and appropriate prevocational skills. Thus it is argued that recreation education not only promotes the process of socialization but also helps prepare the individual for participation in vocational activities.

The aim of socio-recreative programming for the younger retardate is prevention—that is, prevention of social isolation. For the teenage or adult retardate the aim is primarily supportive or remedial—either an extension of the experiences begun earlier or an attempt to overcome social handicaps which may have been caused by isolation and/or rejection. The experiences provided the individual are divided into three phases: "(1) learning social and prevocational skills in a sheltered situation, (2) practicing these skills in realistic social situations, and (3) learning to make independent and appropriate use of as many as possible of the community's resources for recreation" (Avedon and Arje, 1964, p. 2). Socio-recreative programming is appropriate for all age groups, from infant to adult, and all degrees of retardation, from the socially independent to the semidependent child.

Selection of activities for inclusion in a program of recreation and leisure-time education should be based on questions such as these:

1. Does the activity offer ample opportunity for achievement and success?
2. Is the activity adaptable to the individual or group?
3. Does the activity contribute to the need for providing a wide variety of experiences involving many different skills?

4. Is the activity practical for the time alloted and the facilities available?
5. Is the activity relatively safe for the individual—considering his physical and mental abilities and his emotional and psychological conditions?
6. Does the activity invite response to its challenge?
7. To what degree does the activity promote cooperative effort or involve competition?
8. Is the activity socially beneficial?
9. Is the focus on action and participation?
                                                          [AAHPER, 1966, pp. 45-46]

Most recreational activities can be adapted to the level of the trainable retardate. Activities should be analyzed in terms of the basic skills they require. These skills are then taught separately but sequentially as children proceed from mastery of one step to mastery of the next higher one. In this way, the child learns to integrate and coordinate skills and achieves success all along the way. Following such training, even spectator sports will become more meaningful because the retardate will be more capable of following the sequential events in the game. To list the activities which can be taught is unnecessary because of the availability of activities guides (*e.g.*, Avedon and Arje, 1964; AAHPER, 1966; Katz, 1968). However, activities would generally fall under the headings of games and sports, performing arts, fine arts and crafts, hobbies, social activities, and religious activities. More recently, camping and outdoor education have proved valuable in promoting language development, physical development, social experiences, and in stimulating creative activities (Baer and Stanley, 1969; Morlock and Mason, 1969).

Certainly a program designed to meet the recreational and leisure-time needs of the mentally retarded cannot be the total responsibility of the schools. The integration, coordination, and cooperation of all the available services in the community is needed. The community should plan a comprehensive network of

services and facilities to promote the highest level of social usefulness and self-fulfillment in the mentally retarded and their families
(Begab, 1967). Indeed, the community itself remains the key to
successful socio-recreative programming (Avedon and Arje, 1964).
Katz has outlined certain principles underlying community programming for the adult TMR or EMR (1968, pp. 186-188):

1. The retardate should be integrated into the community life
   as much as possible.
2. A comprehensive array of services should be provided.
3. There should be a continuum of services for all ages.
4. There should be a coordination of public and private agencies providing these services.
5. There should be a fixed point of referral for information
   and guidance regarding these services.
6. All sectors of the community should be involved in the
   planning program.
7. Services provided should be of the highest quality.
8. Services should be easily accessible to the retardate.
9. There should be an ongoing program of evaluation.

Such a continuum of services should include physical and mental
health, educational, recreational, and social service organizations
whose facilities would become available to families of all retardates.
Actual coordination of existing services and formation of new but
necessary services by the community frequently require reeduca-
tion of the community. It may be necessary to reeducate it to the
needs and abilities of the mentally retarded in order to break down
traditional misconceptions about the retarded, as well as to under-
line the responsibility of the community toward the retarded individual as a human being and as a citizen of that community. Help
may also be required in adapting and/or extending current programs to include the mentally retarded. In most communities, such
aid can be provided by the local Association for Retarded Children.
    A policy statement adopted by the National Association for

Retarded Children (NARC) in 1964 (Sengstock and Stein, 1967) provides some guidelines in the development of recreational programming. Among these directions are the following:

1. The mentally retarded are entitled to be included in public and community recreation programs. Special programs geared to meet the varying needs, ages, intellectual levels, etc., should be provided for those who find it difficult to participate in the existing community programs.

2. Recreation programs . . . should be under the supervision of professional recreation leaders who have an optimistic insight into the expectations possible with the mentally retarded as well as their limitations.

3. Recreation programs sponsored by associations for retarded children should, wherever possible, be established and operated on a demonstration basis with the objective of involving the appropriate agency in the community at the earliest possible date.

4. The recreation program . . . should encompass as wide a spectrum of activities as is offered in programs for all citizens of the community. Programs should include year-round activities as well as seasonal ones.

NARC has established a Recreation Committee, which is subdivided into groups concerned with: (a) camping, (b) family and individual recreation, (c) youth-serving agencies, (d) community recreation, (e) institutional recreation, and (f) recreation for adults. The primary function of the committee is to encourage local community action in developing recreational programs for the retarded, and to serve as liaison with public and private recreational agencies. Community services which can be extended or adapted to meet the leisure needs of the retarded include day camps and summer camps, YMCAs and YWCAs, boy scout and girl scout organizations, church recreational activities, youth centers, organized park and playground recreational facilities, boys' clubs, and continued education through evening classes in the public schools.

Another means of providing recreative, leisure-time programs for the mentally retarded in the community is the Activity Center. The basic philosophy of such centers is to enable the retarded to develop a sense of human dignity, self-fulfillment, and realization of their potential (Cortazzo, 1967), by providing recreational and social activities which stress independence, self-care, motor skills, communication skills, and social relations (Katz, 1968). The five major objectives of the Activity Center listed by Cortazzo (1967, p. 248) are:

1. to provide the retarded with a socially acceptable behavior pattern for daily living.
2. to help the retardate make the important transition into adult living through training in living skills and adjustment.
3. to work closely with parents and help them understand, accept, and develop the new role of the severely retarded adult in the family.
4. to provide an alternative to institutional living.
5. to prepare the retarded who have the potential in the necessary skills and adjustment for more advanced programs.

Cortazzo speaks of two types of activity centers: Comprehensive Activity Programs, which provide training in the several skills and activities required in adult living and adjustment, and Specialized Activity Programs, which provide training in only one particular area of adult living—recreation or leisure time. An important part of the training received from these programs is in the area of community skills. Training is both general—learning to travel independently—and specific—learning to make use of community facilities such as the zoo, museums, theaters, sporting events, and membership in recreational clubs (swimming, bowling, dancing, etc.). Instruction is also provided in the type of behavior needed for acceptance by others in these community activities (Cortazzo, 1967, p. 269).

Activity Centers thus furnish an extension and continuation of the socio-recreative programming of the schools while meeting the leisure needs of the retarded. At the same time, they provide counseling services for the individual and his family.

Thus, it is recognized that in preparing an educational structure for the mentally retarded it is important to consider recreational activities as a major contributor to successful training. Play and recreational activities stimulate and reinforce growth in all areas—physical, mental, emotional, and social. The relationship of such training to the process of socialization is important as the activities, skills, and interests learned in school carry over into leisure-time activities and provide opportunities to achieve companionship, feelings of worth, prestige, and independence.

# References

American Association for Health, Physical Education, and Recreation. *Recreation and Physical Activity for the Mentally Retarded.* Washington, D.C.: AAHPER, 1966.

Avedon, E. M., and Arje, F. B. *Socio-Recreative Programming for the Retarded.* New York: Columbia University, 1964.

Baer, L., and Stanley, P. "A Camping Program for the Trainable Retarded." *Education and Training of the Mentally Retarded* 4 (1969): 81-84.

Begab, M. J. "Community Planning." In *Planning Community Services for the Mentally Retarded,* edited by E. L. Meyen, pp. 36-41. Scranton, Pa.: International Textbook, 1967.

Cortazzo, A. D. "A Guide to Establishing an Activity Program for Mentally Retarded Adults." In *Planning Community Services for the Mentally Retarded,* edited by E. L. Meyen, pp. 243-270. Scranton, Pa.: International Textbook, 1967.

Dybwad, G. *Challenges in Mental Retardation*. New York: Columbia University Press, 1964.

Farber, B. *Mental Retardation: Its Social Context and Social Consequences*. Boston: Houghton Mifflin, 1968.

Giles, M. T. "Classroom Research Leads to Physical Fitness for Retarded Youth." *Education and Training of the Mentally Retarded* 3 (1968): 67-74.

Ginglend, D. "Recreation Programming for the Adult Retardate." In Project on Recreation and Fitness for the Mentally Retarded. *Programming for the Mentally Retarded*. Washington, D. C.: AAHPER, 1968.

Happ, F. W. "Physical activities for the trainable mentally retarded." Paper presented at the 91st annual meeting of the American Association on Mental Deficiency, May 1967, Denver, Colo.

Katz, E. *The Retarded Adult in the Community*. Springfield, Ill.: Charles C. Thomas, 1968.

Kelly, L. J. "The Special Education Approach to the Importance of Physical Fitness and Recreation in a Curriculum for the Mentally Retarded." In *Proceedings of the Seminars on Physical Education and Recreation for the Mentally Retarded*, edited by S. Auerbach. Washington, D. C.: Joseph P. Kennedy Jr. Foundation, 1967.

Molloy, J. S. *Trainable Children: Curriculum and Procedures*. New York: John Day Co., 1963.

Morlock, D. A., and Mason, B. "Outdoor Education for the Mentally Retarded." *Education and Training of the Mentally Retarded* 4 (1969): 84-88.

Schreiber, M. "Group Work and Leisure Time Needs of Retarded Youth." In Children's Bureau. *Group Work and Leisure Time Programs for Mentally Retarded Children and Adolescents*. A report of a conference, 1 December, 1966. pp. 33-36. Washington, D. C.: Social and Rehabilitation Service, 1968.

Sengstock, W. L., and Stein, J. U. "Recreation for the Mentally Retarded: A Summary of Major Activities." *Exceptional Children* 33 (1967): 491-497.

Sessoms, H. D. "The Mentally Handicapped Child Grows at Play." *Mental Retardation* 4 (1965): 12-14.

# III

# Methods and Techniques

# Introduction

*How* in the provision of learning experiences is as important as *what* and *why*. Reviews of assessment techniques and educational programs for the moderately retarded frequently neglect consideration of methods which can be used in their implementation. Yet this third factor is crucial to the success of training programs. For this reason three complementary methods, Montessori, behavior modification, and discrimination learning are presented in this section. All have proven to be effective in promoting learning in the moderately retarded.

Rather than listing existing studies which show benefits derived from use of the Montessori method with the moderately retarded and rather than making an attempt to specifically direct teachers in their application of the method, Banta introduces the reader first to Maria Montessori and her materials and then presents a succinct analysis of her theory and methods. The analysis addresses consideration to her: (1) developmental theory, (2) educational program and didactic materials, (3) views on "planned" environment, and (4) emphasis on demonstration and interest in the teacher-child relationship.

In his review of behavior principles which can be applied to the training of the moderately retarded, Girardeau considers implementation of the major principle, positive rewards for appropriate behavior, as well as methods for eliminating or decelerating undesirable behavior. Implementation requires identification of the behavior to be changed, advance planning of the steps to be involved in behavior modification, and selection plus consistent use of techniques and procedures.

The need for a structured educational setting that insures that the child attends to relevant aspects of a learning task is emphasized in Gold and Scott's discussion of discrimination learning. Work by Zeaman and House provides a theoretical framework for behavioral rules and techniques useful for sequential training in discrimination learning. Consideration also is addressed to step-by-step application of the method in the establishment of self-care and vocational skills.

# 14

## MONTESSORI AND THE
## MODERATELY RETARDED

### Thomas J. Banta

> I succeeded in teaching a number of the idiots
> from the asylums both to read and to write so well
> that I was able to present them at a public school
> for an examination together with normal children.
> And they passed the examination successfully.
> *(The Montessori Method)*

Four of us, all psychologists, had made arrangements to visit a Montessori classroom in Chicago. We arrived in the late morning, parked our car, walked across the gray dull street, which was marked with the signs of ghetto and public housing living: broken glass, old newspaper, bent tin cans. Then we entered the brightly lit, brightly painted classroom in the Mother Cabrini project. What I saw there was quite interesting. It was quiet. All the children were working individually in their separate chosen areas, some at low tables, some standing, some on the floor on small rugs. When the teacher spoke, her voice was low and gentle and typically directed toward an individual child, addressing him by name, directly, and with total attention given to that particular interaction sequence. Neither the children nor their teacher took notice of the four of us as we entered. Only after the teacher completed her work with an individual child did she come over to greet us.

The equipment in the room was arranged in an orderly way on the shelves, and when children replaced materials they did so carefully. The equipment itself was apparently well made, some of it was brightly colored, some of it was natural wood color. Each child appeared to be using the materials in a definite way, with great intensity of interest and with pleasure. The children appeared to choose their own work, worked alone, and showed very little in the way of dependency in relation to the teacher or other children.

> The children in our schools are free, but that does not mean there is no organization. Organization, in fact, is necessary, and if the children are to be free to work, it must be even more thorough than in the ordinary schools.
>
> *(The Absorbent Mind)*

Maria Montessori, first Italian woman to be awarded the M.D. degree, was born in 1870 and died in 1952. At just about the turn of the century she began to receive considerable attention because she had trained several "feeble-minded" children who subsequently passed a state education examination. By 1907 she moved on to a larger sociological venture, starting the Casa dei Bambini or Children's Houses, in the former slum area of San Lorenzo in Rome. From 1907 until the beginning of the war the schools gained worldwide attention, and by 1916 in the United States there were 189 authorized Montessori schools and over 2,000 schools using her name and perhaps part of her methods without training or permission. By 1925 references to her work became relatively infrequent and in America she lost much ground by comparison with the growing progressive educational procedures of John Dewey and Frances Wayland Parker. A significant factor in the early downfall of Montessori was Dewey's greatest supporter, William Heard Kilpatrick, known as Columbia Teacher's College as the "million dollar professor." He appeared in 1914 before the International Kindergarten Union to point out that, except for her Children's Houses, Montessori's ideas were not new and that he felt she was "some fifty years behind the present development of educational theory." Kilpatrick's writing (Kilpatrick, 1914) was effective—it was read widely and the prestige of Dewey's methods and Kilpatrick's persuasive endorsements effectively reduced enthusiasm for Montessori at that time.

An excellent summary of the historical conditions surrounding the state of psychological and pedagogical theory, then and now, is given by J. McV. Hunt in the Preface to the paperback edition of *The Montessori Method* (Montessori, 1964). Fifty years later, Hunt shows how contemporary psychological theory fits her thinking at many points, and this modern interpretation of her views may in part account for the resurgence of interest in Montessori.

## The Montessori Didactic Materials

Certainly one of the outstanding features of the Montessori method and the one that impresses most persons who view a classroom for the first time is the array of attractive materials. The first impression is that a lot of money has been spent on well-made toys, but further observation shows that they are in fact carefully designed teaching materials, each with a specific purpose. Each piece of material in the graded series was carefully developed through observation of retarded children's reactions. Each piece had to fit the child's hand properly; each item was attractively colored; a set of items was designed to emphasize *one* dimension to be learned, not a distracting or confusing array of stimuli, especially in the elementary materials. In short, the material must *hold the child's interest*, and it must *teach*.

How do materials teach? The major concept Montessori used was that of *error control* built into the materials. That is, each piece of equipment is built so that when an error is made the material itself reveals the error and provides a way for the child himself to correct it through experimentation.

The knobbed cylinders provide a good example of error control. The material consists of ten small cylinders all of the same height, but with a diameter decreasing from thick to thin (Figs. 1a, 1b). The exercise consists of removing all the cylinders, mixing them up and replacing each in its proper place. The child first makes a few trials. Many errors are made; the child attempts to place a large cylinder in a small hole, then he places it in a larger hole. Trying and testing each one, he typically finds that almost all the cylinders have been replaced, but there are one or two that do not fit. Thus it is evident from the material itself that more work needs to be done. Some cylinders have too much room, and this is discovered by the child. The assumption is that the child need not be told, need not be interrupted, in order for him to succeed at a task that interests him.

Once the cylinders have been replaced properly, many children will continue the exercise, repeating it many times. For example, in *Montessori's Own Handbook* (Montessori, 1965), she says, "Little children from three to three and a half years old have repeated the exercise up to *forty* times without losing their interest in it." Not everyone immediately sees the value of such repetition. In one copy of the book I examined, an unsympathetic reader had inserted a comment in the margin: "So what?" This indignant annotation reveals a common misunderstanding about the mental life of the child, and modern psychology is just rediscovering what Montessori became convinced of early in this century—intellectual development comes through sensory development, and it is this expression of triumph that is shown in repetition of an activity. For the child of mental age three, self-initiated repetition is an important avenue to impressing simple concepts upon his mind. At this

Fig. 1a. Knobbed cylinders. These cylinders decrease in diameter only. This is the simplest set; others decrease by height only, with diameter the same; still another set decreases in both height and diameter (see Fig. 6). At mental age two or three the sensorimotor activity of removing the cylinders, mixing them up, and carefully checking, comparing, trying, and correcting, is one of the most attractive. Children typically enjoy repeating this exercise many times over. When other sets of cylinders are later introduced, the child becomes interested in the change of shape and, with renewed attention, proceeds to solve his new serialization problem.

Fig. 1b. Error control is built into the design of the knobbed cylinders. A key idea is that the teacher does not point out errors to the child or show him how to correct them. The teacher demonstrates how the material itself reveals a correct procedure; it is left to the child's own self-directed curiosity and interest, which lead to problem solutions. Note that the small knobs facilitate training in finger-thumb opposition, a precursor to properly holding a pencil for writing and for developing fine motor coordination.

stage of development, repetition is an expression of interest, and Montessori, first and foremost, knew the value of interest in effective educational procedures.

It is always fascinating to note how interested children are in watching the slow, deliberate, knowing demonstration of the teacher. If this were a meaningless exercise in compulsive routine, the child would be the first to let you know it. The proof is in the observation of many children who attend carefully to such instructions and intensively use what they have learned in completing the exercise. It was part of Montessori's genius that she emphasized detail and saw its importance *in light of the child's behavior.* Above all, she was an excellent observer, and would never have retained a purposeless aspect of a lesson if children did not respond to it with interest. That is a good perspective for all teachers—the burden of learning is not on the so-called retardate, but on the teacher and her discovery of good methods.

Another detail should be noted. The solid wood in which the cylinders are inserted has been cut to a shape convenient for a small hand to grasp and hold easily (see Figs. 1a and 1b). Thus, from the very start of the exercise, which involves the child's removing the material from its place on a shelf, he finds that this is an activity which fits him. The act of bringing his own material to his table or rug is not confounded by awkward movements or outsized material. The entire process is guaranteed to arouse the child's interest and intelligence.

Before we leave this example, some further details about the design of this particular exercise should be noted. For example, the knobs on top of each cylinder are not just convenient handles but are designed to help the child develop fine motor coordination—in this case, finger-thumb opposition, similar to that involved in grasping a pencil. Thus the teacher, when demonstrating this material, carefully shows the child how to pick up each piece through use of two fingers and a thumb, rather than in the fist, as some children are at first inclined to do. Each step—grasping the knob, slowly lifting the cylinder, placing it *quietly* on the table, etc. —is given detailed attention by the teacher.

Each and every piece of Montessori equipment was designed to serve the child's natural tendency to work and learn. It is worth examining the range of materials available. The Montessori environment is usually divided in three categories: motor education, sensory education, and language and mathematics. The most relevant material for the trainable retardate is the motor and sensory equipment. Motor or muscular education has reference to the organization and control of the spontaneous movements of the child (which some persons unfortunately still view as "never keeping still," "always getting into something," or "unruliness" and "naughtiness"). Montessori sought to outline exercises that will organize and coordinate such movements so that they will be useful. She saw the relevance of the following procedures for effective development of the retarded child (and the young normal child as well):

Movements of everyday life (walking, rising, sitting, handling objects)

Care of the person

Management of the household

Gardening

Manual Work

Gymnastics

Rhythmic movements

Dressing and undressing is seen as the first step in the care of the person. In Figure 2, one of the several frames for teaching lacing, buttoning, buckling, and snapping is shown.

This exercise, with its own built-in error control, is taken seriously as a precursor to effective intellectual development. Without such motor coordination and impulse control, future development of higher mental processes is not effective. The child is shown,

Fig. 2. Buckling frame. One of a series of frames used to acquaint the child with the many ways of fastening cloth, plastic, leather, etc.: buttoning, hooking, snapping, zipping and various useful ways man has found for fastening material together. The teacher demonstrates the method by fastening very slowly, separating the movements into different parts. Once the process is outlined slowly and deliberately by the teacher, the child tries his hand at it and is soon able to apply what he has learned to his own clothing. Not only can children learn to take care of themselves, but typically prefer to do it themselves. In addition, one will see older, more competent children helping the less able.

slowly and deliberately, how the material must be brought together so that the edges line up from top to bottom; then the teacher shows, step by step, the separate aspects of completing each buckle, button, or other fastener.

Similarly, pouring (Fig. 3), polishing (Fig. 4), and shoe polishing (Fig. 5) are practiced, as well as other relevant household management activities, such as table setting, washing, sweeping, and mopping. There is not space here to describe in detail each of these procedures but it is important to note that these are real, not "play" activities. The table is set because the children are going to eat or have a snack. Mopping is done when something is spilled. Real glass is used rather than plastic since glass when dropped provides its own error control through breakage. But small glasses are used, and mops are scaled down to the child's size; the bucket is suitable for the child to carry.

Singing and rhythmic exercises are likewise used to develop motor coordination and a sense of order and organization. Each

Fig. 3. Pouring exercises. Here children learn the process of coordinating their action. Conveniently, pouring contains its own error control, and this simple task is seen to hold the greatest interest for the child. Water or other material, when spilled, is cleaned up; when the child has finished he completes his work by carefully returning his materials to the proper place on the shelf. The child incidently learns about the way in which volume is conserved—the *same* amount of water may occupy different-shaped containers, and this can be checked by pouring the water back to its original container.

Fig. 4. Metal polishing. Here again, fine motor skills are developed at a task that is both an interesting and a useful practical life exercise.

Fig. 5. Shoe polishing is another popular activity with obvious relevance to care of the person. It is activities such as these that help provide the child, normal and retarded alike, with competence and self-confidence. The more the child can do for himself, the less a burden the child will be on others.

exercise is a meaningful activity; it is done with a sense of purpose, interest, and enjoyment, never as a routine or ritual. *Completion* of work is kept in view. When Montessori first taught retarded children, she herself put everything away when a child finished a task but noted that the children wanted to get up and follow her to the shelves. Montessori capitalized on this curiosity and interest and showed each child how to walk slowly and carefully, carrying each item securely in two hands. Children readily adopted this practice, and in any Montessori classroom, one can see children taking great pains to replace their materials exactly where they belong. There is evidently a level in which competence, however simple it may appear to the adult, is a valuable part of the child's world. There is a manifest sense of pride and satisfaction when the child shows a good finish to his work.

Sensory education and language education are developed through the graded didactic materials. The severely retarded child may show little interest in these materials at first, in which case the directress follows the lead of the child and allows him to work with the practical-life and other motor-education materials. Until he shows a readiness to work in a sustained purposeful way when introduced periodically to the didactic materials, no special emphasis is placed on them. However, when the child shows interest, the teacher nurtures this with individual instruction or includes him in a small group lesson.

There is a wide variety of didactic materials designed to improve perception of touch, hearing, and vision. Other materials emphasize concepts of volume, length, weight, etc. Following is a list of the best-known sensorial materials. For more detail, see *The Montessori Method* (1964), *Dr. Montessori's Own Handbook* (1965a), and *The Montessori Elementary Material* (1917).

*Knobbed cylinders* varying in diameter only (Fig. 1), varying in height only, and varying in both diameter and height (see Fig. 6).

Three sets of solids in graduated sizes including: the *Pink Tower* (see Fig. 7), consisting of ten wooden cubes diminishing from ten centimeters to one centimeter; the *Broad Stair* (Fig. 8), ten wooden prisms painted brown, each twenty centimeters in length; and as with the Pink Tower, the square sides diminish from ten to one centimeter; and the *Long Stair*, ten rods four centimeters square, marked alternately in red and blue and varying in length from ten centimeters to one meter.

Various geometric solids (as prisms, pyramids, spheres, cylinders, cones, etc., in Fig. 9).

Rectangular tablets with rough and smooth surfaces.

Small wooden tablets of different weights.

Colored tablets of varying shades.

A chest of drawers containing plane insets.

A series of cards with outlines corresponding to the geometric shapes of the plane insets (Fig. 10).

A series of cylindrical closed boxes, identical in shape but matched in pairs for sound when shaken.

A series of paired musical bells.

All these materials serve to acquaint the child with basic discriminations learned through systematic sensorial inputs. The geometric solids, for example, are looked at, handled, named, compared. The child is blindfolded and introduced to exercises involving touching, identifying, naming.

It should be noted that materials are interrelated. When the Pink Tower is mastered, the Broad Stair is introduced; still, ordering in terms of volume is the key concept being learned. Similarly the Long Stair involves only variations in length, based on the already familiar unit of ten centimeters, touched and handled while working with the Pink Tower and the Broad Stair.

In using all sensorial material, the principle of organization of lessons is very important. Montessori found that the best order of procedure in every sensory training method was to proceed as follows:

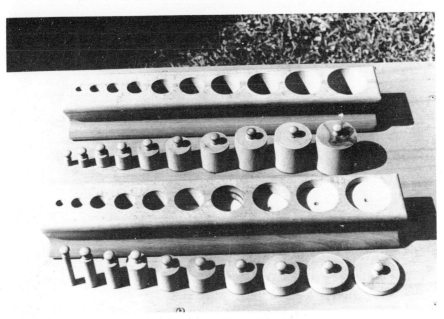

Fig. 6. Knobbed cylinders varying in both height and diameter. After mastering each set separately, the several sets of knobbed cylinders may be combined, mixing up the various forms for a still more difficult learning. The child, through these physical operations, comes to grasp the independent dimensions of height and diameter which go to make up the volume of cylinders.

Fig. 8. The Broad Stair. Each prism is exactly parallel to the dimensions of the cubes in the Pink Tower. After each exercise is mastered individually, they may be combined, placing the Pink Tower in line beside the Stair; thus both differences and commonalities may be emphasized. For the retarded child, the task may be simplified by using only every other prism for easier discriminations.

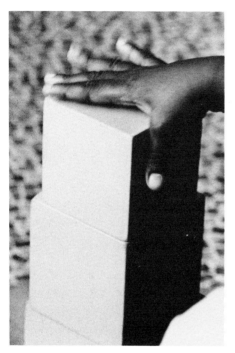
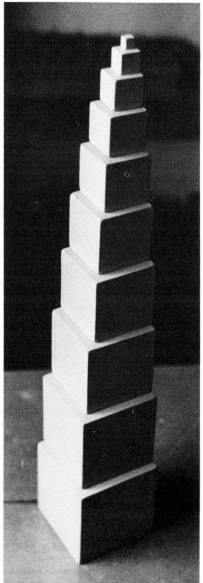

Fig. 7. The Pink Tower. This is another exercise in serializing volumes. With the retarded child, the tower may be simplified by using every other block, thus making size discriminations easier. As the child masters the larger discriminations, the task can be made slightly more difficult by using all the blocks in the set. Many of the materials may be simplified for the trainable. Still, the directress always attempts to let the child correct himself by arranging the materials appropriately for the individual children. Rather than correcting the child, her job is mainly one of preventing disorderly or noisy use of the materials. Glaring errors are not to be corrected; the child should be left to practice by himself. The Pink Tower is somewhat more difficult than the knobbed cylinders in that the control of error is provided by training the eye to make the proper discriminations in selecting the next cube to add to the Tower.

Fig. 9. Geometric solids. This exercise usually begins with the cube, sphere, and cone. Later other forms are introduced. This precedes training in recognition of two-dimensional drawings, where surfaces of the solids are matched with their respective plane representations. Additional skill is acquired by blindfolding the child and handing him one solid at a time. Thus it becomes a verbal exercise as well and encourages the child to use his sense of touch to explore the relation between properties of objects and their names.

Fig. 10. Plane insets and sets of cards with geometrical forms. Grasping each plane inset by the small knob, the child matches it with its appropriate drawing. In this figure the child has a large number of forms spread out before him. The retarded child may work with only a few at first, mastering the simpler, more common discriminations such as triangle, square, and circle. Only later will more subtle discriminations be introduced.

1. Recognition of *identities* (the pairing of similar objects or the insertion of solid forms into places which fit them).
2. Recognition of *contrasts* (the presentation of the extremes of a series of objects).
3. Discrimination between objects very *similar* to one another.

All this provides the basis for moving on to discrimination and judgment involved in the language and mathematics materials. These materials include sandpaper letters to be traced with a finger to familiarize the child with the sensory aspects of letter shapes; colored cardboard alphabets for spelling; sandpaper and cardboard numerals for sensory aspects of numerals' shapes; boxes of sticks for counting; and beads and cubes for counting from one (a 1-centimeter bead) to one thousand (a 10 x 10 x 10-centimeter cube of beads).

Proper use of the materials takes many hours of observation and practice. But good teachers can adopt the parts of the method that appeal to them in their work with the retardate. Ideally one should see these materials and methods in practice (see addresses and references at end of this chapter). One will find that it is the sensorial didactic materials and the practical life exercises that are most useful in dealing with the trainable retardate.

It is now necessary to turn to other characteristics of the method and to review some of the research findings that throw light on the validity of the method.

## Analysis of the Method

Essentially, there are three main areas that provide a basis for analyzing Montessori methods: (1) her developmental theory, (2) her educational program and didactic materials, and (3) her views on the role of the teacher and the teacher-child relationship. All three areas are currently points of controversy between Montessorians and "non-Montessorians." The term "non-Montessorians" is in question because until recently the best alternative label for nursery school practice has been "traditional," a most nonspecific and unhelpful designation. But now we have other systems (Bereiter, O. K. Moore, Nimnicht, and the behavior modifiers) competing for our attention. Some educators have suggested that Montessori ideas have taken hold in part because they are *named*. It has not been very distinguishing or prestigeful to be called a traditionalist or a non-Montessorian.

It is very encouraging to see that Nimnicht, for example, acknowledges some degree of debt to the ideas of Montessori in the development of his New Nursery School curriculum. In some respects Nimnicht's work is more in the spirit of Montessori's experimental ideas than some of the Montessori adherents themselves, who are simply bent on mechanical application of her didactic materials and deification of the *dottoressa*. I cannot believe, however, that Montessori herself was rigid, mechanical, or ritualistic. She was too much a scientist, too sensitive an observer, for that.

> At the Bicetre, where I spent some time, I saw that it was the didactic apparatus of Seguin far more than his method which was being used. . . . The teaching there was purely mechanical, each teacher following the rules according to the letter.
> *(The Montessori Method)*

## Developmental theory

Put simply, Montessori had great faith in the positive growth tendencies of the child, normal and retarded alike. In *The Montessori Method* she says, "To stimulate life—leaving it then free to develop, to unfold—herein lies the first task of the educator." She postulated four normal growth periods. The first is from birth to six years, and this is made up of two subphases—birth to three and three to six. In the first subphase, the child's mind is not subject to direct approach or influence. Certainly she would now change that position in the light of recent experimental findings. The second subphase consists of the same mental type (mainly learning from sensory-motor contact with the environment), but with the possibility of direct adult influence resulting in profound changes in personality. She comments that even under six a child's real interest is to be always at work. Between three and six, nursery school age, she states, the mind begins to control the child and in this period the child needs help in acquiring self-directed concentration and abilities. It is this phase that most nearly resembles the world of the trainable mentally retarded child, and the one in which her most highly developed methods have best application.

> The difficulty of fixing the attention, the general instability, etc., are characteristics which the normal infant and the deficient child have in common.
> *(The Montessori Method)*

Montessori's developmental theory and educational procedures apply to the retarded just as they apply to normal children. The retarded child is simply a human being who comes to be interested in materials that are lower in the graded scale of sophistication, a person who takes longer to move from one level of difficulty to another, and one who may need closer attention from the directress or her assistant. But in no case is the ideal of a child concentrating on self-chosen projects sacrificed. The teacher's job is that of preparing the environment so that the child can prepare himself for life. "Retarded" and "normal" are in a sense, then, inappropriate labels. All are members of the same species; all exist on the same continuum; the differences are a matter of degree.

Montessori's view of retardation is an essentially optimistic one.

Although trained in medicine, she was reluctant to conceptualize retardation in terms of disease or any other relatively permanent status. She said, "I felt that mental deficiency presented chiefly a pedagogical, rather than mainly a medical, problem." How closely this resembles "modern" psychological thought!

> If you watch a child of three, you will see that he is always playing with something. This means that he is working out, and making conscious, something that his unconscious mind has earlier absorbed . . . The hands are the instruments of man's intelligence.
>
> *(The Absorbent Mind)*

The next period, from six to twelve years, brings the flowering of conscience and socialization. Once the concentration and self-direction comes, a child becomes joyful, careful, and conserving of things; responsible toward and loving of his fellows. This is a period of growth unaccompanied by other change; it is a period of calm, health, and assured stability.

The third period, from twelve to eighteen, Montessori says, "is a period of so much change as to remind one of the first." The final period of full maturity is not marked by further physical changes, and Montessori has little to say about the role of later sociocultural effects or adult education.

It is part of Montessori's genius that she was able to profit from what others have seen as "just obvious." She noted that educational theorists have been slow to see that if at six a child can go to school, understand directions, find his way around, etc., that he surely has already learned a great deal and undergone considerable cognitive development. Her aim, then, was to capitalize particularly on this subphase of the first period where adult influence can be felt and during which much useful learning occurs.

Development is a series of re-births.
*(The Absorbent Mind)*

One should note that the Montessori developmental periods not only coincide with the official educational designations but also generally agree with the developmental periods of Piaget: Sensorimotor, Preoperational, Concretely Operational, and Formally Operational (as discussed in Stephens' chapter on cognitive development). Similarly, Montessori viewed these periods not simply as sequential events but as manifesting different psychological types, different ways of viewing the world. To understand the child at each age it is necessary to communicate with him in appropriate mental terms. Thus, when the child repeats and repeats an activity, one does not criticize him for his repetitiveness. The teacher understands that between three and six washing a mirror over and over, for example, is a form of important learning, there being so many learnings about smooth flat surfaces, reflecting surfaces, angles of incidence, rectangular forms, edges, right angles, etc., that are most profitably acquired through repetition of sensorimotor activities.

## Educational program and didactic materials

The "planned environment" is a key Montessori idea. The classroom in every detail is designed exclusively for the child. The weight and size of furniture, the height of washstands and shelves, reflects consideration for the appropriate environmental scale suitable for the three- and four-year old child. Ideally the program permits freedom of movement, requires orderliness, and prevents improper uses of materials. "Improper use" does not mean restrictiveness or discouragement of creative variations. The didactic materials were carefully designed to provide important basic learning for the child; random, disruptive, or destructive uses are looked upon as improper. Thus, careful demonstrations of key qualities of each set of materials are typically provided, either individually or in a group, before the material is made available for free use in the classroom.

The relevance of the care with which Montessori describes her lesson technique for trainable retardates is shown clearly when we summarize the six steps of initiating a new learning with didactic material. Exceptionally good detail is given in *The Discovery of the Child* (Montessori, 1948), in the chapter titled "The Technique of the Lessons."

*Isolating the object* is first: "The child's attention must be isolated from everything but the object of the lesson. She will therefore take care to clear a table of everything else and place on it only the material she wishes to present" (p. 169). Next is *working exactly:* This consists of showing the child how to use the material properly, and typically she "performs the exercise herself once or twice, removing, for example, the cylinders from the solid insets, then mixing them up, and putting them back in position by a process of trial and error." Then she emphasizes *rousing the attention:* Whenever a teacher offers an object to a child, she should not do so coldly but rather display a lively interest in what she is doing and attract the attention of the child to it. *Preventing errors in using the material* is divided into two parts: errors controlled by the material itself, which will be corrected by further development of the child, and are overcome by long and proper use of the material; and errors "due to a kind of ill will, to negligence on the part of the teacher . . . . When material is used wrongly so as to create confusion, or for needs that it cannot satisfy, it is not really used at all. . . . It cannot be said that one learns by making mistakes of this type. The longer one persists in such an error the farther removed he is from the possibility of learning." Then *respect for useful activity* covers the child's tendency to repeat successful learnings: "The teacher will permit him to continue to repeat the same exercise or make his own experiments as often as he wants without interrupting him in his efforts, either to correct slight errors or to stop his work through fear of his becoming tired." Finally, *a good finish:* "When a child has spontaneously given up an exercise . . . the teacher, if need be, can, and indeed must, intervene so that the child puts the material back in place and everything is left in perfect order."

Since one goal of the Montessori curriculum is to communicate specific ideas to the child, the teacher's intervention sometimes is useful to diagnose the degree of learning that has been accomplished. The famous three-staged lesson, originally used by Seguin, has been found useful not only for defective children but for normal young children as well. The first stage consists of associating sense perceptions with names. The teacher says of one surface, "It is smooth," of another, "It is rough." Both object and name should come to the child's understanding at the same time. In the second stage, the teacher checks to see if her lesson has had good effect. Several moments later the teacher asks the child, "Which one is *smooth?*" and "Which one is *rough?*" The child indicates his answer by pointing, and the teacher persists in asking the child many times. If the child does not attend well or is otherwise distracted, the lesson is terminated. In no case does the teacher insist upon the exercise. Learning is the child's choice, and when he makes a mistake it indicates his lack of readiness at that time, not his inability or inferiority. Montessori points out that for the teacher to say "No, you are mistaken," would make more of an impression on the child than the learning of the names. The third stage checks on the child's ability to generate the object-name himself. "What is this?" If the child is ready, "he will reply with the proper word: 'It is *smooth.*' 'It is *rough.*'" If the child does not pronounce clearly, the teacher makes note of it and follows up with corrective exercises in pronunciation at a later time.

The above examples provide some idea of the degree of attention to the small matters of education of the retarded that make a difference. All these teaching procedures are supported by well-designed, didactic materials, which are part of the total educational program. For Montessori, these materials are not just toys, but "learning preparations" to facilitate the child's innate interest in the world when something interesting is provided.

> The first essential for the child's development is concentration. It lays the whole basis for his character and social behavior. He must find out how to concentrate, and for this he needs things to concentrate on.
>
> *(The Absorbent Mind)*

To summarize, the program that is applicable to trainable retardates involves three areas of effort, more or less in sequence:

1. Exercises of practical life: polishing, pouring, buttoning.
2. Sensory discriminations: texture, weight, shape, temperature, rhythm, tones, odors, tastes.
3. Conversion of manual dexterity into simple writing, visual and auditory skills into basic reading, and all of this into physical and basic mathematical concepts.

One is tempted to conjecture that the prepared environment is a good reality-contact "teaching machine." Montessori pointed out that "it is not simply the objects used for the training of the senses and developing habits but the whole environment that is designed to make it easy to correct mistakes. . . . Bright colors and shining surfaces reveal stains. The light furniture, when it is tipped over or noisily dragged over the floor, tells of movements which are still clumsy and imperfect. The whole environment thus becomes a kind of instructor or sentinel always on the alert" (Montessori, 1948).

Thus the *materials* and the *prepared environment*, built to provide error control, along with a *teacher*, demonstrating appropriate use, and a *child*, interested in the world around him, combine to make the effective learning setting. In addition, there is intentionally only one set of materials for the entire classroom. This sets up a condition of necessary cooperation as a means to fair access to these attractive materials. Social skills combined with individual effort are part of the prepared environment's intended effect.

> I was often asked, "But how do you make these tinies behave so well? How do you teach them such discipline?" It was not I. It was the environment we had prepared so carefully and the freedom they found in it.
>
> *(The Absorbent Mind)*

## The teacher and teacher-child relationships

What, then, is the role of the teacher in the carefully prepared environment? Certainly her attitude is one of humility. The word *teacher*, in fact, may carry too much of a connotation from conventional education, centering too much on the accomplishments of the adult, rather than the accomplishments of the child. The translation from the Italian of Montessori's word is *directress*, although this itself is not quite accurate. One of the very fine Montessori teachers, Hilda Rothschild, of Cincinnati, who studied with Montessori, suggested that her teaching is *indirect.* Perhaps *indirectress* is the accurate designation for the Montessori teacher. In any event, her function is that of facilitating learning, not one of pushing, forcing, or insisting.

The teacher may interact freely with new young children to make them comfortable and to allow them time to learn their way around and familiarize themselves with other children and with the new equipment. The teacher ultimately wants to withdraw into a position of being indirective—her job is not to talk but to arrange for the child's emergent motivation, to work with the materials and

model the older or more advanced children's behaviors.
The child is not rewarded, graded, corrected, scolded, or congratulated. He is simply shown. The teacher may divert a child who would otherwise create a disturbance to others. She may prevent destructive actions but she will not punish or scold a child. Montessori's chapter "Discipline" in *The Montessori Method* is a favorite of many teachers, and in it she cautions that the will of the child should be encouraged, not destroyed by punishment.

"So what must she look out for?" Montessori asks, and her answer is clear: "That one child or another will begin to concentrate" (Montessori, 1949, p. 277). First, the new children will be restless, and to the uninitiated this will seem so predominant and so salient that one might wonder if the classroom will ever come to anything at all. But in this first stage such behaviors are to be expected and at this time the teacher's attention should not be focused on the children but on the appearance of the room, the materials, and herself. Her job in this stage, like all stages of the Montessorian education, is to be a good *observer.*

> One who follows my method teaches little, observes a great deal, but rather directs the psychic activities of the children and their physiological development. This is why I have changed her name from teacher to that of "directress."
>
> *(Discovery of the Child)*

The teacher's observations center on signs of the child's interest in work. But the approach is indirect, and the teacher must use her personality and skills in clever ways. Montessori pointed out that "Every action of the teacher's can become a call and an invitation to the children" (Montessori, 1948, p. 279). Thus a lively teacher, interested in those things that attract children, from a walk in the garden to polishing a brass jug, is the beginning of development of interest on the part of the child.

For the child who persistently annoys other children, Montessori recommends a simple tactic. Interrupt him. When the child is involved in work, never interrupt him, but here the procedure is just the opposite—break the flow of his disturbing activity. " 'How are you, Johnny? Come with me, I have something for you to do.' Probably, he won't want to be shown, and the teacher will say, 'All right, it doesn't matter. Let's go into the garden,' and either she will go with him or send her assistant."

The first indication of interest in something by the children is to be carefully noted by the directress. Usually this interest is first shown in the exercise of practical life. Montessori was convinced through experience that starting with the sensorial materials or the more advanced cultural materials is useless and sometimes harmful. She emphasizes that after the child's entrance into the classroom this first step is fragile and delicate, and that any interruptions may set the child back severely. This is a time when many teachers go wrong. In their enthusiasm for this first important step the teacher may say "good" or "fine" and this detracts from the child's own self-directed interest to the point that the task may be abandoned for weeks thereafter.

> . . . as soon as concentration has begun, act as if the child does not exist.
>
> *(The Absorbent Mind)*

The directress must be free of preconceived ideas about the level at which the child is functioning. To this end, the teacher's main job is facilitating the development of concentration and this is in part a social problem. The child absorbed in his work must not be disturbed by his companions, and one of the most important duties of the directress is to maintain order. A well-run Montessori classroom is a peaceful place. Only in this setting, it is argued, can the child perform optimally. A child who disturbs others, or a class-room that is confused and disorderly, is never to be considered the fault of "bad children" but of bad teaching. The Montessori teacher is responsible for the environment. It is she who prepared it, and the ineffective classroom is her responsibility and must be reviewed and evaluated in that light.

> Coins usually have two faces, one being more beautiful and finely chiselled, bearing a head or allegorical figure, while the other is less ornate, with nothing but a number or some writing. The plain side can be compared to freedom, and the finely chiselled side to discipline. This is so true that when her class becomes undisciplined, the teacher sees in the disorder merely an indication of some error that she had made; she seeks this out and corrects it.
>
> *(The Absorbent Mind)*

# Research

Early Montessori education was not followed up in any system-atic way. Only recently have research funds and research interest increased to the point of subsidizing adequately designed studies. No studies of the effect on trainable retardates have been initiated. But some of the data on normal children are helpful in understand-ing the direction of Montessori teaching. At this point, there have been a number of observational studies scattered around the coun-try, but for the most part they have not been designed with suffi-cient care to consider them as more than expressions of opinion. Typically these studies have not been related to any theory, nor have they provided adequate controls or relevant comparison groups.

An excellent exploratory study was reported by Dreyer and Rigler (1967) at the annual meeting of the Eastern Psychological Association. They found plausible results from a comparison of traditional Montessori classroom effects with a "Cooperative nursery school . . . representative of the larger proportion of modern progressive nursery schools with its opportunities for 'unstructured' play." Montessori children in the testing situation were "highly task oriented," while the nursery school children viewed it as "an opportunity to be involved socially with the examiner." Consistent with this observation, Montessori children tended to describe objects in terms of physical characteristics (square, made of wood, green) rather than the *function* served by the object (to play with), spent less time in solving a hidden-figures test (but did just as well), and on the picture-completion test showed some creativity, but significantly less than the nursery school children. Thus they were more object oriented, more efficient, and less creative. It is tempting to "run away" with these data that confirm the stereotype, but it is necessary to withhold judgment since this study applies to one Montessori teacher only and, as will be documented later, great differences abound between Montessori teachers. A lot depends on the teacher, Montessori or otherwise.

A second study was conducted in Chicago under the direction of Kohlberg (Hess and Baer, 1968). This study, which involved just one Montessori classroom during a summer Head Start program, also was compared with two other curricula: one "run by an elementary school teacher stressing readiness for public school," the other "run by a teacher who had previously worked in, and believed in, a permissive child-development oriented pre-school" (Hess and Baer, 1968, p. 105). The permissive classroom showed a significant *decrease* of five IQ points on the Stanford-Binet, while the other two classes increased, but only by two or three points. The permissive classroom significantly increased in distractibility, while the other classes showed a slight decrease. There was a high correlation (.63) between IQ drop and distractibility. The greater the distractibility, the more the IQ decrease.

Kohlberg then studied a year-long Montessori program with ten Negro children who showed a seventeen-point IQ increase between October and January, with middle-class children in the same classroom showing a mean increase of ten IQ points. The IQ increase (.65) correlated highly with ratings of attention (the opposite of the distractibility measure) increase.

In summary, Kohlberg's results, based on only one Montessori teacher, show significant improvement in attention and in conventional cognitive functioning (IQ). In addition he found that these two are highly related to one another.

The Montessori Research Project at the University of Cincinnati was initiated in 1965 (Banta, 1965–1968). The project was oriented toward understanding the development of autonomy in young children and to what extent early education has an effect. "Autonomy" was defined as self-regulating behaviors that facilitate effective problem solving. An important feature of this approach involved the idea of looking at the various strengths of the child, rather than emphasis on a single indicator like IQ (Banta, 1969b). For this reason a test was designed for evaluating early education. The test, the Cincinnati Autonomy Test Battery (CATB) provides scores on fourteen variables. The subtests do not favor Montessori methods and do not contain any materials which resemble those of Montessori. Detailed description of the tests and testing procedures is provided in the writer's chapter, "Tests for the Evaluation of Early Childhood Education: The Cincinnati Autonomy Test Battery (CATB)" in a book titled *Cognitive Studies* (Banta, 1969b).

A brief summary of findings is presented from our first two-year study, based upon close study of Cincinnati Montessori classrooms. Of the three classrooms, one was highly structured, one was less structured, and the third was very permissive. This serves to indicate the wide range of personal choice involved in the teacher's management of a Montessori classroom.

When you open the door of a highly structured classroom, you do not hear much noise; children are seated quietly working with didactic materials; group activities are limited; children are organized and controlled sometimes by obvious instructions ("Now go over and get something to work with"), and sometimes by subtle directions (a look of disapproval when materials are used improperly). When you walk into a highly permissive classroom, you hear many sounds; children singing or furniture being moved about to construct forts or houses; some children are working by themselves while others are organizing a march or a family; the teacher may be holding a child or leading songs; the teacher is more of a participant than a detached observer; there is much more body contact between teacher and child. The highly structured classroom is class oriented while the highly permissive classroom is fantasy oriented and free play oriented.

Both kinds of classrooms occur within Montessori philosophy and Montessori training, because the teacher brings to the teaching situation a whole life history of relationships with children. It would be strange psychology indeed if one were to expect that a few months or years of training would modify basic patterns of structure or permissiveness on the part of the teacher. The teacher's personality has a direct bearing on what will happen (or what cannot happen) in the classroom.

The two classrooms which were compared showed that the actual amount of time children used the didactic materials varied tremendously from class to class, even though all classes were run by Montessori-certified teachers. Based on forty-two hours of observation, we found that the highly structured classroom spent from 10 to 21 percent of their time daily in didactic activity, while the relatively unstructured classroom ranged from only one-half of one percent to 7 percent didactic activity (Banta, 1969). The CATB was administered to the lower-class Negro children in each of these two classrooms and to pupils in a relatively high-tuition school for white middle- and upper-class children. In addition some comparisons are based on control groups of lower-class Negro children who did not attend preschool classes. Here are four provisional generalizations about types of classrooms and their different effects on disadvantaged children.

1. *Innovative behavior is lacking among the lower-class children; it can be modified through prekindergarten experience, but the upper-class children have a considerable head start. The highly permissive classroom showed the greatest improvement.*

2. *Field independence (or analytic thinking) can be trained in structured prekindergarten classrooms, but again the upper-class child has the advantage.* The greatest improvement was found in the highly structured classroom.

3. *Learning processes are greatly improved through kindergarten experience, and under certain conditions lower-class children do slightly better than upper-class children.* There are two kinds of learning: intentional, ability to master a task set by an adult for the child, and incidental, learning aspects of the problems incidental to the main task. In intentional learning, the prekindergarten children, upper- and lower-class, did much better than children who did not go to school. In incidental learning, lower-class children did at least as well as upper-class children, and lower-class prekindergarten children did slightly better. The prekindergarten experiences greatly improved the lower-class child, regardless of whether they were highly structured or highly permissive Montessori classrooms.

4. *Highly structured classrooms reduce curiosity motivation and exploratory behavior.* Although training in analytical thinking was accomplished in highly structured classrooms, this type of environment did not promote growth in exploratory behavior.

In summary, we have found that classrooms function on an either-or basis: either analytic thinking *or* curiosity and innovative behaviors are improved. But at present, we cannot have everything. All classrooms do appear to improve conventional learning processes. It is our hope that we can eventually develop procedures that will produce not only improved conventional learning processes, but improvement in analytic thinking *along with* maintenance of curiosity motivation, exploratory behavior, and innovative behavior. At the present time it appears that teaching practices do not improve *all* factors in autonomous problem solving within one classroom. Educational innovations are sorely needed which optimize autonomous functioning in all areas.

Another line of evidence comes from a study we have been conducting on the effects of continuing Montessori education into the primary grades. One group of children had the benefit of Montessori preschool experience and were then enrolled in a nongraded Montessori experimental classroom in the public school. It appears that this is a very beneficial arrangement. When compared with three other groups of children in the same school (matched on age and sex and from the same socioeconomic background) the Montessori class obtained the highest average scores on nine of the ten tests administered. The results, however, should not be taken to unequivocally support the Montessori method. One of the comparison groups came in a very close second and obtained higher scores on one. This comparison group was also a nongraded primary class which had had the benefit of preschool experience, but had at no time been exposed to Montessori methods.

The general configuration of the results went like this: Montessori continuity from preschool to primary grades did best, but *non-*Montessori continuity from preschool to primary grades did very nearly as well; a group of children who received *no* preschool exposure and who then went on to a *graded* primary class did poorest; finally, another group, *with* preschool experience but *graded* primary exposure showed results intermediate between the top two nongraded classes and the lowest group that did not have preschool.

In summary, nongraded primary combined with preschool experience showed the best overall results; subtracting either preschool or nongraded practices reduced the progress of the children.

Before summarizing the specific changes which occurred, it is important to clarify the meaning of the above results. When one observes and analyzes the educational experiences of the Montessori and the non-Montessori nongraded primary classes, one is impressed with the commonalities more than the differences. If Maria Montessori were to visit the very skillful work of the so-called non-Montessori nongraded class, she probably would endorse its freedom for the children (moving about, working alone), its planned environment (innovative methods with tape recorder, live rabbit, etc.), its nonpunitive character (an "incorrect" answer deserves help, not anger; original answers are reinforced, but other answers are pursued), and its emphasis on concentration (the children can sustain activity without supervision for relatively long periods of time). This class is more teacher oriented than Montessori might perhaps approve of, since there are frequently group lessons and little equipment that emphasizes individual effort. Thus, there is no reason to believe that many aspects of Montessori thinking cannot be incorporated into the teacher's personal style in a useful and effective way. One might say that the teacher manifests his particular genius through selective reading and use of Montessori ideas and methods, which are varied and rich indeed.

The Montessori continuity group had, since preschool, exposure to a relatively indirect teaching method combined with materials that were well suited to individual work. Whatever slight edge the group had in our study might be tentatively attributed to this feature.

The specific results were as important as the overall outcome. The significant advantages of the nongraded primary groups showed up not only in terms of innovative behavior, but even more strongly in what we call conventional intelligence measures: the ability to repeat sentences accurately after hearing them read just one time; or the ability to match objects which are conventionally thought to go together, like a gun and holster, or a bottle with a baby. This was important in terms of the children's ability to *shift* from conventionally intelligent functioning to innovative functioning. Such shifting ability gives the child flexibility in his attack upon problems; he can draw on traditional, culturally sanctioned answers, or he can move out with novel solutions when the task demands it. This is a key idea in the theory of autonomous functioning (Banta, 1965–1968; Hartmann, 1947, 1958).

## Summary and Prospects

An attempt has been made to present a sympathetic description of the Montessori method which originated at the turn of the century as a method for training retarded children. It has subsequently been applied to the education of normal, sometimes privileged children, and has recently been used with culturally deprived children in Negro ghettos and public housing settings.

Systematic evaluation has just begun, but results show that in a general way the gains from Montessori education are significant. Research has started to help clarify what the effects are and how long-lasting they may be. The Montessori method is at best an ideal; actual practice varies from teacher to teacher, and in fact, some non-Montessori classes share many of the theoretical advantages of the method itself. There is no reason to believe that Dr. Montessori herself would resent this; to all indications she would have been at the forefront of change due to technological innovations like those of O. K. Moore and Glen Nimnicht, who use electric typewriters, the Language Master, films, and other cognitive, sensorial, and audiovisual techniques.

Finally, the writer's own view is that whatever persuasion a teacher may become dedicated to, it is a great learning to have at least read extensively in Montessori's writings. Dr. Montessori was a keen observer and provided us with important insights into the nature of self-directed and self-sufficient growth tendencies in children which we in academic psychology have only recently taken seriously. After much more research is in, it is not likely at all that only one acceptable method will remain. Developments are taking shape rapidly and the variety of approaches is good for the experimentally minded; it provides freedom to try different things, and it provides the teacher with the good possibility of finding a method of approach congenial to her own personal style and capabilities. It is almost a certainty that we will emerge with a variety of methods in this field, and that our main task will be to match up the right teacher personality with the best method to fit that personality.

However, the Montessori method itself has several strengths, which should be carefully considered.

1. A frequently hypothesized deficiency of the retardate is his lack of attention and persistence. The Montessori method, with its carefully developed materials and its graded difficulty, provides the child with a maximum probability of success at tasks which are interesting and attractive. The materials have been selected and

developed over the years precisely because they induce good attention and emphasize persistence. Furthermore, the classroom procedure is designed so that there is a minimum of distraction and an atmosphere of work and purposeful activity. This socially facilitates the goal of attention and persistence.

2. Most people have as a minimum goal for trainable retardates skills in daily living and self-sufficiency. Surely one of the central trends in Montessori education deals directly with these developments. All children, normal or retarded, begin with the "exercises of practical life," and the classroom is oriented around the child's participation in housekeeping and maintenance of an orderly, predictable environment. Polishing shoes, setting table, washing dishes, and peeling carrots are all part of learning in a Montessori classroom.

3. A common observation is that the retardate does not initiate his work, but sits idly until told or cajoled to do something. By designing the prepared environment, the Montessori teacher provides attractive materials and a permissive environment, which encourages the retardate to start and finish work on his own, which is scaled to an appropriate level of difficulty for him.

4. Finally, teachers of trainable retardates should benefit from the open-minded, optimistic working assumptions of the Montessori method. No child is condemned to live with a label (retarded, deficient, etc.) but rather each child is looked upon as having developmental potential within him; he is never prejudged, but new ways of preparing work for him, along with respect for his abilities, at whatever level he may be functioning, are utilized to facilitate his learning. The "indirectress," as observer, uses the method diagnostically as well, to discover the strengths of the child so that these may be emphasized to help develop good self-image and a sense of competence.

# Training Centers, Films, Slides, Readings

## Montessori centers for trainables.

Alquin Montessori School, Chicago, Illinois. An interesting combination of Montessori and the controversial Doman-Delacado techniques. In addition they have integrated retarded children with lower-middle-class children in the same classroom. This is in keeping with the idea of nongraded classes with more and less advanced children providing models and mutual help.

Dale Rogers Center, 2501 N. Meek Drive, Oklahoma City, Oklahoma. One of the largest groups of retarded children trained by Montessori methods in the country. The children are divided in three classes according to readiness for Montessori materials. In a nearby building teenage and young men and women are given simple paid work to do, providing them with a good degree of self-sufficiency and purpose. There is a great deal to learn from this staff and their experiences.

The Rubella Nursery, Child Study Center, 601 N.E. 18th, Oklahoma City, Oklahoma. A very courageous attempt to work with severely multihandicapped babies born to mothers who had contracted German measles in a rubella epidemic in the spring of 1964. Problems presented by these children in varying degrees of severity include blindness, deafness, brain damage, mental retardation, cardiac disorders, and other anomalies. A stated goal of the program is to plan a program for dealing with behavioral problems which are the result of sensory deprivation. Combinations of approaches have to be worked out and experimental media used in order to establish means of communications between the child and his environment. Montessori-trained directress Ann Ramey shows the method at its best—flexible, child oriented, nonritualistic.

Mrs. Peggy Loeffler, Cassady Demonstration School, Oklahoma City, Oklahoma. Here is another instance of adventurous exploratory work within the Montessori framework. The electric typewriter and the Language Master are both used to work with language development in retarded children. A variety of diagnostic categories are present, ranging from Down's syndrome (mongoloid) children, to autistic, emotionally disturbed, and extreme brain damaged, plus various combinations. The work is simultaneously diagnostic and treatment oriented. Normal children are brought in to work with the other children on Monday afternoons. This is most interesting and is one of the more promising experiments under way.

In Cincinnati, there are two persons that would be very helpful to anyone wishing to pursue the Montessori method in relation to the moderately retarded pupil: Mrs.

Hilda Rothschild has films of her own Montessori class of upper- to upper-middle-class culturally advantaged children (she is willing to share the films with interested persons), and Dr. Sylvia Richardson, a pediatrician, educator, and trained Montessori teacher who has had extensive experience around the country with the development of training and diagnostic programs for the retardate.

In addition, one can write to Mrs. Lean L. Gitter of the Montessori Society of Greater Washington, 3130 Pennsylvania Avenue S.E., Washington, D.C. 20020. She has been one of the outstanding proponents of Montessori applications in this area over a span of many years and has written extensively on the topic.

The American Montessori Society has prepared a list of other Montessori applications to trainables. The addresses and short descriptions are reproduced here in the hope that more communication will result among interested parties.

Northwest Michigan Child Guidance Clinic, John H. Young, M.D., Director, Munson Medical Center, Traverse City, Michigan 49684. An affiliate of American Montessori Society (AMS) since 1966 when Marie Shaw was brought in as a Montessori teacher to work with ten students with minimal brain dysfunction.

The Hilary School, Josephine Peoples, 505 W. Market Street, Newark, New Jersey 07107. School added a class in 1968 for mentally disturbed using Montessori techniques.

New York Institute for the Education of the Blind, Helen Ziegel, 999 Pelham Parkway North, Bronx, New York 10469. Teachers of multihandicapped children at this institute are beginning to use Montessori.

St. Joseph's School for the Deaf, Miss Francis Cronin, 1000 Hutchinson River Parkway, Bronx, New York 10465. Has used Montessori techniques for four years with blind children.

Katzenbach School for the Deaf, Elizabeth F. Titsworth, Assistant Superintendent, West Trenton, New Jersey 08625. School has used Montessori techniques in classes for over two years.

Laboratory Class, Theodore F. Naumann, Ph.D., Washington State College, Ellensburg, Washington. With Bobbie N. Parson as Montessori teacher, demonstration and research are being carried out at the college. In addition, Dr. Naumann received a National Institute of Mental Health Grant to study thirty-five persons, age six and over at the Yakima Valley State Institution for Non-Ambulatory Severely Retarded. No report available on the project yet, but results should be forthcoming.

Lafayette Clinic, Mrs. Lela A. Llorens, Head, Occupational Therapy, 951 E. Lafayette, Detroit, Michigan. Clinic utilizes Montessori methods in occupational therapy program for emotionally disturbed children. A manual presently is being written as this goes to press.

Department of Studies, Montreal Children's Hospital, Miss Joyce Wood, Director, 2300 Tupper Street, Montreal 25, Quebec, Canada. Montessori-trained teacher works with group of cerebral palsied five-year-olds.

Preschool for Visually Handicapped and Partially Sighted Children, Mrs. Joseph I. Speyer, Director, 2119 W. 73 Terrace, Kansas City, Mo., has made film of kindergarten and use of educational equipment, including Montessori materials. Will loan to those interested.

## Films and Slides

To my knowledge no films of work with trainables have been made. For an overview of the method, the best available film is probably "Montessori, A Demonstration of the Method," 16mm color, silent, but with a great deal of written materials, two reels, 45 minutes each. The teacher whose class is seen in this film worked with Dr. Montessori. Children range in age from four to six. Address inquiries to: D. Hazel M. Lambert, Fresno State College, Fresno, California 93726.

More Montessori visual aids are available from Mrs. George Obolensky, 184 Edgewood Avenue, Pleasantville, New York. These materials include (a) 160 slides describing sequential steps involved in sensorial materials, (b) 300 feet of color movie film showing points to be emphasized in demonstrating the material, (c) 44 slides showing the organization of material for use, the exercise itself, and the clean-up, (d) 68 slides covering traditional Montessori language materials, (e) 103 slides showing steps involved in using mathematics materials, and (f) 160 feet of color movie film showing the number beads with base-ten exercises, functions of addition, multiplication, and subtraction.

## Readings

The best comprehensive bibliography on Montessori is given in Nancy McCormick Rambusch's *Learning How to Learn* (Helicon Press, Baltimore, 1962). The references are a thorough compilation of writings by and about Montessori from

1909 to 1961, including references to reviews and obituaries relevant to Montessori and her writing.

For an overview of the history and method of Montessori, Rambusch's book, might be supplemented with Montessori's writings; for example, *Dr. Montessori's Own Handbook* (New York, F.A. Stokes, 1914; Schocken paperback, 1965) or *The Montessori Method* (F.A. Stokes, 1912; Schocken paperback, 1964). The new introduction to the Schocken edition of *The Montessori Method* is particularly valuable in that it was written by an eminent psychologist, J. McV. Hunt, and constitutes a reevaluation of Montessori's ideas in light of recent psychological theory and research evidence.

# References

Banta, T.J. "The Montessori Research Project: Project Reports." Mimeographed. University of Cincinnati, 1965 to 1968.

Banta, T. J. "Is There Really a Montessori Method?" *American Montessori Society Bulletin* (1969a).

Banta, T.J. "Tests for the Evaluation of Early Childhood Education: The Cincinnati Autonomy Test Battery (CATB)." In *Cognitive Studies*, vol. 1, edited by J. Hellmuth. Seattle, Wash.: Special Child Publications (1969b).

Dreyer, A., and Rigler, D. Personal communication and paper presented at the 1967 annual meeting of the Eastern Psychological Association.

Hartmann, H. *Ego Psychology and the Problem of Adaptation.* (English Translation) New York: International Universities Press, 1958.

Hartmann, H. "On Rational and Irrational Action." In *Psychoanalysis and the Social Sciences*, vol. 7. New York: International Universities Press, 1947.

Hess, R., and Baer, R.M. *Early Education.* Chicago: Aldine Publishing Co., 1968.

Kilpatrick, W.H. *The Montessori System Examined.* Boston: Houghton Mifflin, 1914.

Montessori, M. *The Montessori Method.* New York: F.A. Stokes, 1912. Reprint. New York: Shocken, 1964.

Montessori, M. *Dr. Montessori's Own Handbook.* New York: F.A. Stokes, 1914. Reprint. New York: Shocken, 1965a.
Montessori, M. *Spontaneous Activity in Education.* New York: F.A. Stokes, 1917. Reprint. New York: Shocken, 1965b.
Montessori, M. *The Montessori Elementary Material.* New York: F.A. Stokes, 1917.
Montessori, M. *The Discovery of the Child.* Madras, India: Theosophical Publishing House, 1948.
Montessori, M. *The Absorbent Mind.* Madras, India: Theosophical Publishing House, 1949.

# 15

## THE SYSTEMATIC USE OF BEHAVIORAL PRINCIPLES IN TRAINING AND TEACHING DEVELOPMENTALLY YOUNG CHILDREN

### Frederic L. Girardeau

> A journey of ten thousand miles starts with a single step.
> —A Chinese proverb often quoted by John F. Kennedy

All people who interact repeatedly with children modify to some degree the behavior of the children. When we interact with children we change their behavior—we train and teach them—whether we realize it or not. These changes in behavior occur because of the way we arrange their physical surroundings and because of the way we react, or do not react, to their behavior. Children are greatly influenced by their external surroundings, and our structuring of their environment (both physical and social) is crucial to their development. We can do much to improve their surroundings, thus making them happier and more productive members of our society. A knowledge and proper use of well-established behavioral principles is important in this endeavor.

All of us try to modify or change the behavior of children in ways that will make them happier, more "intelligent," more productive, and more creative. But with some children we have found this to be a difficult task. These children are difficult for their parents and the schools; many end up in institutions where they sit on the floor in a back ward and others are given only a second-rate education. These are children on whom many have given up hope. Whether in the community or in the institutions, they are not allowed to learn the necessary behavior to help themselves or others.

Although these children are currently functioning at a behavioral level much lower than their chronological age peers, they are capable of vast improvements in self-help and social and academic behavior. No longer must they remain untrained or uneducated because of outmoded notions about what they cannot learn. We *can* do something. By systematically using well-established principles of behavior we can do much to help prevent and remediate retarded behavior. There is still much to be learned about changing behavior, but we do have some procedures which can help today. These procedures will not solve all the problems, but a systematic use of them by innovative teachers will contribute a great deal in helping the severely and moderately retarded rise to levels of achievement heretofore considered impossible by many people.

The purpose of this chapter is to review some of the behavioral principles which can readily be applied to training and educational situations. Since they are concerned with modifying behavior, these principles and the procedures based on them are sometimes referred to as *behavior modification* principles. They are derived, in most part, from research stimulated by the functional analysis approach to behavior proposed by Skinner (1953, 1968). The basic principles are not new in the sense that many have used them for years. But today we have a better understanding of specific details. Most of the applied work has occurred in the last five years, and the *Journal of Applied Behavior Analysis* was begun in 1968 so that work in this area could be reported regularly. It is not necessarily suggested that behavior modification procedures be used every hour of every day for every child but that a more thorough knowledge and careful use of them will greatly benefit many children.

## The Major Principle: Positive Rewards for Appropriate Behavior

If we want to help a child learn, we must prompt the correct response and reward him for his attempts to produce the correct response. As soon as he makes the correct response, we should immediately follow it with something that the child finds pleasing. This "something" can be praise, an opportunity to go to the next task, a drink of orange juice, a piece of candy, or anything he wants to do. This something can be a check mark or an aluminum token indicating a correct response, providing the check marks or tokens can be traded in later for something else the child chooses. *The major principle in the development of behavior, then, is that a positive reward immediately following some bit of behavior increases the likelihood that the behavior will occur in that context again.*

The principle of giving a positive reward or reinforcer *immediately* following appropriate behavior cannot be overemphasized because it is the foundation of much complex behavior. We can also reward approximations to the desired behavior and build up slowly to the correct response. This procedure, called shaping, is tedious but sometimes necessary. Also, it is still something of an art and there is much to be learned about the details of shaping. But the point is that new behavior *can* be developed in this manner. A quicker procedure than shaping is one in which the teacher gives the correct response and asks the child to imitate it; later the child gives it with less and less prompting. Baer, Peterson, and Sherman (1967) have used positive reinforcement principles in developing imitative behavior by retarded children. Imitative behavior is *not* the final goal, but it is a beginning for some children who have never talked or responded much to their environment. McLean (1970) used imitative behavior as the initial step for developing correct articulation by retarded children in more complex verbal situations.

## The Subprinciple of Immediacy of Reward

You might have noticed that the word *immediately* was used several times. Immediacy is important. The effectiveness of a reinforcer drops off rapidly as a function of time since the response. In fact, if we wait too long, other responses may occur and the reward will strengthen them. Unwittingly, by waiting we might strengthen behavior which is not appropriate to the situation. Therefore, the reinforcer should follow as quickly as possible the desired behavior.

## The Subprinciple of Occasional Rewards

Once we have the correct behavior started, we do *not* have to reward it each time it occurs. Fortunately, we can require more and more correct behavior before we provide a reward. For some, this may seem implausible. But there are literally hundreds of well-controlled studies which show that behavior can be maintained at great strength with only an occasional reinforcer. The point is that, contrary to popular belief, a person does *not* come to rely more and more on the reward but, if properly scheduled, will do more and more with less and less extrinsic reward. It is best to be generous with our rewards in the early stages of behavior development, but we know that our rewards can be given less frequently as the behavior becomes better established. Many people believe that children will come to depend upon rewards, but this is true only if the parent or teacher sets the situation up in a dependent manner.

Rewards should be given always after the behavior occurs and should not be used in a bribe-type manner. In some cases, however, contracts may be set up (Birnbrauer, Bijou, Wolf, and Kidder, 1965). The child might occasionally ask for a reward, but the teacher can ignore the request when he asks, giving it only when the teacher deems it appropriate. We can also require longer and longer behavioral episodes before we give a reward. For example, we might give a token or check mark at first for hanging up a coat upon entering the room. Then, after this is well learned, we would require the child to hang up the coat, get a puzzle from the rack, and successfully complete the puzzle before we give the reward. Thus, we can put simple behaviors together to build more complex behavior.

## The Subprinciple of Individualizing Rewards

In the past many people who have used rewards for developing behavior have tried to use the same reward for all children. As adults we know that what appeals to us might not appeal to others and that what appeals to us at one time might not at another time. We now have good evidence that we should individualize our rewards, allowing the child to tell us what will be rewarding at the time it will be given. What is desired by one child might well be unacceptable to another, and we should be very careful in making this judgment. Many classrooms and training projects that utilize reward systems have a little store with fruit, ice cream, candy, and toys from which the child can select his reward. Addison and Homme (1966) have developed a "reinforcing event menu," a picture book of rewards, from which a selection can be made. Toy books and mail-order catalogs can also be quite useful.

The best way to individualize rewards is probably through the use of a token system. Tokens are anything that can be redeemed for merchandise of some kind or for the opportunity to engage in certain behavior. Check marks, teacher drawings of smiling faces, silver and gold stars, trading stamps, foreign coins, metal washers, and specially designed "money" have been used as tokens. There are many other token-type rewards that teachers occasionally use, such as little Valentines stamped on the page, written comments ("Very good, Karen!"), and even bits of construction paper. Tokens have several advantages which recommend them for use in educational situations.

1. A token system allows each child to earn the kind of object or activity that is most rewarding to him. He can spend his tokens for small objects, save them for larger ones, or purchase an activity or free period.

2. The token system approximates the monetary system and gives experience in trading tokens for things. Furthermore, the token system may be used to teach certain arithmetic facts and the care of valuable personal property.

3. The delivery of a token does not interfere with certain educational tasks (e.g., oral reading) as would other rewards, such as candy.

4. Tokens can be given and withdrawn. If one wants to set up a situation where a reward is lost for an error, then food (if consumed) and social reinforcers cannot be used.

5. A token system permits the use of powerful reinforcers which cannot be dispensed in the educational situation, e.g., trips to the zoo, use of a record player or typewriter, twenty minutes of watching cartoons. Thus, small bits of behavior can be rewarded in an economical manner and, if the parents so desire, the back-up rewards for the tokens can be given at home.

6. If records are desired, it is probably easier to record the number of rewards given in group situations when tokens are used, since each child's tokens can be counted at the end of the session. Hence, recording does not interfere with ongoing educational situations. Such records are quite important in that they indicate the extent

of each child's participation in the program, if the tokens are delivered in an objective manner. Checks should be made to see that the tokens are being given appropriately.

7. The token is not as dependent on deprivation states as are many other rewards. Not all children view candy, ice cream, or soda pop as a reward.

Token systems of one type or another have been used by some teachers for many years. As we learn more about their effectiveness and how to make them fit in with the natural classroom and home environment, they will be adopted by more and more teachers and parents. Teachers and parents can cooperate in a system in which the teacher gives tokens at school and the parents redeem the tokens at home. Many innovations and improvements undoubtedly will be made, and teachers can contribute a great deal to progress in this area.

### Research and Demonstration Programs Using Token Rewards

Several programs which systematically use token rewards have been developed, and the tokens have been demonstrated to be effective in improving a wide variety of behaviors. Ayllon and Azrin (1968) have worked with adult psychotics and some adult retardates. Wolf, Giles, and Hall (1968) developed an extensive remedial program for children in an inner-city ghetto area and thoroughly evaluated the effectiveness of the tokens (check marks given immediately and traded in later).

The two most extensive programs with retarded persons were conducted at Rainer School in Rainer, Washington, by Birnbrauer, Bijou, Wolf, and Kidder (1965) and at Parsons State Hospital and Training Center in Parsons, Kansas, by Girardeau and Spradlin (1970), Lent (1968), and Lent, LeBlanc, and Spradlin (in press). The beginning effort is reported in the following paragraphs, but one should read the Lent (1968) and Lent, *et al.* (in press) reports to appreciate fully the expansion and improvement made in the Parsons program. The film "Operation Behavior Modification," listed at the end of this chapter, shows this program in operation. Although carried out in a state institution, much of the program can be adapted to the classroom by an innovative teacher.

The program at Parsons began in a cottage of twenty-eight adolescent girls with an IQ range of 20 to 50. The girls ranged in chronological age from twelve to sixteen years and presented a wide variety of training and educational problems. Before the training program was started a simple evaluation of the behavioral level of each girl was made. For about ten days following the evaluation period tokens were given for behaviors common to the daily life of these girls. They were allowed to trade these tokens immediately in a small store set up in the cottage. The store had a wide variety of items including candy, gum, fruit, soda pop, perfume, lipstick, lace underwear, crayons, paper, and picture books. Following the ten-day period of establishing the reward value of the tokens a reward scale was set up as a guide for the two assistants who were delivering tokens. A sample of the activities that were rewarded and the reward amounts are given in Table 1.

Improvement in behavior was stressed as the basis for reward. Another important principle was that one should not expect immediate, gross improvement but that small improvements in behavior should be rewarded and that complete mastery of a task would occur gradually in most cases. Tokens were given on an individual basis. There was one immediate problem: the girls became so motivated that it was difficult to create tasks fast enough for them! A classroom was set up to work on beginning academic skills. The classroom work has been greatly expanded with marked success by Lent and LeBlanc (in press).

A bank was set up and girls began to save for larger purchases. The program has expanded to several other departments and nu-

## Table 1
### A SAMPLE OF THE BEHAVIORS TO BE REWARDED
### AND APPROXIMATE REWARD AMOUNTS

| Behavior | Reward Amount* |
| --- | --- |
| Making up bed | 1 token |
| Dressing for a meal | 2 tokens |
| Brushing teeth | 2 tokens |
| Taking shower properly | 2 tokens |
| Helping clean cottage | Quite variable |
| Setting hair | 4 tokens |
| Straightening bed drawer | 2 tokens |
| Trimming and filing nails | 2 tokens |
| Combing hair | 1 token |
| Washing hair | 2 tokens |
| Group play (30 minutes) | 5 tokens |
| Coloring | Quite variable |
| Work placement in institution | 10 tokens per day |
| Cleaning goldfish bowl | 5 tokens |
| Feeding goldfish | 1 token |
| Cleaning bird cage | 5 tokens |
| School readiness tasks | Quite variable |
| Being on time at work or speech therapy | 4 tokens |
| Shining shoes | 5 tokens |
| General proper use of leisure time (20 minute period) | 4 tokens |

* The numbers of tokens listed are only approximate. They are given on an individual basis and may vary a great deal from girl to girl. As an activity becomes established, the reward is changed from a continuous schedule (every time the behavior is performed) to an intermittent one (only occasionally when the behavior is emitted). This change is a very gradual one, however.

merous improvements have been made. More extensive programs are being developed, and better recording of behavior has been introduced. The program has demonstrated that trainable retarded persons can do much more than many people would predict.

## Eliminating or Decelerating Undesirable Behavior

In some sense it would be nice if our only job were developing behavior and we could concentrate on that. However, there are many times when a child has behavior that is detrimental to his physical well-being or behavior that is incompatible and interfering with the development of appropriate behavior. Some examples of undesirable behavior are head banging, certain kinds of stereotyped behavior, "dawdling," tantrums, and getting out of seat. Fortunately, there are methods for dealing with these and other undesirable classes of behavior. The following techniques or procedures may be used to decelerate undesirable behavior.

### 1. Physical Restraint

In some cases, such as thumb sucking, head banging, and getting out of seat, physical restraint may be used. This procedure, though, has an undesirable effect in that the person cannot utilize the restrained body part to perform desirable activities. Therefore physical restraint probably should be used only as a last resort for extremely undesirable behavior.

### 2. Satiation with Rewards

If a person is emitting a behavior which results in a reward, it may be possible to provide a lot of the reward at other times and thereby reduce its potency as a reward. If a child hits another child and receives teacher attention for it, then teacher attention given at other times may result in a reduction of the hitting. Unless coupled with a behavior development program, though, this procedure is effective for only short periods of time.

### 3. Change in Constant Stimulus Conditions

Sometimes a child will stop emitting a behavior when there is a sudden change in the environment (*e.g.*, sudden noise), but the effect is usually only short-lived and not very useful in educational situations.

### 4. Punishment

One type of punishment involves the delivery of an aversive event following a behavior. When this is done, the rate of the behavior drops off quickly, depending on the severity of the aversive event. There are natural punishment situations built into the physical environment (*e.g.*, not maintaining a proper balance results in falling, and looking in a different direction results in running into a door), and many punishing situations have been added (*e.g.*, spanking, scolding, etc.). Although punishment can be quite effective, it may lower the rate of other behaviors occurring at the same or nearly the same time and it also results in the deliverer becoming aversive. Hence, the child does not approach the teacher or parent as readily as before the punishment.

### 5. Remove Positive Reward

Another type of punishment is one in which a pleasant event is terminated when a behavior occurs. For example, television cartoons can be turned off when thumb sucking occurs and the result will be a reduction in thumb sucking (if watching cartoons is a positive reward for the child). This procedure probably also has the same undesirable effects as the delivery of an aversive event.

## 6. Extinction

If you can determine the reinforcer maintaining some behavior, you can remove the reinforcer and behavior will decrease in frequency. Sometimes it is social attention (by peers, teacher, or parent) that is maintaining the behavior. In such a case, if you ignore the behavior and the environment does not change following the behavior, then the behavior will occur less and less frequently. This is an effective but sometimes time-consuming procedure in that the behavior may occur many times before there is a quite noticeable reduction in its frequency. Also, if you ignore the behavior several times and then reward it (with attention, for example), you now have the behavior on an occasional positive reward schedule and it will be much more difficult to eliminate. If you decide to use extinction, by all means do not give up too early or you have intensified your problem.

## 7. Substitute Desirable Behavior and Positively Reward It

In most educational situations, this procedure is probably the most desired, both from the standpoint of its effectiveness and from the view that you are concomitantly developing desirable behavior. Good teachers and parents have been doing this for many years; very calmly they show the child an appropriate behavior, get him to emit it, and then reward him heavily. Pretty soon the undesired behavior is no longer occurring; it has been replaced by the desired behavior. Where possible every teacher should try to use this procedure rather than those procedures which simply eliminate behavior.

We want the child doing something but something which is constructive in terms of *his* future development.

## Steps in Behavior Modification

The application of behavioral principles in solving educational
problems, like good teaching, proceeds by deliberate, well-planned
steps. Advance planning is required in terms of materials and
procedures. Furthermore, the behavior undergoing change is specified precisely and records of the behavior are maintained. Objective records are necessary if we are to make certain that our
procedures are having the desired effect. Precise records are the
hallmark of good teaching; they provide the basis for educational
decisions. Lindsley and his students at the University of Kansas are
developing "precision teaching" methods for classroom teachers.
The emphases in precision teaching are on the precise specification
of the behavior to be modified ("pinpoint the behavior") and on the
keeping of precise records on the occurrence of the behavior.
Where possible, they are teaching the children to keep their own
records. A good example of precision teaching is reported by Slezak
(1969).

The general activities involved in implementing a behavior
modification procedure can be summarized in six steps.

### 1. Decide and Specify Precisely the Behavior to Be Changed

Too often we fail in achieving an educational objective because
we do not specify our objective clearly enough. To say that we want
Jimmy to "put on his clothes better" or "add numbers faster" is not
precise enough. The reason that such statements are not precise
enough is that it would be difficult to decide when or if we had

reached our goal. What does Jimmy have to do to put on his clothes better or add faster? In every case we must formulate our objectives in such a manner that we can tell when that objective is reached. (Then we can set other objectives and pursue them.) In terms of the dressing behavior example we should specify that we want Jimmy to "put on short pants, button them, put on short-sleeve shirt, button shirt, and put on socks and shoes (but not tie them) in three minutes." Of course, many times we would begin with a portion of the above and build up to the more complex behavioral objective later, as exemplified in the training of the profoundly retarded by Breland (1965) and Bensberg, Colwell, and Cassell (1965). In terms of "adding numbers faster" we should specify that the objective is for Jimmy "to add two, two-digit numbers not requiring carrying at the rate of ten problems correct per minute." Anyone interested in improving the precision of his educational objectives for children would benefit from the short paperback book by Mager, *Preparing Instructional Objectives* (1962).

## 2. Measure the Present Rate of the Behavior

*Before* beginning a procedure to change behavior it is important to have an accurate count of the frequency of the behavior in question, how many correct responses and how many incorrect responses and the time period in which they occurred. We call this a "before" or *baseline* against which the success of our procedure will be judged. This is a very important step because it tells about the success or failure of our procedures; without this baseline step we can only guess, sometimes erroneously, about the outcome of our efforts. The behavior of children needing our assistance is too important to be left to guesswork. We should *not* rely on our general impression; it is not specific enough.

## 3. Decide on an Appropriate Modification Technique

In choosing a modification technique we rely a great deal on the child's previous behavior in telling us what will be successful. If our objective is improving an academic behavior, we choose curriculum materials at or slightly below his current level. We *do not* give him materials on which it is likely that he will fail ("to challenge him") since it is quite likely that many children needing our systematic assistance have been through many failure experiences and they are no longer challenging, if they ever were.

The child also tells us what type of consequence (reward or punisher) will be effective for him at this time. We might give him five extra minutes of recess or free time each time he does twenty problems correctly in fifteen minutes. Or we might give him tokens which he can trade for dessert at lunch, candy, toys, or activities (such as the use of a record player, radio, etc.). The innovative teacher can probably come up with hundreds of inexpensive items and activities that can be used as rewards following improvement in behavior. Always remember it is important to let the child select the reward since the probability of its being effective is greatly increased.

Also to be determined is the frequency with which the rewards are to be given. Remember that early in a modification program it is best to be lavish with our praise or other rewards; we can give them less frequently as the behavior improves.

## 4. Introduce the Modification Procedures

Once we have a "before" or baseline record of the behavior and have settled on a modification procedure, we are ready to implement the procedure. *Consistency in this phase is very important.* We should not, at this point, change our procedures too quickly. Rather, we should give them some time to take effect. Occasionally there will be immediate, dramatic effects but more often the behavior in question will improve gradually. Frequently there will be a quick improvement in "motivation" and "attitude" and small improvements in the academic, self-help, or social behavior itself. Learn to accept small improvements; they lead to larger ones.

If changes have to be made in the procedures, be certain to note the exact time that the change occurred so that its effect can be noted.

## 5. Continue Measurement During the Modification Procedure

Be certain to continue measuring and recording the scores during the time the procedures are in effect. The difference between the behavior now and the baseline ("before" phase) is the principal measure of the effectiveness of the procedure. The record can be used to show the effect of our modification procedure and we can compare the effects of the current procedure with other procedures.

## 6. Continue Measurement Following the Modification Procedure

As long as it is feasible, continue recording the behavior after you have discontinued your modification procedure in order to determine if the behavior is maintaining (or is still at a low rate in the case of eliminating undesirable behaviors) in the absence of your specific treatment. If the behavior returns to the original rate, you may want to reintroduce your modification procedure or try a different one. In research situations, sometimes the behavior is intentionally returned to the original level to show that the specific modification procedure was responsible for the behavior change.

When a return to the original level is not possible or not desirable, other techniques are used, such as recording two behaviors but applying the modification treatment to only one, while continuing to record both.

### 7. Don't Give Up: Try, Try Again

Too frequently in working with the retarded we give up too easily and conclude that it cannot be done, by anyone, ever. Perhaps we should more often conclude that we just haven't found an effective procedure yet but that we will keep searching for one. We should not make decisions hastily about what will *not* happen in the future. Be realistic about the present but optimistic about what might happen in the future.

One example of a record sheet that can be used by teachers is given in Figure 1. From this record the daily performance can be plotted on graph paper (*e.g.*, see Slezak, 1969).

## Teacher Attention

The attention given children by adults is a positive reward for most children. It can be used, however, to help or hurt the child's development. It is important to remember that positive rewards work as well in increasing *undesirable* behavior as they do in increasing desirable behavior. Therefore we must be careful with our attentiveness to children since it can be so easily and indiscriminately given.

The teacher has many opportunities to provide or withdraw attention in the classroom. When Johnny is out of his seat bothering Susie, it is very tempting to go over and lead him back to his seat. This attention, however, can result in Johnny's getting out of his seat more often. In the long run, a better procedure is to watch

## Figure 1

## RECORD SHEET

(One possible example which can be modified to fit a teacher's specific purpose.)

Child_____Observer_____

Teacher_____School_____

Behavior being recorded: Correct adding of addition problems

| Date & Time | No. of Times Behavior Occurred | Consequence | Contingency |
|---|---|---|---|
| 3–1 9:30–10:00 | 90 correct, 20 incorrect | Tokens | One token for each 10 correct. |
| 3–2 10:00–10:30 | 70 correct, 30 incorrect | Tokens | One token for each 10 correct. |
| | | | |
| | | | |
| | | | |
| | | | |
| | | | |
| | | | |
| | | | |
| | | | |
| | | | |

Johnny closely and go over and praise him when he is in his seat and doing his academic work. This latter procedure takes time to become effective (and, in some cases, may not work) but if the teacher can be patient and consistent, her efforts will be rewarded by Johnny's improved behavior. Too often we pay attention to children only when they exhibit undesirable behavior.

In a very readable booklet designed for inservice training, Hall (1969) discusses the numerous possible uses of teacher attention in school situations. He reports quite a few examples of situations in which teacher attention can be misused, and how, with only a slight change in procedure, the attention can be used in a constructive way to eliminate discipline problems and accelerate desirable classroom behavior, both academic and social. Hall's experience as a teacher and principal and his current work in assisting teachers give him a perspective on behavior modification procedures that is not found in some sources. This booklet is highly recommended for teachers who are interested in using their attention in an effective manner.

## Summary

Behavior modification procedures, if properly handled, can be used to improve greatly the behavior of developmentally retarded persons. The most important principle is the systematic use of positive reinforcers immediately following desirable behavior. Tokens combined with teacher attention are a very useful and feasible procedure in most classroom and home situations. Records should be kept so that the effects of procedures can be evaluated and progress (or the lack of it) noted. Although a great deal of progress has been made in developing behavior modification procedures in the last five years, there is still much to be learned about their application in classroom and home situations. Teachers and parents can contribute substantially to the continued improvement of these procedures. Most people already use these procedures but not consistently. It is the systematic use over a period of time that results in the greatest behavior improvement of retarded persons.

# References

Addison, R. M., and Homme, L. E. "The Reinforcing Event (RE) Menu." *National Society for Programmed Instruction* 5 (1966): 8-9.

Ayllon, T., and Azrin, N. *The Token Economy: A Motivational System for Therapy and Rehabilitation.* New York: Appleton-Century-Crofts, 1968.

Baer, D. M.; Peterson, R. F.; and Sherman, J. A. "The Development of Imitation by Reinforcing Behavioral Similarity to a Model." *Journal of the Experimental Analysis of Behavior* 10 (1967): 405-416.

Bensberg, G. J.; Colwell, C. N.; and Cassell, R. H. "Teaching the Profoundly Retarded Self-Help Skill Activities by Behavior Shaping Techniques." *American Journal of Mental Deficiency* 69 (1965): 674-679.

Birnbrauer, J. S.; Bijou, S. W.; Wolf, M. M.; and Kidder, J. D. "Programmed Instruction in the Classroom." In *Case Studies in Behavior Modification,* edited by L. P. Ullman and L. Krasner. New York: Holt, Rinehart, and Winston, 1965.

Breland, M. "Foundation of Teaching by Positive Reinforcements." In *Teaching the Mentally Retarded: A Handbook for Ward Personnel,* edited by G. Bensberg, pp. 127-141. Atlanta, Ga.: Southern Regional Education Board, 1965.

Girardeau, F. L., and Spradlin, J. E., eds. "A Functional Analysis Approach to Speech and Language Behavior." American Speech and Hearing Association Monograph, no. 14, 1970.

Hall, R. V. *Improving Teaching Skills.* Chicago: Science Research Associates, 1969.

Lent, J. R. "Mimosa Cottage: Experiment in Hope." *Psychology Today* 2 (1968): 51-58.

Lent, J. R.; LeBlanc, J. M.; and Spradlin, J. E. "Research of Rehabilitative Culture for Moderately Retarded Adolescent Girls." In *Control of Human Behavior,* vol. 3, edited by R. Ulrich, T. Stachnik, and J. Mabry. Glenview, Ill.: Scott, Foresman & Co. (in press).

Mager, R. F. *Preparing Instructional Objectives.* Palo Alto, Calif.: Fearon Publishers, 1962.

McLean, J. E. "Extending Stimulus Control of Phoneme Articulation by Operant Techniques." In "A Functional Analysis Approach to Speech and Language Behavior, edited by F. L. Girardeau and J. E. Spradlin. *American Speech and Hearing Association Monograph,* no. 14 (1970).

Skinner, B. F. *Science and Human Behavior.* New York: MacMillan, 1953.

Skinner, B. F. *Contingencies of Reinforcement: A Theoretical Analysis.* New York: Appleton-Century-Crofts, 1968.

Slezak, S. "Two Years of Precision Teaching with Orthopedically-Handicapped Children." Master's thesis, University of Kansas, 1969.

Wolf, M. M.; Giles, D. K.; and Hall, R. V. "Experiments with Token Reinforcement in a Remedial Classroom." *Behavior Research and Therapy* 6 (1968): 51-64.

Additional Readings

Bensberg, G. J., ed. *Teaching the Mentally Retarded: A Handbook for Ward Personnel.* Atlanta, Ga.: Southern Regional Educational Board, 1965.

Bijou, S. W. "A Functional Analysis of Retarded Development. In *International Review of Research in Mental Retardation,* vol. 1., edited by N. R. Ellis. New York: Academic Press, 1966.

Birnbrauer, J. S., and Lawler, J. "Token Reinforcement for Learning." *Mental Retardation,* 2 (1964): 275-279.

Buddenhagen, R. G. "Issue at Point: Toward a Better Understanding-Part II." *Mental Retardation,* December 1969, 63-65.

Hamilton, J. "Environmental Control and Retardate Behavior. In *Unique Programs in Behavior Readjustment,* edited by C. Richards. Elmsford, N. Y.: Pergamon (in press).

Haring, N. G., and Lovitt, T. C. "Operant Methodology and Educational Technology in Special Education. In *Methods in Special Education,* edited by N. G. Haring and R. L. Schiefelbusch, pp. 12-48. New York: McGraw-Hill, 1967.

Hollis, J. H., and Gorton, C. E. "Training Severely and Profoundly Developmentally Retarded Children." *Mental Retardation* 5 (1968): 20-24.

Mackay, H. A., and Sidman, M. "Instructing the Mentally Retarded in an Institutional Environment." In *Expanding Concepts in Mental Retardation*, edited by G. A. Jervis, pp. 164-169. Springfield, Ill.: Charles C. Thomas, 1968.

Malott, R. W., and Whaley, D. L. *Elementary Principles of Behavior.* Ann Arbor, Mich.: Edwards Brothers, 1969.

Martin, G. L. "Operant Conditioning at the Manitoba School: A Description of Program Development." *Manitoba School Journal* 1 (1969): 3.

Orlando, R.; Schoelkopf, A.; and Tobias, L. "Tokens as Reinforcers: Classroom Applications by Teachers of the Retarded." IMRID Papers and Reports, George Peabody College, vol. 4, no. 14.

Spradlin, J. E., and Girardeau, F. L. "The Behavior of Moderately and Severely Retarded Persons." In *International Review of Research in Mental Retardation*, vol. 1, edited by N. R. Ellis, pp. 257-298. New York: Academic Press, 1966.

Watson, L. S., Jr. "Application of Operant Conditioning Techniques to Institutionalized Severely and Profoundly Retarded Children." *Mental Retardation Abstracts* 1 (1967): 1-18.

Zimmerman, J.; Stuckey, T. E.; Garlick, B. J.; and Miller, M. "Effects of Token Reinforcement in Multiply Handicapped Clients in a Sheltered Workshop." *Rehabilitation Literature* 2 (1969): 34-41.

## Films

The following films would be particularly useful to those interested in learning more about behavior modification principles.

Title:            *Spearhead at Juniper Gardens,* 40 minutes, 16mm, black and white, sound, released 1968.

Purpose:          To demonstrate a preschool and remedial education research project conducted by the University of Kansas Bureau of Child Research in a deprived community of Kansas City, Kansas.

Description:        The Juniper Gardens Children's Project is a program of research conducted in a deprived area of northeast Kansas City, Kansas. Behavioral scientists and teachers from the University of Kansas Bureau of Child Research operate two preschool classes and a remedical education class within the community. Reinforcement principles are used to develop the language of preschoolers, and to motivate slow-learning grade school children. Community cooperation is stressed. The teaching staff from one of the preschools is in fact comprised of mothers from the community. They are trained as teachers by the project staff. The remedial education section in the film demonstrates the use of incentives in remedial education. The children attend three-hour sessions each day in which they compete for points which are exchangeable for a variety of reinforcers. Other aspects of the project include a regular program of medical service, a well-child conference program, home counseling conducted by the project staff, and research in the public schools where public school teachers learn to apply reinforcement principles to modify the behavior of dawdling or disruptive children. The film was produced by the KU Bureau of Child Research under research and demonstration grants from the National Institute of Child Health and Human Development and the Office of Economic Opportunity.

Available From:     The University of Kansas
                    Bureau of Visual Instruction
                    6 Bailey Hall
                    Lawrence, Kansas 66044

The Special Education Instructional Materials Center
1115 Louisiana Street
University of Kansas
Lawrence, Kansas 66044

Title:        *Operation Behavior Modification*, 40 minutes, 16mm, black and white, sound, released 1967.

Purpose:       To demonstrate the systematic application of behavior modification techniques in the rehabilitation of institutionalized, trainable retarded girls.

Description:    The training received by girls in Mimosa Cottage is designed to enable them to look and act as much as possible like girls of the same age who live in the community. Positive reinforcement of desired responses is the primary behavior modification technique applied by the demonstration project staff. A different reinforcer is used with each of three groups. The film traces the progress of 20-year-old Ellen H. through the various training programs to eventual placement in the community as a nurse's aid.

Available From:   The National Medical Audiovisual Center
Chamblee, Georgia 30005
Attn: Film Distribution

The University of Kansas
Bureau of Visual Instruction
6 Bailey Hall
Lawrence, Kansas 66044

Title:        *Research with Disadvantaged Preschool Children*, 10 minutes, 16mm, color, sound, released 1969.

| | |
|---|---|
| Purpose: | To demonstrate language development research at the Juniper Gardens Children's Project in Kansas City, Kansas. |
| Description: | This film demonstrates research at the Juniper Gardens Children's Project of the University of Kansas Bureau of Child Research. The film was made in Turner House in northeast Kansas City, Kansas, where the Bureau of Child Research conducts behavioral research with disadvantaged preschool children. The Turner House Preschool is designed to develop and investigate child behavior, particularly language behavior. The purpose is to find out what skills these children need to prepare them for success in the public school system, and to find out which of these skills can be taught to disadvantaged children in the course of a three-hour preschool day during one school year. The objective of the work is to bring about behavioral changes, particularly in the area of language, so the children will have a real chance for success once they enter the public school system. |
| Available From: | The University of Kansas<br>Bureau of Visual Instruction<br>6 Bailey Hall<br>Lawrence, Kansas 66044 |
| Title: | *Operant Audiometry with Severely Retarded Children*, 16 minutes, 16 mm, color, sound, released 1968. |
| Purpose: | To demonstrate the use of operant conditioning in testing the hearing of severely retarded children. |
| Description: | This picture was produced by the Parsons State Hospital and Training Center and the University of |

Kansas Bureau of Child Research. The film demonstrates the use of positive reinforcement discrimination techniques in the audiologic assessment of a severely retarded subject. It traces the progress of a 13-year-old boy through several clinical sessions designed to detect and diagnose hearing impairments. It demonstrates how the child is conditioned to wear a headset, and how reinforcement techniques are employed to train the child to respond to auditory stimuli.

Available From:
The University of Kansas
Bureau of Visual Instruction
6 Bailey Hall
Lawrence, Kansas 66044

Title:
*Achievement Place,* 30 minutes, 16 mm, black and white, sound, released 1970.

Purpose:
To demonstrate a special behavioral management foster home for predelinquent boys.

Description:
This film concerns a home for predelinquent boys in a university community. Achievement Place is a foster home for boys assigned by court action after they become involved in acts which bring them to the continuing attention of law enforcement officers. The home was established and is still supported largely by funds from local civic organizations and private contributions. The motion picture was supported by a research grant from the National Institute of Mental Health Center for Research on Crime and Delinquency.

Six to eight boys live at Achievement Place under the supervision of foster parents, who maintain a token reinforcement system designed to help the boys get off the road to prison and back on the road to achievement. Every privilege in the home is earned by the accumulation of points for appropriate behavior. Each boy carries a points card with him at all times when he is in the home. As each boy engages in appropriate behavior he accumulates points on his card. Once a week these points are totaled and the boys exchange what they have accumulated for privileges in the upcoming week.

Available From: The University of Kansas
Bureau of Visual Instruction
6 Bailey Hall
Lawrence, Kansas 66044

Title: *Out of the Shadows*, 17 minutes, 16 mm, color, sound, released 1969.

Purpose: To demonstrate an institutional intensive training program for severely handicapped children.

Description: This motion picture demonstrates a special education project at Parsons State Hospital and Training Center. About fifty severely retarded children are taken into an intensive care program and trained to bring them up to the level of less severely retarded children in the hospital. No child in the program has an IQ above 40, and when most of them come to the program they require constant nursing supervision. After a year in the program they are able to feed themselves properly, they are toilet trained, and most of them can find their way around the hospital grounds without supervision. Through a well-organized reinforcement system these children, who would otherwise have continued to exist in a custodial environment, learn the motor skills, color perception, and the basic speech formation which allows them to participate in regular hospital programs which are geared to the moderately and mildly retarded.

Available From: The University of Kansas
Bureau of Visual Instruction
6 Bailey Hall
Lawrence, Kansas 66044

Title: *Shift of Stimulus Control,* 30 minutes, 16 mm, color, sound, released 1969.

Purpose: To demonstrate the uses of recently developed stimulus shift techniques in articulation and language training for handicapped children.

Description: The film was made over a period of a year in dozens of clinical sessions with two retarded children. It shows the general strategy of the stimulus shift techniques in which new speech responses are developed under precise stimulus control and are made functional for the child in a systematic programmed clinical procedure. The scenes show this developing through a series of programmed stimulus presentations which evoke and support new responses and then systematically shift their occurrence to the control of new types of stimuli which are more like those found in a normal social environment.

Available From: The University of Kansas
Bureau of Visual Instruction
6 Bailey Hall
Lawrence, Kansas 66044

Journals That Have Behavior Modification Articles

*Journal of Applied Behavior Analysis*
*Behavior Research and Therapy*
Occasional articles appear in *Mental Retardation* and the *American Journal of Mental Deficiency.*

# 16

## DISCRIMINATION LEARNING
## Marc W. Gold and Keith G. Scott

The retarded child is surrounded with a variable environment and from it he must select those features that are relevant to the activities in which he is engaged. This means some events must be attended to while others are ignored. One of the characteristics of the retarded is a reduced ability to independently select the relevant aspects of a task. Their teachers must arrange the educational environment first to attract the child's attention to the relevant aspects of tasks and second to help him learn to do this for himself. This chapter is concerned with ways to accomplish these goals.

## General Principles of Attention

Before we turn to specific training procedures it is necessary to define terms and principles relevant to discrimination learning. The theory behind these ideas is the extensively researched Attention Theory of Zeaman and House (Zeaman, 1965). Attention refers to

*Preparation of this chapter was supported by Grant MHO7346 and by a career award K4HD46370 to Keith G. Scott.

the process by which a child focuses on some aspects of the stimuli to which he is exposed (Zeaman and House, 1963). *Attention in this context, and in this chapter is concerned with what the child looks at rather than the length of time a child spends doing something.*

## Discrimination and generalization

All learning requires that the child detect some differences in the events he hears, sees, or touches. Thus, in learning to recognize letters the child must discriminate differences in position of the vertical stroke to discriminate a *d* from a *b*. Similarly, some aspects of the letters must be ignored such as the slope *b* and *d*. In a social setting the child learns to attend to certain physical characteristics such as body shape and facial features to discriminate men from women. With current fashions and styles some features such as length of hair must be ignored. Learning to detect the relevant dimensions of variation is necessary before the child can respond to differences. In our examples this would involve saying *b* or *d* or responding in the socially appropriate way to a man or a woman.

Once a child has acquired a discrimination he must learn to transfer the training. The discrimination must be generalizable to new situations. Thus, having learned to discriminate between one male and one female, the child must *generalize* his learning to apply to other individuals as well. However, the generalization may be too great. Behavior that is the appropriate social response to a young women teacher might not be appropriate with an older woman or grandmother. If the child gave the same response to all people regardless of age or sex we would say that he had *overgeneralized* and was not discriminating. At first the young child commonly calls all men "Daddy." He had learned to discriminate men from women but overgeneralizes in attaching the label to all men. Later he will learn that some men are daddies and others are not, and that one particular daddy is his. Further, "My Daddy" is a particular person who may wear different clothes and sometimes be pleased and sometimes angry. Despite these variations in mood and appearance he is still "My Daddy." Generalization needs to be sufficiently broad to permit acceptance of unimportant or irrelevant details about Daddy while other critical aspects can be sharply discriminated so that he is not confused with other men. *We need to engineer the pupil's attention so that he learns to attend to those aspects of the situation that are relevant to his learning and to ignore those that are irrelevant* (Scott, 1966).

There are two important kinds of stimulus variation to consider in engineering a pupil's attention and discrimination. First, there is simple discrimination. Here a child who learns to discriminate red from green may at first overgeneralize and confuse red and orange. With repeated training where only red is reinforced this confusion will be removed. However, in other ways his learning one color discrimination will also aid in learning other color discriminations. The child learns that there are also systematic dimensions of variation in the world. This second kind of stimulus variation is called *mediated generalization.* Not only does the child distinguish between the particular colors red and green, he also learns that color is a dimension on which things in the world vary. As he plays with his blocks the child learns that one way to sort them is in terms of their color. Another way to sort the blocks is in terms of their form or shape. The child, in making a discrimination, must learn to attend to the dimensions on which things differ as well as, and perhaps before, he can see differences between particular stimuli within those dimensions. He must learn the dimensions of difference that are relevant to discriminations among people, among blocks, or among letters and words.

## Attention Theory

A major postulate of attention theories of discrimination learning has been that solving a discrimination consists of learning a chain of two responses (Zeaman and House, 1963). *First the child must learn to attend to the relevant dimension of difference between the stimuli and then choose the particular stimulus that is correct.* An apparatus, called the Wisconsin General Test Apparatus, shown in Figure 1, has been used in the laboratory to investigate this result. With this apparatus the tester sits behind a one-way vision screen and arranges two stimuli, *e.g.*, a red square and a green square, so that they cover two holes in the sliding tray. Under one of the colored squares is hidden a small reward object such as a candy. The tester slides the tray forward and the child now tries to find the candy by moving one of the squares to uncover the hole. The child, to be scored correct, must find the candy on his first try.

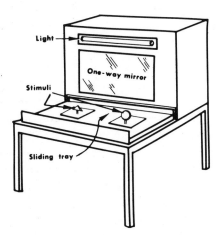

Figure 1 The Wisconsin General Test Appartus, or WGTA

The traditional view of learning was that the child acquired the discrimination between the red and green stimuli slowly by building up little increments of habit. In this view, retarded children's slowness in acquiring habits is due to their acquiring smaller than normal increments each time they make a correct choice and are reinforced (Scott, 1970). This view of normal-retardate differences is illustrated by the hypothetical curves, shown in Figure 2, which show learning of a habit as gradual and incremental. Research in discrimination learning has shown that learning is not a matter of building up little bits of habit, and that these curves, commonly seen in some older writings, are created by inappropriate methods of grouping data which mask the shape of the individual curves (Zeaman and House, 1963).

A more accurate view of the course of learning and of the difference between normal and retardate learning is shown in Figure 3.

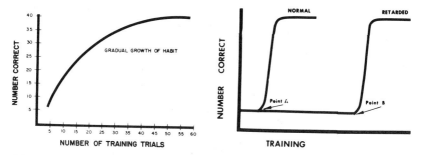

Figure 2 Schematic diagram of the course of learning when the growth of a habit is seen as gradual. The curve should be compared with those in Figure 3, which are more representative of the performance of an individual subject.

Figure 3 The course of learning for normal and retarded children as training progresses. As can be seen, after they reach a critical point, *i.e.*, attend to the relevant stimuli, the children learn at the same rate (A for the normals and B for the retarded). The diagrams are schematic.

Here we see that *learning consists of an initial period of responding at chance followed by a sudden onset of learning, or a point* (labeled A and B in Figure 3) *where the child makes an insightful solution to the problem.* An important point can be seen in Figure 3. *The difference between normal and retarded children lies not in the rate at which performance increases but rather in the length of time it takes the retarded child to reach the point where he begins to learn.* More detailed analyses of data show very clearly that the retarded child takes longer to attend to the relevant dimension, and thus begin learning, than does a normal child (Zeaman, 1965).

Once the retarded child attends to the relevant dimension he learns very rapidly and essentially at the same rate as his normal peer. It follows that a large part of the teacher's job in facilitating the learning of retarded children consists of arranging the teaching material so as to direct the child's attention to the relevant dimensions of the problem.

## Dimensions and shifts

A useful way to conceive of a dimension is as a meaningfully related group of items. Thus, the various colors—red, green, blue, orange, and so on—make up the color dimension. As learning theorists study learning about groups such as animals (*e.g.,* bird, bear, dog, and so on), they have often called the groups or dimensions "clusters." The general point is that to make learning about things efficient the adult or child must achieve some organization of the material into effective groupings. This has at least two major effects. First, it allows the child to focus on the critical features by directing his attention to what is relevant. Second, in remembering the material later it provides for direction of his memory search.

When a child learns one color discrimination and subsequently is taught another but different color discrimination, his learning of the second problem is much faster than of the first. That is, in learning the first discrimination he learns both that color is a relevant dimension and which particular color is correct. In learning the second problem, since he is already attending to the color dimension, the child has only to learn to pick which of the new colors is correct. The second problem is then said to involve a shift of attention within a dimension and is called an *intradimensional shift*. If the second problem involves a shift of attention to a new dimension, such as form, it would be described as an *extradimensional shift* (Wolff, 1967). In Figure 4 schematic learning curves are

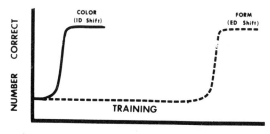

Figure 4 Schematic diagrams showing the effect of introducing new problems on a previously trained dimension (color) and a new dimension. Such problems are known as intradimensional (ID) and extradimensional (ED) shifts.

shown for children who, having learned one discrimination, are now learning a second discrimination. The solid line would represent the curve for a child who, having learned one color problem, is now learning another color problem (intradimensional shift). The dotted curve is for a child who, having learned one color problem, is now learning a form problem (extradimensional shift). As can be seen, when the second problem is solved using the same dimension as the first, learning is much faster.

# Some Specific Concepts About Attention

## Redundancy

Sometimes a problem can be learned in more than one way. Such problems are said to be *redundant*. An example would be the discrimination between a red square (the correct choice) and a green triangle. A perfect solution could be achieved by selecting the red object without looking at its shape. Alternatively, a perfect solution could be made by selecting the square while ignoring the color. When two dimensions or stimuli are always together they are thus said to be *redundant*.

Different effects of redundancy have been investigated (Zeaman, 1968). One important finding is that learning occurs more rapidly as the number of redundant relevant dimensions increases. The more cues a pupil has to help solve a problem (within reason) the faster he will solve it. A child will learn to pick the large, yellow triangle more quickly than to pick the triangle. Having three relevant and redundant dimensions makes the task easier.

## Irrelevant cues

Related to redundancy is the finding that when variable irrelevant dimensions are fewer, the child will learn more quickly (Zeaman, 1965). Irrelevant dimensions may be variable or constant. If a child is learning a problem where form only is relevant, then all other dimensions are irrelevant. If all of the forms (stimuli) are the same color and size, then color and size are *constant* and *irrelevant*. If the forms are different colors and sizes and change for each form from trial to trial, then color and size are *variable* and *irrelevant*.

If the child is learning to discriminate triangle from square, then having different colors and sizes of triangles and squares would impede learning. Having all triangles and squares the same color and size would not get rid of the color and size dimensions. However, holding them constant does not impede learning. *In summary, retarded children can take advantage of more than one relevant and redundant cue at a time to help solve a problem. They also learn faster when irrelevant information is kept to a minimum.*

### Fading

One other use of cue redundancy occurs "in a technique called *fading* (Terrace, 1966; Moore and Goldiamond, 1964). Here an already established discrimination is used as a crutch to aid in the acquisition of a new and more difficult discrimination. For example, let us suppose that a child can already distinguish between a red and a yellow stimulus but cannot do this for a circle and an ellipse. At the start of training both colors and forms are made redundant. That is, the circle is always yellow and the ellipse always red. This problem could be solved by the use of either color or form. At first, knowing the color discrimination, the child will use it to solve the problem. Gradually, through the course of training, the difference between the red and yellow is decreased until both are orange while the forms remain constant. If the rate at which the crutch cues (colors) are faded is not too great, then the child will proceed through the course of learning with few or no errors. This procedure is thought to minimize frustration and is one method of facilitating the acquisition of difficult tasks. When using fading, one should also avoid fading so slowly that time is wasted and the child is put through many unnecessary and boring trials.

## Clustering

The way in which stimuli are grouped can affect the ease with which they are learned and remembered. Thus in learning lists of words, items that belong to a category or *cluster* are more readily recalled (Bousfield, 1953). For example, a list of words that consists only of animals, vehicles, or people's names would be recalled better than a list of unrelated words. Children or adults tend to remember by grouping words from the same category. In order for this powerful facilitator of remembering to operate the child must, of course, possess the concept that the items do belong to a class or group. It can be seen that this process, called *clustering*, has much in common with the concept of a dimension. To cluster is much like attending to the relevant dimension.

## Criterion

Learning is generally said to have occurred when the child has achieved some criterion of performance. For example, an experimenter might decide that *criterion performance* (learning) for a particular experiment is six consecutive correct responses. This is an arbitrary decision. But when the child makes six consecutive correct responses, the experimenter assumes that the child has learned the task. Whether or not the criterion is appropriate is determined by observing the child's performance following criterion. If there are many errors after criterion, it is an indication that the experimenter's criterion was not appropriate and that learning, or the elimination of errors, has not taken place. In such a case, the criterion would be changed and reevaluated.

## Overlearning

A concept closely related to criterion is overlearning. *Overlearning* is defined as trials beyond criterion. This does not mean correct trials only. However, frequent errors in overlearning usually indicate that a too weak criterion has been selected. Overlearning is important in two ways. First, retention is greatly influenced by the degree of original learning (Belmont, 1966). That is, if a child is brought to a strong criterion and/or is given some degree of overlearning, this will increase his retention of the material. Second, overlearning facilitates transfer on an intradimensional shift. This means that the child who gets overlearning on a problem where the form dimension is relevant will rapidly learn subsequent form problems even though the specific forms change.

## Easy-to-hard sequences

Another finding from research on discrimination learning involves the use of easy-to-hard sequences. *A sequence of easy-to-hard problems is learned more quickly than hard problems alone* (House and Zeaman, 1960; Zeaman and House, 1963). If, for example, you wanted a child to learn to sort a pile of two different-length bolts where the difference was one-eighth inch, he would learn best by starting with a pile of bolts where the difference in length was one-half inch, then moving to a one-fourth inch difference, then one-eighth. This procedure helps the child identify the relevant dimension, length, because he starts out with large differences on that dimension. When the differences get smaller he will be attending to the relevant dimension, greatly increasing his chances of solving the problem. The child who must learn to attend to a dimension where the differences are small to begin with has a much more difficult problem to solve (Shepp and Zeaman, 1966).

## Failure sets

Still another important finding is the powerful detrimental effect of failure sets. Retarded children who experience prolonged failure on difficult problems often will fail to solve even very simple problems (Zeaman, 1965).

This formation of a *failure set* is the result of the child's ceasing to attend to any of the relevant cues in the learning situation. Thus when the teacher or experimenter makes some change in the problem to bring it within the child's ability, it makes no difference. The child is not oriented to the task and does not observe the change. Materials and procedures should be programmed so as to minimize the child's experience of failure. The technique described in the lesson plans that follow illustrate some methods of attack. Also, when the child makes the wrong choice from two or more possibilities, he should be told to try another way instead of being told he is wrong (Gold, 1969). This method emphasizes where he can go to succeed instead of where he has failed.

## Novelty

Most teachers are well aware of the attention-attracting features of a novel event. *Novelty* is a powerful controlling variable in directing attention and can be defined as some discrepant occurrence in a pattern or sequence of events or stimuli. Children who have formed deep failure sets will sometimes start to attend to a novel stimulus suddenly introduced in the series of learning trials. In general, unless an adequate level of stimulus variability is maintained during a training session, children will cease to attend. Often they are said to be "daydreaming" or "bored."

The question then can be asked, What is the optimal level of variability that will maintain attention? (Berlyne, 1960). One clear answer is that the task should differ from what the child has been doing by a margin just wide enough to hold the child's attention. In practice this may be difficult to judge. However, the two extremes—for a task to be either totally repetitive or so difficult that the child cannot solve it—both lead to the extinction of attention and can be readily detected. Unfortunately these extremes frequently are rampant in the workshop and classroom.

# Special Training Procedures

Some training techniques which are related to discrimination learning are useful in training the retarded.

## Match-to-sample

One such technique is called *match-to-sample* and is sometimes used in discrimination learning experiments (Heal and Bransky, 1966). This technique consists of presenting an object (stimulus) and having the child select from a group of objects (response choices) the one that matches. This technique is not unfamiliar to the classroom teacher. Using some of the concepts described, this procedure can be used to program many kinds and levels of learning. By controlling the number of relevant and variable irrelevant dimensions a series of easy-to-hard problems is not difficult to achieve.

## Oddity

A similar procedure involves *oddity* (Brown, 1970). That is, three or four objects are displayed before the child. All but one of them are alike. He has to tell which one is different. The ways in which the stimuli are alike and different can vary greatly. For instance, if you are teaching the concept of male-female, a child might start out with problems where there are two identical pictures of a boy and a picture of a girl. After he chooses the odd picture, with sets like these, six consecutive times, say, give him cards on which there are still two boys and a girl, or vice versa, but where the two alike pictures are not identical. Following successful solution, or criterion, on that set, you could change to pictures of adults or pictures where the sex differences are more subtle. The same idea, of course, can be used with the match-to-sample technique. The important thing is to know how to control the relevant and irrelevant dimensions, which in turn do much to control the level of difficulty of the task.

### Task analysis and sequencing

The lessons to be described utilize lesson planning rules and concepts such as task analysis and sequencing. *Task analysis* refers to breaking a task down into its component parts. The steps listed in sample Lesson 1 are an example. The concept of task analysis is very important for teaching retarded children. Using task analysis, we find that tasks that are usually seen as consisting of two or three difficult steps are really twenty or thirty simple steps. Examples of this are folding a piece of paper in half, tying shoelaces, walking to the store, and calling the telephone operator in an emergency. *Sequencing* merely refers to putting the steps into a logical order.

## A Note on Perceptual-Motor Learning

Tasks such as tying shoelaces are frequently called perceptual-motor. This has been thought to describe the supposed reliance on visual perception of the task details and the use of particular dexterous motor movements. When a child cannot learn such tasks, we usually attribute his failure to one or both of two causes. The first is the inability to perceive rather than to discriminate. The second is the failure to make certain movements instead of learn a sequence of movements. *It should be emphasized that most of the moderately retarded have difficulty in learning where to put the lace and when to move the fingers rather than being unable to see the lace holes or to make the component specific movements.* Observation of a child eating will often allow simple confirmation of his development. Discrimination between foods of different color and texture can be observed as the child systematically eats one food rather than another. His skill in manipulating utensils is also apparent. If the child did not possess the necessary perceptual-motor abilities, he could not make the discriminations involved. If such a task is seen as a discrimination learning problem, then we begin to see the task as a sequence of discriminations to be taught rather than relying on some perceptual or motor ability that requires large-scale general training. That is, conceived of in terms of discrimination, the teaching program is one of training a specific task sequence.

## The Application of Some Principles in the Sheltered Workshop

The potential of Zeaman and House's Attention Theory was demonstrated recently in a study on the acquisition of a complex assembly task by retarded adolescents by Gold (1969). This was the first reported study utilizing the Zeaman theory in an applied setting. Procedures developed from Attention Theory were used to train sixty-four moderately and severely retarded adolescents with an average IQ of 47, who were enrolled in four sheltered workshops, to assemble a 15-piece and a 24-piece bicycle brake. One-half of the subjects worked with the parts of the 15-piece brake as they came from the factory. That is, in order to decide which way a part went on, the subjects had to attend to the form dimension (the shape of the part). The other subjects worked with parts that were color coded. Coding consisted of painting red that surface of each part that is facing the subject when it is placed in the proper position for assembling. This constituted a cue redundancy, making form and color relevant and redundant. All subjects also worked with the parts of the 24-piece brake as they came from the factory (form only). Sixty-three of the sixty-four subjects reached a criterion of six correct out of eight consecutive trials on both brakes. The one subject who failed reached criteron on the training brake only. The results of the experimental procedures were dramatic. First, the subjects who had cue redundancy on the 15-piece brake learned it in half the trials needed by the group that had only the form dimension relevant. The average number of trials needed to reach criteron on the 15-piece brake was thirty-three for the form-only group and seventeen for the color-form group. On the 24-piece brake the average for all groups was twenty-two. Second, the use of very systematic programming of the task meant that virtually all subjects learned to assemble the brakes. None of the directors of the sheltered workshops expected any of the clients to be able to learn the tasks at all.

## Sample Lessons

To illustrate the principles involved in discrimination learning two sample lesson plans for the moderately retarded are presented. One involves the techniques that are used in teaching a child to tie his shoes, the other demonstrates the sequence of activities encountered in sorting bolts. Reminder is made that these are illustrations and are not to be followed rigidly. Varying situations and individudals may necessitate additions to or rearrangement of the sequence.

## Lesson 1

*Purpose:* To promote opportunity for the child to learn to tie shoe-laces.

*Materials:* The child's shoes, long laces, or a lacing board.

*Techniques and concepts to be illustrated:* Criterion, cue redundancy, task analysis, overlearning, fading.

*Procedure:*

A.  List the steps in tying shoes. The descriptions used here are for you and, in most instances, should not be used with the child. Follow these steps with a shoe in front of you.

1.  Get shoes.
2.  Put on shoes (correctly? maybe not yet) which already have laces in them.
3.  Pull tongue up and straight.
4.  Hold a lace end in each hand.
5.  Pull them tight. (More steps might be needed here if lower part of lace is loose.)
6.  Release laces.
7.  With palms facing up, pincer grasp one lace in each hand, approximately one-third the distance from the shoe to the end of the lace.
8.  Cross the laces so that the lace on top moves into the other pincer grasp.
9.  Let go of that lace.
10.  Grasp the other lace, which is the one behind.
11.  Bring it toward you, then, with the thumb, push it through the hole.
12.  With the same hand, let go.
13.  Grasp the same lace behind the hole.
14.  Pull it so that you now have one lace in each grasp.

15. Pull both laces tight.
16. Let go.
17. With a pincer grasp (always the same hand, but let the child choose which hand) lift up the lace opposite the hand used, one-third of the distance from the shoe to the end.
18. With the other hand grasp the two parts of the lace together, at the shoe, so that the two parts of the lace that are between the two grasps are equal and taut. This leaves one-third of the lace free.
19. Release the grasp that is away from the shoe (step 10).
20. With the free hand grasp the other lace one-third the distance from the shoe.
21. Bring the lace all the way around your side of the loop extending above the other grasp.
22. Release the grasp on that lace.
23. Grasp the two parts of that lace and push the longer part so that it shows between the shorter part and the loop being held in the other grasp.
24. With the forefinger of the hand holding the loop, push the part showing, through the hole, letting go with the other grasp.
25. Grasp the end of the long loop.
26. Let go of the grasp that has been close to the shoe since step 11.
27. Grasp the part of the lace which was pushed through the hole in step 17.
28. Pull both loops tight.
29. Let go. (Note: Many of our friends who know how to tie shoes suggest alternatives to our procedures. May we suggest that you use your own method, but task analyze and teach it using the techniques presented here.)

B. Establish criterion: When the child has tied his shoes correctly

ten times without help we will assume he has learned the task.
C. Decide on ways to direct child's attention to the relevant dimensions of the problem. Make the two halves of the lace different colors. This will be a cue redundancy because the actual relevant dimension for this task is position—position of the laces and of the fingers. The addition of a color should help. You might also put a black spot on each lace one-third the distance from the shoe to the end of the lace.
D. Decide on a training procedure. The training procedure tells how to teach the task and should not be confused with the steps of the task itself.

1. Teach the child to respond to the command "pinch here," so that before he actually begins tying shoes he knows how to make a pincer grasp where you tell him.
2. Teach him to respond to the commands "pull tight" and "let go here." For the other movements use as little talking as possible.
3. With his shoe on and the laces fairly loose (or with the lacing board) say out loud to yourself, "pinch here," pointing to a point on one of the laces. Then you make a pincher grasp at that point.
4. Point to the same place, give the same command, and ask the child to do it.
5. When he is able to make a pincher grasp at the right point for approximately five consecutive correct times, continue the same procedure for the other commands.
6. In the classroom you would probably begin with Step 4 (grasp a lace end in each hand). Pointing to both laces say, "pull tight" (5). Then, "let go" (6). These two steps are probably best learned together until the child can do them correctly five consecutive times. Then with your commands, tell him to "do it by yourself" and have him do

Steps 5 and 6 to a criterion of five consecutive correct times without verbal assistance.

7. On the next trial, when he finishes Step 6, say, "hold your hands like this (palms up), pinch here (wait for him), and pinch here" (7).

8. Without saying "let go," say "good, let's try that much again." Take his hands away from the laces.

9. Tell the child to go ahead (Step 4). Bring him to a criterion of five consecutive correct trials where you give him verbal assistance only on Step 7. Five consecutive trials without any help should follow.

10. On the next trial, with the child grasping the laces, you mimic Step 8 and say "go like this." The purpose of this is to determine which lace the child naturally places in front. Once you know this you can show him how to do it and watch to see that he is consistent. By moving his hands, show him how to do Step 8. Then, pointing to the top lace, say, "let go here" (9).

11. Again, take his hands away from the laces without saying "let go" and use the procedures described in Step 9. Bring him to criterion on Steps 4 through 9.

12. Use the same procedures for the rest of the steps.

13. When the child has reached criterion on the entire task, give him several days or weeks of overlearning.

14. Then remove the color cue. If the child's performance drops, try using the original procedures, but without the color cue, bringing the child again to criterion.

15. It might be necessary to reinstate the color cue. If so, either give the child more overlearning trials with the color before removing it again, or try using a fading procedure. This might consist of making the two colors more and more alike, or making just the very ends of the laces different colors.

*Evaluation:* By having a predetermined criterion, you will know if the lessons are successful. The teacher must be prepared to make changes in the procedures in order to meet the individual needs of the children. The lesson described is not seen as *the* way to teach children to tie shoes. It is seen as one way. You will have to modify it. The reason the lesson is included in this chapter is to demonstrate how to use some of the techniques and concepts described.

## Lesson 2

*Purpose:* To assist the child in learning to sort bolts into categories of size, length, and head shape.
*Materials:* Several hundred bolts with the following characteristics:
1. Hexagon head, 1 inch x ⅜ inch (all bolts standard thread)
2. Hexagon head, 1 inch x ¼ inch
3. Hexagon head, ¾ inch x ⅜ inch
4. Hexagon head, ¾ inch x ¼ inch
5. Hexagon head, ½ inch x ⅜ inch
6. Hexagon head, ½ inch x ¼ inch
7. Round head, 1 inch x ⅜ inch
8. Round head, 1 inch x ¼ inch
9. Round head, ¾ inch x ⅜ inch
10. Round head, ¾ inch x ¼ inch
11. Round head, ½ inch x ⅜ inch
12. Round head, ½ inch x ¼ inch

The bolts described have differences on three dimensions—head shape, length, and width.
*Techniques and concepts to be illustrated:* Criterion, cue redundancy, easy-to-hard sequence.

*Procedure:*
   A. To teach the vocabulary for the bolts and for the directions, refer to the article by Gold (1968).
   B. Establish criterion: When the child sorts the pile twice without errors it will be assumed he has learned the task that is represented by that pile.
   C. Present the child (or children) with a pile containing the hexagonal, 1 inch x ¼ inch bolts and the round, ½ inch x ⅜ bolts. In doing this you have provided a task on which there are three relevant and redundant dimensions.
   D. Either use labels and commands the child knows or, non-verbally, remove one kind of bolt and put it in one place (container) and put the other bolt in another container.
   E. Ask the child to start. If he has difficulty, you start slowly sorting the pile and encourage him to do the same.
   F. Following criterion, change the task to each of the following establishing criterion each time.

     1. Make all dimensions relevant and redundant. That is, sort hexagonal 1 inch x ⅜ inch from round ½ inch x ¼ inch bolts.
     2. Keep one dimension constant and irrelevant and sort for the other two. That is, use one head shape and sort 1 inch x ⅜ inch from ½ inch x ¼ inch bolts. Or use one length and sort hexagonal 1 inch x ¼ inch from round 1 inch x ⅜ inch bolts.
     3. Keep two dimensions constant and irrelevant and sort for the third. That is, sort hexagonal 1 inch x ⅜ inch from hexagonal 1 inch x ¼ inch bolts, and so on.
     4. Do steps 1 and 2 above using the ¾ inch with the 1 inch and/or the ⅜ inch bolts. This will constitute a move toward a finer discrimination.
     5. Use all bolts and sort on all relevant dimensions (twelve

piles). You might need to start without ¾ inch bolts. In this case there would be eight piles.

6. Use all the bolts and have variable irrelevant dimensions. That is, sort all of the hexagonal bolts from all of the round bolts. In this case length and width would vary but would not be relevant.

7. Use other combinations, remembering the rules about cue redundancy, relevant and variable irrelevant dimensions, and easy-to-hard sequences.

*Evaluation:* If the child is able to perform at criterion given any combination of categories, he has not only learned to sort bolts but has developed a sorting skill that will transfer to many other tasks.

## Summary

Retarded children learn rapidly once they attend to the relevant stimuli and dimensions in a learning situation. A major task of the teacher of the developmentally young is to program the instructional materials in a manner which will direct and maintain attention and thus facilitate learning.

Research on discrimination learning provides a number of key concepts, *e.g.*, the dimensional organization of stimuli, that have led to theories about attention. This theoretical framework in turn provides the teacher with the language, behavioral rules, and techniques to plan carefully sequenced training. Not only is learning made easier for children, but in addition, the teacher is able to avoid unfortunate side effects, *e.g.*, the formation of failure sets.

The procedure is illustrated by a report of research demonstrating the assembly of complex mechanical equipment by retarded adolescents. Also two model lesson plans, and the procedure by which they are developed, are outlined. The chapter thus provides a systematic plan for programming the acquisition of relevant tasks in terms of specific training as an alternative to planning a broad and vague program aimed at "perceptual-motor abilities."

# References

Belmont, J. "Long-Term Memory in Mental Retardates." In *International Review of Research in Mental Retardation*, vol. 1, edited by N. R. Ellis, p. 219-255. New York: Academic Press, 1966.

Berlyne, D. *Conflict, Arousal, and Curiosity.* New York: McGraw-Hill, 1960.

Bousfield, W.A. "The Occurrence of Clustering in the Recall of Randomly Arranged Associates." *Journal of General Psychology,* 1953: 229-240.

Brown, A.L. "Subject and Experimental Variables in the Oddity Learning of Normal and Retarded Children." *American Journal of Mental Deficiency,* 1970 (in press).

Gold, M. "Classroom Techniques: Preworkshop Skills for the Trainable: A Sequential Technique." *Education and Training of the Mentally Retarded,* 3 (1968): 31-37.

Gold, M.W. "The Acquisition of a Complex Assembly Task by Retarded Adolescents." *Final Report,* Project No. 8-8060. University of Illinois Champaign-Urbana Library, May 1969.

Heal, L.W., and Bransky, M. L. "The Comparison of Matching-to-Sample with Discrimination Learning in Retardates." *American Journal of Mental Deficiency,* 71 (1966): 481-485.

House, B., and Zeaman, D. "Transfer of a Discrimination from Objects to Patterns." *Journal of Experimental Psychology* 59 (1960): 298-302.

Moore, R., and Goldiamond, I. "Errorless Establishment of Visual Discrimination Using Fading Procedures." *Journal of the Experimental Analysis of Behavior* 7 (1964): 269-272.

Scott, K. G. "Engineering Attention: Some Rules for the Classroom." *Education and Training of the Mentally Retarded,* 1 (1966): 125-129.

Scott, K.G. "Learning and Intelligence." In *Psychometric Intelligence,* edited by C. Haywood. New York: Appleton-Century-Crofts, 1970 (in press).

Shepp, B., and Zeaman, D. "Discrimination Learning of Size and Brightness by Retardates." *Journal of Comparative and Physiological Psychology* 62 (1966): 55-59.

Terrace, H.S. "Stimulus Control." In *Operant Behavior: Areas of Research and Application,* edited by W. K. Honig, pp. 271-344. New York: Appleton-Century-Crofts, 1966.

Wolff, J.L. "Concept Shift and Discrimination-Reversal Learning in Humans." *Psychological Bulletin* 68 (1967): 369-408.

Zeaman, D. "Learning Processes of the Mentally Retarded." In *The Biosocial Basis of Mental Retardation,* edited by S. Osler and R. Cooke, pp. 107-127. Baltimore, Maryland: The Johns Hopkins Press, 1965.

Zeaman, D. "The Law of Redundancy." Paper presented at Gatlinburg Conference on Research and Theory in Mental Retardation, Gatlinburg, Tennessee, March 1968.

Zeaman, D., and House, B. J. "The Role of Attention in Retardate Discrimination Learning." In *Handbook of Mental Deficiency,* edited by N. R. Ellis, pp. 159-223. New York: McGraw-Hill, 1963.

# INDEX OF NAMES

# INDEX OF SUBJECTS